T0390739

Thailand's International Meditation Centers

This book explores contemporary practices within the new institution of international meditation centers in Thailand. It discusses the development of Thai Buddhism, the evolution of Western views about Thai Buddhism, and relates Thai Buddhism to contemporary processes of commodification and globalization. Through an examination of how meditation centers are promoted internationally, the author considers how Thai Buddhism is 'translated' and taught to international tourists. Shedding new light on global religious practices, and raising new questions concerning tourism and religion, this book focuses on the nature of cultural exchange, spiritual tourism, and religious choice in modernity. With an aim of reframing questions of religious modernity and an emphasis on all of the actors involved in the promotion of meditation and new forms of religiosity, each chapter offers a new perspective on the phenomenon of spiritual seeking in Thailand. Offering an analysis of why meditation practices appeal to non-Buddhists, this book contends that religions do not travel as whole entities, but instead that partial elements resonate with different cultures and are appropriated over time.

Brooke Schedneck is Lecturer in Buddhist Studies at the Institute of Southeast Asian Affairs at Chiangmai University, Thailand.

Routledge Religion in Contemporary Asia Series
Series Editor
Bryan S. Turner, *Professor at the City University of New York and Director of the Centre for Religion and Society at the University of Western Sydney*

1 **State Management of Religion in Indonesia**
   Myengkyo Seo

2 **Religious Pluralism, State and Society in Asia**
   Edited by Chiara Formichi

3 **Thailand's International Meditation Centers**
   Tourism and the global commodification of religious practices
   Brooke Schedneck

Thailand's International Meditation Centers
Tourism and the global commodification of religious practices

Brooke Schedneck

LONDON AND NEW YORK

First published 2015
by Routledge
2 Park Square, Milton Park, Abingdon, Oxon OX14 4RN

and by Routledge
711 Third Avenue, New York, NY 10017

Routledge is an imprint of the Taylor & Francis Group, an Informa business

© 2015 Brooke Schedneck

The right of Brooke Schedneck to be identified as author of this work
has been asserted by her in accordance with sections 77 and 78 of the
Copyright, Designs and Patents Act 1988.

All rights reserved. No part of this book may be reprinted or reproduced or
utilised in any form or by any electronic, mechanical, or other means, now
known or hereafter invented, including photocopying and recording, or in
any information storage or retrieval system, without permission in writing
from the publishers.

Trademark notice: Product or corporate names may be trademarks or
registered trademarks, and are used only for identification and explanation
without intent to infringe.

British Library Cataloguing in Publication Data
A catalogue record for this book is available from the British Library

Library of Congress Cataloging-in-Publication Data
Schedneck, Brooke, author.
Thailand's international meditation centers : tourism and the global
commodification of religious practices / Brooke Schedneck.
pages cm. — (Routledge religion in contemporary Asia series ; 3)
1. Meditation—Thailand—Buddhism. 2. Globalization—Religious
aspects—Buddhism. 3. Tourism—Thailand. 4. Buddhism—Thailand.
I. Title.
BQ566.S28 2015
294.3′443509593—dc23
2014045177

ISBN: 978-0-415-81958-9 (hbk)
ISBN: 978-1-315-69728-4 (ebk)

Typeset in Times New Roman
by Swales & Willis Ltd, Exeter, Devon, UK

To my two favorite guys: P'Win and Nong Jet!

Contents

List of figures	viii
List of tables	ix
Acknowledgments	x
Transliteration of Thai terms	xii

1	Imagining Buddhism	1
2	Theravāda Buddhism and the history of modern *vipassanā*	24
3	The field of international engagement with Thai meditation centers	45
4	Narratives of international meditators' experiences	75
5	Meditation for tourists in Thailand: commodifying a universal and national symbol	103
6	Pedagogical techniques for translating *vipassanā* meditation	124
7	Embodying meditation	149
8	The future of Thailand's international meditation centers	169
	Bibliography	178
	Index	192

Figures

3.1	Map of Thailand	46
3.2	Meditation hall, Diphabavan	56
3.3	Rules and regulations at Wat Kow Tahm	57
3.4	Accommodation at Wat Kow Tahm	57
3.5	Buddha cave, Wat Tam Doi Tohn	60
3.6	Sign outside Wat Pah Tam Wua	61
3.7	Mae Chii chanting, Wat Chom Tong	63
4.1	Scenic view, Wat Pah Tam Wua	80
4.2	Almsround, Wat Rampoeng	94
4.3	Bathing wells, International Dhamma Hermitage	98
4.4	Meditation hall, International Dhamma Hermitage	100
7.1	Meditation clothes	157

Tables

3.1	Temple regions	47
3.2	Statistics	47

Acknowledgments

In order to conduct this research, I first needed the consent and willingness of the teachers and participants in Thailand's international meditation centers. Therefore, I am most indebted to all of the international meditation center teachers who supported my project, taught me about their meditation program and teachings, and made the time to answer my questions in formal interview settings. I also must thank all of the international meditators I encountered who were happy to share their stories, motivations, reflections, and experiences with me. I use actual names for those meditation teachers who are public figures but rely on pseudonyms for other teachers and international meditators.

The first incarnation of this work was my dissertation, so a special thanks goes to the support I received from professors and colleagues at Arizona State University. My advisor, Juliane Schober, always offered gentle encouragement and constant enthusiasm for my project. Her mentorship has extended beyond the dissertation and book to include all aspects of academia. I would also like to extend my gratitude to Joel Gereboff, Tracy Fessenden, and James Rush, who greatly encouraged and supported my work. Discussions with colleagues Seth Clippard, Semiha Topal, Smita Kothari, Jean-Marie Stevens, Samsul Maarif, Sadia Mahmood, and Bret Lewis about religious studies theories and methods enhanced my thinking and the quality of my fieldwork and writing. During previous graduate work at Harvard University, classes with Anne Blackburn and Christopher Queen influenced my thinking about Buddhist studies. As well, Professor Donald Swearer's enthusiasm for Buddhism in Southeast Asia sparked my own, and I would like to thank him for encouraging my interest in this field.

I have benefited from financial support from a Fulbright grant for my research in Thailand. My work was also furthered though funding during the writing phase from Arizona State University Graduate College, the Empowering Network for International Thai Studies, and the Philanthropic Educational Organization. I am indebted to these organizations for their support during this writing period. My writing and thinking during the course of this project was also fostered through conferences where I presented my work. In particular, feedback from participants in the International Association of Buddhist Studies (2011) in Taiwan, the Sakyadhita Conference (2011) in Thailand, the Fulbright Mid-Year Enrichment Seminar (2010) in the Philippines, the Southeast Asia Graduate Conference (2011) at the University of Michigan, and the Western Perspectives on Buddhism conference at Ludwig-Maxilian University in Munich (2011), was useful in developing the framework and structure of the manuscript. Especially important in this regard is the Henry Luce Foundation for its support of my participation in the Theravāda Civilizations Dissertation Workshop. For their comments during this workshop I thank Steven Collins, Anne Hansen, Christoph Emmrich, and Justin McDaniel. I wish to acknowledge the staff of the Ecole française d'Extrême-Orient in Chiangmai including Piyawit Moonkham and Rosakon Siriyuktanont, for their friendliness and interest during my many days of writing in their beautiful library.

My friends and colleagues in Chiangmai, Thailand, my base while researching this book, have also helped to shape some of my thinking about international meditation centers. Charlotte Trenk-Hinterberger, Steve Epstein, Miskaman Rujavichai, Tidarat Jitsook, Apinya Feungfusakul, and Alan Lopez provided valuable ideas and clarifications. Since 2010 my Thai teacher, Potjanee Manipantee, or Kru Oo, has not only taught me new vocabulary and sentence structures, but also provided valuable perspectives and information about Buddhism and meditation in Thailand. My students and colleagues at my current institution, the Institute of Southeast Asian Affairs at Chiangmai University, have encouraged and provided intellectual support. Students in my "Buddhism in Thai Society" course at Chiangmai University and "Buddhist Meditation" course at Payap University have offered useful conversations about their encounters with Thai Buddhism and meditation. I particularly appreciate my students who attended meditation retreats and discussed their experiences with me. My colleague Adam Dedman has supported this project since its inception, always helping me to connect with scholars and interested meditators. I thank him especially for his thoughtfulness and friendship.

Julia Cassaniti, Alan Lopez, Thomas Borchert, Bhikkhu Gavesako, Will Yaryan, Udom Tan, Juliane Schober, and Erik Braun all read parts of the manuscript and offered valuable feedback. Julia Cassaniti in particular offered crucial advice in a gentle and caring way. Alexandra Dalferro provided the cover photo and Arkadiusz Slanda created all figures in this book. Bryan Turner, editor of Routledge's Contemporary Asian Religions series and Peter Sowden, Routledge editor, have shown great interest and enthusiasm for this project and I thank them for their careful reading and comments. Earlier versions of Chapter 4 appeared in *Rian Thai Journal* and Chapter 5 in the *Journal of Contemporary Religion*. I thank them for permission to use these as a basis for my book.

My thanks and love also go to my parents and sister, Jillian Schedneck, a creative non-fiction author and academic herself, who took time out of her busy life to read and comment on chapters during the early and finishing stages of manuscript writing. My parents' belief in my goals was never doubted. I thank them for their interest and support in this project. My little guy, Jet Pasha, came into this world during the final year of writing this book. He brought much joy to my life during this time and some much needed distractions from the manuscript.

And most of all I thank my husband, William Starner. Not only did he move with me to Thailand, but he has always supported me in whatever I felt I needed to do to complete my research and writing. His easygoing and light-hearted manner eased any stressful moments and I will always be grateful for his time, patience, interest, and partnership during the course of this project. Not everyone is lucky enough to be married to their best friend as well as a great research assistant and proofreader.

Transliteration of Thai terms

The Romanization system I use follows a simplified version of that used by the Library of Congress. For example, for the consonant čh I use j and I do not indicate long vowels or tones. A number of Thai transliteration systems exist and in some cases references use a different spelling from the ones I use in the text. In these cases I have kept the original Romanization. When using Thai words derived from Pāli, I use the Thai Romanization. For temple and monastic names I have used the most popular spellings.

1 Imagining Buddhism

It's hard to sit in a room where there is nothing to do but be in silence with yourself. It's time to face your deeper feelings, fears and wonders. No more excuses or distractions. The challenge is on the table, probably the biggest challenge I have ever faced. I had to conquer myself, my habits, my determination, my thoughts and dreams. And I didn't know if I would make it.

(*International Meditator and research participant, Wat Rampoeng, Chiangmai, Thailand*)

Tourists, expatriates, and other non-Thai visitors in Thailand often arrive at meditation temples alone, not knowing much about meditation or living in a temple. Committing to a meditation retreat in a foreign country for at least ten days can seem quite daunting. These visitors, whom I call international meditators,[1] report feeling trapped, confused, nervous, anxious, and excited all at once. Although I had read extensively and understood intellectually about meditation and the purposes of the retreat program in preparation for ethnographic fieldwork of international meditation centers in Thailand, I often felt this same mix of emotions during my research. I was jealous of the Thai meditators who usually came in groups and had friends to commiserate with and activities to participate in besides meditating. When I learned that one temple where I was staying would have a celebration for Kathin, the robe offering ceremony which marks the end of the holiest time of year for Theravāda Buddhists, I rushed to call my husband, telling him he could join me the next day. I was thrilled to have his company, after days of being alone. The retreat experience is incredibly isolating, and yet that is the point. Even if one arrives with friends, each person meditates independently and must 'conquer' his or her own mind.

Of course, there were also times when practicing meditation during fieldwork when I had a rush of energetic sensations throughout my body—known as *piti* or joy, a side effect of deep concentration. There were evenings when I came back to my room after a challenging day meditating in the meditation hall, ate my snack of yogurt and Ovaltine,[2] nodded to my fellow meditators, and felt like I had established a satisfying routine. I learned that most meditators feel this way at some point. They are able to slow their minds, become accustomed to the long days,

2 *Imagining Buddhism*

and eventually understand the benefits of the isolation and loneliness. However, the quote at the start of this chapter highlights many of the initial conceptions held about Buddhism and meditation by international meditators in Thailand. They are often confused and nervous but also excited that they are about to undertake such an endeavor.

International meditators are a diverse group of travelers who can teach us about how Buddhism is constructed in global contexts, within interaction and exchange. They have much to tell us about modern ideas of religion, popular imaginaries of Buddhism, and the role of transnational travel in modern religiosity. Because this book is located in the Buddhist center of Thailand but discusses international travelers, I engage scholarship and ideas from both Theravāda Buddhist studies scholars and scholars of global Buddhism. There have been many studies about Buddhism outside of Asia, in America (Cadge 2005; Tweed 1992, 2002; Prebish 1999; Queen & Williams 1999; Wilson 2009), Canada (Harding et al. 2010, 2014), Australia (Spuler 2003; Rocha & Barker 2011), New Zealand (McAra 2007), Europe (Baumann 1994, 1995, 1997, 2001, 2002), Brazil (Rocha 2006), and Africa (Clasquin 1999). These studies have been useful in noting how Buddhism adapts in these peripheries, highlighting especially the creation of diasporic communities and interactions with new converts. However, religious centers also adapt and create new transnational communities based on international visitors. It is not just a one-way arrow from the center but a number of interlinked flows. Transnational encounters also occur within centers, not only peripheries, as religions come into new contexts. Buddhism is not only being exported and adapted to new cultures but also continues to be reconstructed within Asian centers to account for interactions with new ideas and encounters. However, scholarship on this topic is bifurcated to include either studies focusing on Buddhism adapting to Western countries or studies concerning Buddhism in Asian countries. This bifurcation is unrepresentative of reality as Buddhist practitioners continually oscillate between East and West.

Thailand is an ideal location to situate such a study on transnational Buddhism, as it is one of the few Asian countries which offers a range of possibilities to English-speakers interested in learning about Buddhism and experiencing meditation. Information on meditation sites in Thailand is increasingly easy to obtain through websites, guidebooks, and pamphlets promoting international meditation centers where English-speakers are welcome. Increased interest in Buddhism and appeal of meditation lead travelers to explore further learning opportunities while traveling in Asian Buddhist countries. With the rise in popularity of lay meditation by Thai Buddhists, many temples and meditation centers have sought to accommodate an international audience through teaching in English.

This book takes the reader through a tour of the world of international meditation centers in Thailand through the experiences of international meditators and their teachers. I examine the meaning of these experiences in the context of the commodification of meditation through promotional materials, the cultural translation performed by international meditation center teachers for international meditators, and the ways international meditators embody meditation within the retreat format.

Using over sixty conversations and interviews with international meditators and their teachers, this book offers an ethnography of the phenomenon of international meditation centers in Thailand. These international meditators are sometimes tourists, sometimes long-term residents, or somewhere in between, but all undertake the meditation retreat programs in Thailand through English instruction. Therefore they are not a homogeneous group as they come from various backgrounds, experiences, and a diversity of level of participation in Buddhism. However, I follow the international meditation center teachers I spoke with who constructed these non-Thai participants in their retreats as a group, noting their common ideas and ways of accessing the retreat. As we will see, international meditators have separate teachers, interview times, orientations, opening rituals, and even completely separate retreats from their Thai counterparts. I discuss the tendencies and common themes of this group from my own observations along with international meditators' experiences and their teachers' interpretations. Because of this focus, the present work is primarily a study of how Buddhism is imagined and experienced in contemporary settings.

With the increasing global appeal of meditation, alternative modes of religiosity have arisen, whereby divisions between secular and religious become blurred. Employing the recent revisions of the secularization theory (Casanova 1994; Asad 2003; Smith 2003), I demonstrate that the study of religion in modernity should not center on measuring people's increase or decrease in religious behavior, but instead on the decontextualization of religious practice from its institutional framework. Decontextualization is a key theme within this book as I highlight the ways meditation is disembedded from its Thai Buddhist context, becoming a global religious practice. Instead of this Thai Buddhist context, for international meditators, meditation is situated within modern discourses of individual preference, science, Romanticism, psychology, secularism, and universalism. One of the most pressing issues for scholars of religious studies are the mechanisms by which religion maintains its relevance in contemporary times. Important manifestations of religion and modernity are developing through decontextualized religious practices, temporary or partial religious engagement, transient communities, and international travel. By investigating these manifestations in Thailand, this book argues that decontextualization from the traditional worldview and recontextualization of modern discourses can help us understand the ways religions negotiate modernity and allow for change, and how new members come to learn and practice. In this context I argue that it is more important to discuss experimentation and sampling of religious practices than conversion or religious identity.

In addition to analyzing the consequences of decontextualized meditation, this book also details the historical conditions that have led to persisting interpretations of Buddhism by tracing the continuities between Orientalist interpretations and modern-day spiritual seekers. Spurred by interest in Edwin Arnold's (1879) publication of the now classic *The Light of Asia* and *A Buddhist Bible* by Dwight Goddard (1966 [1938]), Buddhism entered the popular imagination of English-speaking societies for the first time. The world of Buddhism described in these books—and other ideas, values, and images of Buddhism that quickly became

4 *Imagining Buddhism*

public knowledge through various routes—presented a challenge to audiences as it confounded the characteristics of other known religions. Alternately celebrated and derided for stepping outside the fixed religious categories known to the Western world, Buddhism has continued to be a particularly contentious religious and philosophical category in Western countries. Orientalists admired the 'pure,' rational and scientific origins of the Buddhist tradition (Lopez 1995), while late nineteenth century Americans derided the belief system as nihilistic (Tweed 1992). Buddhism was praised, in contrast with Christianity, for its atheism and descriptive rather than revelatory doctrines. However, Buddhism was also commended for its similarities to Christianity, such as having a personal founder, religious texts, and ethics. Scholarly attention has been directed toward colonial readings of Buddhist thought (Lopez 1995; Almond 1988; Prothero 1996), yet Buddhism continues to be reimagined in the modern era. Just as early scholars and popular audiences constructed various readings of Buddhism in the late eighteenth and early nineteenth centuries, modern religious seekers represent the most recent iteration of this search for religious meaning. Although many people were interested in Buddhist philosophy and related Asian culture in the nineteenth century, it is only since the twentieth century that meditation has held a powerful influence over cultural trends with many people using the practice as a supplement or alternative to their own faith.[3] New translations, associations, and connections are created through international meditators' varied interactions and engagements with Thai Buddhism, in dialogue with international meditation center teachers. I explore these constructions by tracing social discourses about Buddhism and meditation practices and interactions on the ground in Thailand.

In this work, I have tried not to overgeneralize this group of international meditators and their contrasts with Thai meditators. There are no clear divisions between the two groups as their opinions and ideas about the retreat programs certainly overlap. There is no clearly defined category of Thai Buddhist practice, as similarly, there is no bounded or defined way to describe international meditators. The ideas of both of these groups are constructed, rendering one no more real or authentic than the other. As such, I don't want to suggest that these two groups have opposite goals or in any way reify their supposed contrasts. There are Thai Buddhists who have similar motivations to international meditators and vice versa. Therefore, I do not discuss two separate Buddhisms but rather the prevailing ideas of the groups in order to reflect on the phenomenon of international meditation centers. Before describing further the international meditation center, it is important to examine previous ethnographies of meditation and possible methodological strategies for investigating this mostly silent, internal practice.

The anthropology of meditation

The anthropology of meditation is a difficult task as the ethnographer does not have access to the inner content of participants in a retreat. For this reason I draw from Noel Salazar (2010) and Arjun Appadurai (1986) in my analysis of international meditation centers. Salazar (2010) offers one approach of a 'global ethnography,' which follows the dissemination of knowledge and imaginaries by tour guides. His field sites are the diverse settings of Indonesia and Tanzania, and he argues that this diversity helps us to understand how ideas move and circulate. Giving attention to human agency within everyday life, as well as the historical and institutional contexts in which they are embedded, he illuminates the interplay between global and local discourses and exchanges (Salazar 2010, xvii). Appadurai's approach follows the flows of commodities as opposed to the flows of people and ideas, investigating how commodities change in meaning and value as they move through and across various cultures. Appadurai looks at how commodities divert from their paths and are "transformed culturally, economically, and socially by the tastes, markets, and ideologies of larger commodities and politics of value" (Appadurai 1986, 26). These diversions create new desires and demands so that the commodity changes with those it comes into contact with (Appadurai 1986, 27). Here I combine these approaches, looking at both tourist flows of ideas within historical contexts and the trajectory of the commodity of meditation itself in order to illuminate the various imaginaries this practice occupies. The fieldwork sites for this study are the numerous international meditation centers of Thailand. I did not confine my research to one space but participated in fieldwork at sites throughout the country, following networks of actors and teachers. This approach works well when researching contemporary practices and the impact of tourism.

A major concern of the anthropology of religion concerns the ways practitioners' subjectivities are formed. Joanna Cook (2010) has written about the ways monastics make themselves embody Buddhist doctrines. Similarly, my work investigates the opportunities and possibilities for international meditators to come to learn from and form themselves into subjects of the meditation retreat. I focus on translation practices and dialogue between international meditators and their teachers. Analyzing intercultural dialogue as a set of double processes, I examine how international meditation center teachers learn international meditators' expectations and assumptions, and in turn, how international meditators learn not only how to meditate but in some cases how to live in a Thai Buddhist temple. They learn, to various extents, how to interact with Thai Buddhists and monastics, observe Buddhist codes of morality, and about Buddhist and Thai culture. I illustrate the impact of these interactions through pedagogical strategies of the teachers as well as narratives of the meditators' experiences. Illuminating and distilling the voices of international meditators and their teachers, this ethnography contributes to the anthropology of religion, tourism, and meditation.

I was motivated to undertake this study because of my long-term interest in understanding religious change and adaptation in modernity. During my last semester as an undergraduate I conducted field research at meditation centers in the Boston area for a seminar paper comparing contemporary meditation practice with the first Buddhist communities. Through this experience I also developed an interest in meditation and a desire to study this global phenomenon more closely. In addition to this academic interest, I had also participated in learning meditation at the Cambridge Insight Meditation Center just outside Boston, Massachusetts.

6   *Imagining Buddhism*

Here I joined their youth group for meditators under thirty and took a basic beginners' course on meditation. At this time, however, I had not yet taken part in an extended retreat. Academically, I was drawn to topics concerning religion in modernity and began to research biographies and memoirs of Buddhist converts from English-speaking countries. At the same time the diversity and complexity of Buddhism in Southeast Asia and the modern practice of meditation held my attention. This project was a perfect blend of these interests.

In the summer of 2008 I conducted preliminary research in Thailand. During this time I discovered the rich field of international meditation centers available for investigation. I began to uncover the diversity of meditation instruction geared toward English-speakers and non-Buddhists. During that summer I participated in two retreats in order to sample what the field research would demand. Through this practice and meeting some of the international meditation center teachers, I developed contacts that would prove to be valuable during my research period. In August 2009 I returned to Thailand and began visiting sites, attending retreats, making contacts, and conducting interviews, a process which lasted over thirteen months. This multi-sited field research was complex at times but ultimately rewarding for the range and quality of data I was able to collect.

These portraits of international meditation centers are based on interviews with over thirty international meditation center teachers and thirty international meditators from visits to over twenty sites for varying lengths of time from August 2009 to September 2010. During this time I used fieldnotes written during and after retreats as a way to analyze both the experiences of international meditators as well as myself. To this end, I utilize some of my own experiences in this work as an international meditator, albeit one who visited many centers and practiced varying methods. My fieldwork experiences include ten-day retreats at long-running and well-attended international centers as well as visits to sites throughout Thailand, which have shorter histories and house English-speaking meditation teachers and small groups of international meditators. I selected sites that consistently host international meditators and are the most popular among travelers and foreign residents, a process discussed further in Chapter 3. At these sites, I investigated how English-speakers learn about both Thai Buddhism and the practice of meditation. Through participant observation I delved into the ways teachings are received by and presented to the international meditators. I did not focus on any particular lineage or school of meditation, but rather the pedagogical strategies of the teachers and the ways they utilized the physical environment of each site. Although lineages are an important organizing feature of Theravāda Buddhism, and indeed of meditation methods in Southeast Asia, there are other structures in place for international meditation centers. As we will see, some international meditation centers are established based on tourism and demand as much as they are through established lineages with charismatic teachers. In this way lineage is not the only organizing principle for centers that cater to international meditators.

During this fieldwork period I expressed my observations and fieldwork analysis via my research website, "Wandering Dhamma."[4] This website aided me in a number of ways. Besides starting the process of writing my findings, I came into

Imagining Buddhism 7

contact with many present and future international meditators. They commented on my posts and engaged in dialogue about meditation in Thailand. Some of them followed my website and added their comments about meditation centers in Thailand. Through this web presence, I often received emails asking me to point prospective travelers to a suitable retreat for them after listing a number of criteria. The characteristics of meditation retreats that were most desirable in these email correspondences provided interesting data to analyze. In addition to international meditators, monks, nuns, and lay meditation teachers also appreciated my website. They were happy that accurate information about their meditation temples was being disseminated through the Internet for a large audience. They were also glad that research was being conducted by a person who was practicing and participating in the meditation retreat. Through one-on-one open-ended interviews with monks, nuns, and lay meditation teachers, I was able to understand what they wanted to communicate to potential international meditators and I became a conduit to bridge information between these two groups. A few meditation teachers even read my posts and clarified some information, adding useful data to my findings. These connections through my website contributed to my ability to conduct an ethnography about meditation.

Within the anthropology of religion there have been a few scholarly works on meditation in which scholars have utilized various methods to obtain data. The first scholarly work of this kind is by Gustaaf Houtman (1990), who wrote his dissertation on meditative traditions in Burma.[5] Houtman attempted ethnographic work in meditation centers and found it challenging, if not impossible. He writes that he obtained remarkably little information of ethnographic value about *vipassanā* while spending ten days at the International Meditation Centre in Heddington, England or in two weeks at the Mahasi Thathana Yeiktha in Yangon, Burma. Being a foreigner, he was grouped with other international meditators. Because of this he was isolated from the Burmese practitioners and what he considered authentic ethnographic data. He was denied concrete information about the organization of the centers or the lives of the teachers or meditators. He also could not combine meditation with ethnographic observation as the center forbade speaking, reading, or writing. Houtman relates how his curiosity about the daily functioning of the center hindered his ability to meditate, and he could not convince his teachers he was making progress. When he tried talking to Burmese meditators and administrators they were either busy meditating or teaching. He found that the Burmese meditators did not have the time or inclination to sit around socializing. Social pleasantries were a distraction to meditation and there were few occasions for small talk. Houtman therefore couldn't have written his dissertation if he had only meditated, and if he were strictly a researcher he would have been unable to gain access to the teachers and meditators he wished to interview. He writes, "Academic anthropology, I concluded, was irreconcilable with meditation" (Houtman 1990, 132).

I had a markedly different experience in the Thai meditation centers, mostly because I was looking for other kinds of information. For the most part, the monk and lay teachers of the international meditation centers I visited understood that

8 *Imagining Buddhism*

I was doing research, but were also happy I decided to meditate as they thought my research would have no value without the practice component. We agreed that I would meditate and report to them as a regular meditator, but at the end of my retreat I could conduct research interviews. This arrangement worked out well in many of the centers. Of course my meditation could have progressed further had I not been interested in talking with the international and Thai meditators, and attending the evening and morning chanting sessions with the *mae chii*[6] and female Thai meditators. However, many meditation teachers understood that I was interested in the 'Buddhist' aspect of living at a center and encouraged a deeper understanding of this as long as it did not interfere too much with my meditation. Therefore many of the Thai meditation centers are not as strict as Houtman's experience at the Mahasi Thathana Yeiktha, and were more flexible in terms of their evaluation of academic knowledge. They found my research a valuable pursuit of knowledge, but of course, not as valuable as attaining liberation.

Ingrid Jordt (2007) was more successful than Houtman in conducting ethnographic fieldwork at the Mahasi Thathana Yeiktha. Jordt had a personal background and interest in meditation and was ordained during her fieldwork. Along with observations at the Mahasi Thathana Yeiktha, she also interviewed members of the government ministries and high-ranking monks. She found her status as a meditator helped her to gain access to high-level information because her visas issued from the Ministry of Home and Religious Affairs, and it allowed her to stay for longer periods than other visitors. Jordt admits that conducting ethnography in this context is difficult. She writes:

> [F]rom an ethnographic point of view, meditation presents a challenge as a subject of study . . . Although the conditions for this practice are carefully structured at MTY [Mahasi Thathana Yeiktha] and one can refer to this structure in a tangible way, the inward encounter is less accessible. The challenge to the ethnographer is immediately obvious on entering a meditation hall.
>
> (Jordt 2007, 56)

The challenge that Jordt is referring to is the fact that the meditators are all sitting straight-backed with their eyes closed in absolute silence. In considering how to connect social scientific research techniques to this phenomenon, she aligns her study with other ethnographies of interiority, such as ones that study ritual, embodiment, and artistic expression (Jordt 2007, 58). I agree with the difficulty such an interior practice as meditation creates for the anthropologist; however, for my research focus and questions, I am not primarily interested in the inward experience. My observations concern the interaction of the international meditators and their teachers, reflections of the meditators, teachers' strategies for instructing their students, and the presentations of meditation and Buddhism to these meditators.

Joanna Cook (2010) was successful in carrying out an ethnography of meditation among monastics in Thailand. She ordained as a *mae chii* and participated in the retreats required for all monastics in Wat Bonamron, the meditation temple where she resided. Cook found that experiential knowledge of meditation "was of paramount importance if [she were] to have any understanding of how meditation becomes meaningful and why people commit themselves to what is often a grueling practice" (Cook 2010, 19). She considered her ordination to be central to her research and also a personal commitment that was understood as a demonstration of respect for monasticism and the monastic project. It was known in the monastery that she would be doing anthropological research but also that she was committed to ordination and meditation. Although I did not ordain and conducted a multi-sited ethnography, Cook's experience resembles the balance I was able to achieve. International meditation center teachers, for the most part, value and feel proud when a non-Thai is conducting research at their temple. If the researcher also participates in meditation, this shows her respect for the tradition and is thought to enhance the value and accuracy of the information collected.

I chose a variety of sites that would illuminate the practices of international meditators in Thailand. I found that each of the sites I researched captured different aspects of their experiences and that each context is different, so I had to adjust accordingly. But each site is also similar in the issues that emerged— translation, commodification, and ways of learning and embodying meditation. My methodology varied slightly depending on the context of the retreat. In some cases, I could interview the teachers during the retreat, but in others I was required to wait until after the closing ceremony. Because I lived in Chiang Mai I could visit local teachers frequently, but in trips to Southern and Central Thailand I had to make sure I made all my contacts and conducted interviews before leaving. With permission from the international meditation center teachers, I was able to connect with other international meditators inside and outside of retreat sites. Depending on the structure of the retreat, there is often time during the orientation and closing periods for discussion with participants. In those cases I used this time to describe my research and make contacts with other meditators. At some of the less strict centers that do not require silence, I was able to communicate, interview, and discuss the motivations and reflections about the meditation experience in Thailand with international meditators during the retreat period. Much of this data, I found, related to the ways Buddhism is imagined by these meditators.

Imaginaries of meditation

Because meditation has become synonymous with Buddhism in popular culture, it has its own set of imaginaries that come into play when international meditators enter a retreat. Drawing from Noel Salazar's work (2012) we can think of these imaginaries as "socially transmitted representational assemblages that interact with people's personal imaginings and are used as meaning-making and world shaping devices" (Salazar 2012, 2). Using this idea of imaginaries from tourism studies is appropriate because many international meditators are also tourists and the retreat is part of their tourist itinerary. These imaginaries are transmitted in promotional materials and through any visual or textual medium about a place,

10 *Imagining Buddhism*

including novels, art, movies, postcards, memoirs, and blogs. Imaginaries of meditation have also become known through popular film and TV references, museum collections of meditating Buddha statues, and numerous popular manuals of meditation. Once the imaginary of one location becomes branded through these means, it can be operationalized and enacted by tourists and tourism providers. Imaginaries of meditation are important to the world of international meditators, the work of tourist institutions, and the instruction of international meditation center teachers. I highlight here the imaginaries of meditation and how this is one facet of the broader imaginary of Buddhism and Thailand that influences the retreat experience of international meditators, discussed more explicitly in Chapter 4. There is a historical context to these imaginaries of meditation, and to this end I first discuss Orientalism and its lingering effects on imaginaries of Buddhism, meditation, and Thailand.

Within the context of colonialism, Buddhist religious teachers aligned their tradition with discourses of modernity, such as rationality and science through Rational Orientalism, hoping to build their authority and legitimacy. These leaders also molded their religious practices to fit with Romantic Orientalist ideas of a 'mystical' and 'ancient' Eastern spirituality. Throughout this book we will see that both poles of Orientalism, the Rational and Romantic, are still operationalized in tourist imaginaries as well as in tourism promotional materials of a Thai Buddhist meditation retreat. Buddhist leaders often sought to fit both molds, reinterpreting their religion to embody a rational, modern aspect as well as a timeless, exotic allure. Many Theravāda Buddhist countries were affected by colonialism[7] when their religions became measured and compared with other religions on a large-scale for the first time. In this way, religion became a way to claim modernity. Although Buddhist teachers were able to construct their own ways of using these discourses for propagating their religion, the control and power over these discourses came from Orientalist scholars and the wider colonial project. This Orientalism, scholars have argued, persists in academic circles (King 1999, 155) but also in the popular imagination of Buddhism.

Tourism imaginaries typically reproduce Orientalist representations, rather than offering a source of resistance (Ahmad 2011, 171). Tourism, therefore, is an important intermediary in the reproduction and maintenance of Orientalist discourses and representations. Although never formally colonized, Thailand's imaginaries are similar to those of colonized Asian nations. Scholars have commonly depicted Siam's colonial period[8] as exceptional, as a result of the monarchy having managed to avoid direct colonization.[9] However, it is clear that Thailand occupied a subordinate position during the colonial period (Jackson 2010, 39). Because of this, there are many arguments that cast it as semi-colonial or crypto-colonial, and therefore it can be considered in part a postcolonial nation (Harrison 2010, 4). Rachel Harrison finds that the West had the most significant impact "on forms of knowledge and modes of representation in Thailand, both locally in Thai language discourses and internationally in European language accounts" (Harrison 2010, 10). Thailand was not formally colonized but this did not stop the country from being constrained by Western imperial powers – mainly British and French – in ways reminiscent of what colonized nations suffered . . . it was as though the *farang*, [white foreigner] more than the Indian or the Burmese or the Malay or the Chinese or the Cambodian or the Lao, was *the* Other against whom the modern person measured himself or herself.

(Chakrabarty 2010, ix)

At the same time as the West was the primary Other for Thais, for colonialists, and Orientalist scholars, Asian culture and religion was marked as the Other. Cultural and religious symbols of Asia did not signify modernity for Westerners but a commodity that could be sold. Early travel writers from Europe made sites famous where this Other could be imagined, noting points of exotic cultural difference that could be consumed. Tourist imaginaries of Asian countries often express the desire for exoticism. This exoticism "is deeply ambivalent because it relies simultaneously on giving value to the Other because it/he is different, while taking value away from the Other, who is fundamentally an inferior being in the colonial civilization scheme" (Peyvel 2011, 227). This ranking and creation of sites during colonialism "which are held to embody difference continues to inform the shaping of tourist itineraries" (Edensor 1998, 24). Tourism meditation publications in Thailand draw on constructions of meditation as an escape from modernity. Advertisements about meditation for the international community imagine Thailand as an exotic Other and its meditation practice as a marker of difference.

International meditators, their teachers, and institutions in Thailand that promote tourism and Buddhism all are involved in the production of imagined cultural and religious difference. These individuals and sources facilitate the ways in which international meditators create their expectations and filter experiences in the meditation retreat. International meditation center teachers as well as larger institutional bodies associated with tourism in Thailand are able to evaluate tourist expectations and imaginaries. A specific imaginary discussed throughout this book involves a Romantic, peaceful, isolated experience in a natural setting. A rational, nondogmatic technique for living is another imaginary of meditation utilized for therapeutic benefits. These expectations are commoditized in brochures and publications so that monks, Thai Buddhists, and the temple setting are expected to embody these imaginaries of Buddhism and meditation. Tourist imaginaries of Buddhist Thailand generate ideas of glittering stupas, chanting monks in robes, and of course a lone meditator seated near or a pond or in the forest with a peaceful smile. Within Thailand's international meditation centers, teachers and tourism promoters draw on these images to create worlds of associations for understanding, teaching, and promotion. However, imaginaries of meditation serve to create expectations for international meditators that are not always met. These materials show more about the imaginative construct of Buddhism and the meditation retreat than the actual experience. The resulting contradictions serve, in some cases, to enhance learning about the self and others, and in other cases cause a lack of engagement due to perceived 'inauthenticity.' The chapters in this book illuminate the ways international meditators react to the retreat programs

12 *Imagining Buddhism*

based on imaginaries of Thailand, meditation, and Buddhism. Imaginaries of meditation form and shape the initial encounter and understanding of the retreat experience for international meditators. This is reinforced through promotional materials concerning meditation in Thailand.

Tourism, religion, and commodification

As various Buddhist institutions promote meditation retreats, meditation becomes commodified while it is shaped into a desirable experience. Scholarship, as well as popular ideas concerning religion and commerce, often assumes that this mixing rings a disingenuous note. The critique of consumer culture and capitalism appears especially in regard to religion, with the idea that consumption practices invade, intrude, and threaten the sentiment of the religious domain leading ultimately to its disgrace and domination by the vulgarity of market forces (Marx 1912; Ward 2003; Miller 2005). A critical portrayal of consumption is premised on the view that consumer culture negatively changes one's relationship to religious beliefs and practices through its emphasis on hedonism and worldly pleasures (Featherstone 2007, 111). Yet, a negative relationship between commodities and religiosity is a false assumption. I argue that commodifying the sacred does not necessarily lead to a decrease in religiosity, but rather shows how religious practice is reconfigured in its relationship with the market and leads to new social spaces (Hefner 1998; Tambiah 1984; Taylor 2008). In Chapter 5, I argue that tourism creates new possibilities and opportunities for sampling and experimentation, which are both prominent features of modern religion. As I investigate the ways that Thai Buddhism is mixed with the market, I argue that this is one of the ways religion adapts and creates new communities. I am not evaluating this commodification but examining the dynamics of promoting meditation, the actors involved, discourses used, and how this relates to imaginaries of meditation.

Tourism which incorporates religious learning and practice is contributing to a postmodern religiosity. Religious tourism, in this context, is not a substitute for organized religion but is instead a space where tourists are encouraged to sample a number of religious practices and possibly integrate them into their lives (Vukonic 2002). Thomas Tweed finds that "sometimes tourism overlaps with pilgrimage as consumers of aesthetic pleasures and leisure diversions invest their travel with spiritual significance" (Tweed 2008, 131). Tourism, therefore, constitutes another avenue for new forms of religiosity. For some the search for the sacred has been replaced by a search for the exotic cultural other. Meditation is especially significant in this regard because it offers an experience and practice that can be consumed.[10] Literature about meditation was instrumental in creating a modern desire for the practice, which is advertised as a way to deal with or escape from modern disenchantment and malaise. Because modernity is often defined by increased secularization, urbanization, and rationalization, a search for reenchantment marks much of the commodification of meditation. Modern man sees value in a timeless era, and tourist materials evocatively draw on this when promoting Thailand's international meditation centers.

Therefore religious movements and practices that connect with commerce are complex expressions of religiosity within daily life. Robert Hefner argues that

> [T]here is a relationship between market growth and religious revival . . . Religion is not being everywhere pressed toward individualistic or hedonistic ends, as some might predict in an era of rising affluence and detradition-alization. Nor is it being uniformly used to mobilize resistance against the individualizing or alienating tendencies of capitalism and urban life.
> (Hefner 1998, 26–270)

Thus there can exist a middle ground where religious traditions neither lose their sense of discipline and asceticism nor do they resist consumerism and exit society altogether. Religious traditions, such as that of Thai Buddhism, when mixed with international tourism, commodifies certain practices that capitalize on reified images of the elements of that tradition, in this case meditation. The commodification of meditation demonstrates how Thai Buddhists, in conjunction with international meditators and other interested tourists, connect with consumer markets as they provide a decontextualized product tailored to this specific audience.

Modern Buddhism

Along with imaginaries of meditation, modern Buddhism is the context within which international meditators engage with the meditation retreat program. Today, modern Buddhism constitutes the foundation for intercultural dialogue examined in the international meditation center settings. Modern Buddhism has become the international or metalanguage of Buddhism, suggesting how to interpret elements of the tradition and position them within modern contexts (McMahan 2008, 259). International meditation center teachers use this language when translating the retreat program for their international guests. The role of modern Buddhism highlights the historically contingent imaginaries of Buddhism as well as the range of imaginaries that international meditators draw from.

Modern Buddhism describes particular forms of practice within specific historical contexts. In the Buddhist traditions of Asia, the teachings of the Buddha developed in differing ways depending on numerous factors such as the religio-cultural and social contexts in which the tradition entered. With relatively limited contact between Buddhist traditions in premodern times, each context in which Buddhism developed occurred autonomously. During the nineteenth century this development entered a new phase with the introduction of colonialism, Christianity, and modernization. Buddhist responses to these transformations have been labeled modern Buddhism. Modern Buddhism has been molded by the colonial encounter, Orientalist scholarship, rise of the nation-state, comparisons with Christianity, as well as internal Buddhist dialogue. The shaping of modern Buddhism continues through new Buddhist movements and increased engagement with the international

14 *Imagining Buddhism*

community. Modern Buddhism develops in varying ways depending on the socio-cultural and political factors of each nation-state.

When considering the term modern Buddhism in this book I draw from Donald Lopez (2002) and David McMahan (2008). Lopez (2002) traces the history of this movement throughout Asia, focusing on institutions and transnational networks of actors. Asserting that a new consciousness was being raised about the history and distinctness of Buddhism, the need to protect it became crucial. Lopez argues that trends of modern Buddhism, although they began in disparate locations in response to modernity and continue today, have formed a new sect of Buddhism (Lopez 2002, xxxi). This new sect, Lopez argues, is characterized by rationalism and empiricism, concern for social justice, placing universal over the local and the individual above the community, a focus on equality and the increased role of women, a rejection of ritual, and a return to a pristine past of the tradition (Lopez 2002, ix). I do not consider modern Buddhism to be a new sect but the characteristics he lists I find constitute a large portion of the imaginary of Buddhism for international meditators. These characteristics have made their way to non-Buddhist countries and it is this form of Buddhism that is most popular internationally and most recognized within the international community. Most international meditators of course do not have a detailed understanding of all these aspects of modern Buddhism. However, they are aware of the basic ideas of Buddhism as a rational, empirical tradition with meditation practice at the core.

I have drawn on several aspects of McMahan's (2008) approach to the study of modern Buddhism. He describes the encounter of Buddhism and modernity both spatially, as he looks at Western and Asian Buddhist contexts, and temporally, as he pays attention to the pre-encounter that established how Buddhism was received in the West and the result of that encounter today. His work demonstrates that in the encounter with new cultural contexts a religious tradition becomes a hybrid that must recreate itself in terms of the prevalent discourses of a society. McMahan treats this hybridity in a complex way, illustrating that a tradition doesn't simply conform to new contexts but engages in a process of reconfiguration and negotiation. McMahan lists three discourses of modernity—scientific rationalism, Romanticism, and Christianity—that he describes as the major facets and connection points of modern Buddhism. He elucidates how each of these has resonated with different aspects of Buddhism, highlighting some parts and occluding others. In my case I am not focusing only on North America but on the dominant discourses of international meditators in Thailand. I find, however, that McMahan's arguments are compelling in this regard and I draw from them throughout the chapters of this book.

Buddhism is imagined in unique ways in the modern era, with modern Buddhism constituting one of the most recent imaginaries. Modern Buddhist actors and practices have formed in Thailand as well. Thailand's form of modern Buddhism was established by similar characteristics noted by Lopez, discourses of modernity described by McMahan, and distinct formations relative to the particular modern history of Thailand. Thailand's version of modern Buddhism was reformulated in an attempt to illustrate the country's modernity in the context of

Imagining Buddhism   15

colonialism and international encounters. This history continues to provide the backdrop for the context of international meditation centers.

Modern Buddhism in Thailand

Modern Thai Buddhism gives us background into the modern Buddhist framework of the international meditators and the project of the international meditation center. This modern construction of Thai Buddhism, however, is one aspect of a larger religious complex. Much of Thai Buddhism is not concerned with modern trends but remains diversely informed by multiple internal and external dialogues. In Chapter 4, I discuss this diversity in terms of the ways Thai Buddhists access the meditation retreat. Here I discuss one aspect of Thai Buddhism articulated within a particular historical moment, which has affected both the mass lay meditation movement in Thailand and how international meditators access the retreat.

Although modern Buddhism has occurred across the Buddhist landscape, each society encountered a particular engagement with this phenomenon.[11] In mid-nineteenth century Siam,[12] the intellectual atmosphere of the elite expressed more concern with modern sciences than traditional beliefs. The elite began to see certain Buddhist practices and beliefs as superstitions, while they strove to appear modern and civilized. A particular interpretation of Buddhism emerged as a way to demonstrate Siam's modernity (Winichakul 2000). During the three reigns of Rama IV, V, and VI,[13] prominent Siamese attempted to demonstrate that at its core, the essence of Buddhism is rational and dependent on empirical analysis.[14] These developments occurred within particular circumstances of colonialism, Christian missionization, and universal discourses of science and rationality. Therefore modern Thai Buddhism developed through particular historical situations and social factors.

Unlike Western modernity where Christianity was usually contrasted with secular rationality, in Siam ritual and protective aspects of Buddhism were counter posed by rational forms of Buddhism. Modern Buddhists were interested in separating themselves from both foreign religions and nondoctrinal and unorthodox forms of Buddhism. Craig Reynolds asserts that "the modernizing tendencies that gained strength during the nineteenth century tended to undercut the traditional cosmological orientations within Buddhism, at least among certain segments of the elite" (Reynolds 1977, 273). The following examples show how Siamese Buddhists created the idea of a modern Buddhism in light of these historical circumstances.

Before ascending the throne, Prince Mongkut created a reform sect called the Thammayut in 1829. Since the eleventh century, reform movements within Theravāda sought to establish pure ordination lineages from abroad and locate reliable texts (Thanissaro 2005, 10). Mongkut was no different and chose to follow Buddhist practices from the Mon people of Burma, whom he acknowledged as inheritors of a strict discipline, with a pure ordination lineage, and accurate ways of wearing monastic robes and holding the almsbowl. Besides this emphasis on correct practices, this discipline also included forest meditation

16　*Imagining Buddhism*

practices revived from the Pāli Canon, and a strict adherence to the Pāli Vinaya (Thanissaro 2005, 5). This sect followed this traditional pattern while also exemplifying a modern form of Buddhism, which focused on rational doctrine, disparaging local folk practices. Mongkut emphasized study of the Pāli Canon in understanding Buddhism and rejected popular texts such as the Jataka tales, stories of the Buddha's previous lives (Buswell & Lopez 2013, 696). Mongkut attempted to develop a kind of Buddhism consistent with Western science; therefore rejecting any teaching that makes supernatural claims and does not follow a scientific and universal truth. Nature and science became separated from religion and because of this some aspects of Buddhism came to be viewed as superstition and myth. One could determine which parts of the Pāli Canon fit these criteria through a deep knowledge of these scriptures, using rationality and critical analysis as a guide (Dhammasakiyo 2010, 30). King Chulalongkorn (Rama V) and King Vajiravudh (Rama VI) continued to promote this rationalized form of Buddhism that could face the Christian missionaries' critiques (Tiyavanich 1997, 213). In this way, the Thammayut sect emphasized textual fundamentalism, rationalism, and what they determined were the essentials of the Buddha's teachings (Reynolds 1972, 125).

An example of modern Buddhism at the state level can also be found in the writings of Vajiravudh (Rama VI). Vajiravudh has argued that the country's primary religion, Theravāda Buddhism, is superior, from an intellectual point of view, to religions practiced elsewhere. He compares Christianity unfavorably to Buddhism, saying that his tradition does not foster such incredible beliefs as virgin birth (Greene 1999, 72). Here we can see Vajiravudh is using categories of science and rationality to place Buddhism above other religions, thus constructing a particular kind of Buddhism that is appealing from a rational modern point of view. We will see throughout this book that an argument for the rationality of Buddhist meditation continues in publications of international meditation centers, assumptions of international meditators, and the teachings of international meditation center teachers.

Another early Siamese modern Buddhist, Prince Wachirayan, the supreme patriarch of Siamese Buddhism from 1910 to 1921 under King Chulalongkorn, inherited the rationalism with which Mongkut (Rama IV) applied to the Buddha's teachings. These new ideas about Buddhism became engrained in the minds of the elite men of Wachirayan's generation after Mongkut (Rama IV) set the stage with his reform movement. Wachirayan sought to distinguish what he deemed as 'original' Buddhism from later 'accretions,' and distrusted any aspect of Buddhism that did not stand up to rational explanation (Reynolds 1972, 144). In Wachirayan's *Biography of the Buddha*, he likens the Pāli Canon to a mangosteen with both the flesh and the rind. The duty of the scholar is to locate and extract the flesh based on the principles of rationalism, and discard the rind consisting of stories and miracles (Thanissaro 2005, 11). Wachirayan believed early Buddhism existed without any magical practices and sought to return to this particular understanding of the Buddhist tradition. In his autobiography, Wachirayan describes the shift in thinking toward a more rational understanding of the teachings. He writes:

Imagining Buddhism   17

[O]ne work which struck me was the Kalama-sutta which taught one not to believe blindly and to depend on one's own thinking. My knowledge and understanding at that time were typical of the modern dhamma student who chooses to believe some things but not everything.

(Reynolds 1979, 30)[15]

Thus some parts of the Buddhist tradition do not cohere with modern values and these were the passages that Wachirayan chose not to believe. Some passages he considered to have been inserted by later generations, and other incredible passages he interpreted as allegories and metaphors (Reynolds 1979, 30). He selected those elements, which he deemed reasonable and used them in his creation of a centralized monastic education system.[16]

Presbyterian missionary Henry Alabaster presents an international example of modern Buddhist writing at this time in *The Wheel of the Law*. This study of Siamese Buddhism was published in London in 1871 and based on Alabaster's many conversations with Minister of Foreign Treasury, Chao Phraya Thipakorawong. Alabaster wrote that in his work he sought to "give a glimpse of the reasonable religious teaching and beautiful morality which lie buried among the superstitions of corrupted Buddhism" (Alabaster 1971, 247). The work reveals that Thipakorawong was critical of Siamese Buddhist beliefs, which contradicted empirical testing and logical rationality (Alabaster 1971, 2). Thipakorawong followed in the tradition of Mongkut and posited a form of modern Buddhism that was influential for Siamese and foreigners. His 1867 book *Kitchanukit* (A Book Explaining Many Things), and Alabaster's translation of part of this titled *Modern Buddhist*, gave both Thai and English-speaking audiences a particular version of Buddhism that was again meant to be based on science and rationality, and what Thipakorawong deemed 'universal' modern truths. Another modern Buddhist in the lineage of Mongkut was Supreme Patriarch Sa Pussadevo, who wrote *Pathamasambodhikatha*, a life story of the Buddha that stripped away all supernatural elements, demythologizing and humanizing his life (Dhammasakiyo 2010, 38).

These descriptions of early Siamese modern Buddhism show the impact of international encounters as well as the shifting ideas about religion and interpretations of Buddhism among the influential Siamese of this period. As Justin McDaniel points out, however, there is still a great diversity within Thai Buddhism. The effect of the Thammayut sect was not to copy the West or control all of Thai Buddhism (McDaniel 2011, 130). Nevertheless, international meditators imagine Buddhism through this same modern Buddhist lens. These early modern Buddhists in Thailand and throughout the world helped to shape the imaginings of Buddhism that are present today. International meditators often hold these ideas of modern Buddhism and utilize them when in dialogue with their teachers during the retreat program.

Studying international meditators

International meditators arrive in Thailand mostly from North America, Europe, and Australia.[17] Some East Asian meditators join English-speaking retreats, but

18   *Imagining Buddhism*

they are a small minority. In fact, in my interviews, international meditation center teachers often spoke of their international students as being mainly from the West, calling them *khon farang* or *khon dawaan dok*. These teachers also characterize some of their students as having book knowledge about Buddhism with some exposure to Buddhist practice. However, for the most part the teachers characterize the students as having limited understanding of Buddhism and meditation. Their relatively superficial knowledge thus begs the question: Why study this group of people?

For any religious tradition or system of thought there will be specialist and lay understandings. Most Buddhist laity realize that monks and other specialists understand more than they do about the religion, but this does not mean that lay Buddhists or international meditators are not worthy of research. But at the same time we cannot define Buddhist practices by the ways international meditators understand them. Julia Cassaniti (2006) argues for the importance of the individual for understanding Buddhist experiences and perspectives. In this way there are no correct or incorrect, authentic or inauthentic forms of Buddhism, only different understandings. She writes that "from contextualized experiences one interprets Buddhism in personal ways according to social positions and individual perspectives" (Cassaniti 2006, 84). Nancy Eberhardt concurs that "we cannot define Buddhism or any other complex tradition solely on the basis of what its virtuosi believe and do" (Eberhardt 2006, 9). I have utilized these insights by focusing not only on Buddhist leaders and teachers, but also on individuals who are engaging with Buddhism for a limited but intense period.

In fact international meditators are doing just that—engaging with Buddhism, rather than practicing religiously. Most often they participate in a meditation retreat as part of an eclectic spirituality. Courtney Bender (2010) has thought the most clearly about this type of religious engagement through her analysis of spiritual metaphysicals in Cambridge, Massachusetts. Spirituality is free floating, individualistic, and lacking some organization but it is entangled within "various religious and secular histories, social structures, and cultural practices" (Bender 2010, 182). This focus on practice and spirituality is an increasingly important way to analyze religious cultures. Bender asserts that even though spiritual practices are organized differently and learned in different ways, this does not make them less religious (Bender 2010, 183). Instead of seeing international meditators as superficial practitioners, I find that their imaginaries as well as relationships with meditation practice and exchanges with their teachers illustrate processes of historically embedded dialogues and relationships, as discussed above. International meditators are conscious and reflexive about their choices to enter into a retreat program and how it fits within their own worldviews.

Similar to connections with studies of spirituality, studying international meditators is comparable to the scholarship of popular Buddhism, which until recently was often considered a superficial undertaking. Pattna Kitiarsa (2012), Justin McDaniel (2011), and Donald Swearer (2010) have argued for the significance of studying popular Buddhism in Thailand, noting the importance of amulets, merit-making, magic monks, and ghost stories within the everyday lives of Thai

Imagining Buddhism 19

Buddhists. I incorporate all of these views as I describe the engagement with Buddhism of international meditators. Kitiarsa describes popular Buddhism as "a vast, real and imagined religio-social space, encompassing monastery, marketplace, media and private home altar. Its beliefs and practices span the past and the present. Its market value is highly dynamic. Its membership is enormous" (Kitiarsa 2012, 1). Popular Buddhism is also distinguished by its loose organization, dominant charismatic personalities, pragmatism, and this-worldly orientation rather than towards scriptures or attainments (Kitiarsa 2012, 2). Within popular Buddhism, practitioners are continually responding and giving feedback to processes of modernization and globalization. Rather than passive objects of larger structural forces, popular Buddhism contributes to dynamic processes of Buddhist change and adaptation (Kitiarsa 2012, 6).

Thai Buddhists creatively utilize the means available to them to understand their world and participate in modern religiosity (McDaniel 2011). McDaniel discusses how the popularity of magic monks and ghosts has escaped the attention of scholars as legitimate subjects. He argues that these topics are worthy of attention and analysis because they matter to people. McDaniel writes that "if we are going to learn from the various Thai ways of being Buddhist, then it is more useful to look at what complex technologies people actually employ to solve problems" (McDaniel 2011, 12). Swearer (2010) also takes into consideration the discrepancy between the highest ideals of Buddhism and the current everyday practices that are observable in Thai Buddhist religious life. He writes that any scholarly work on Thai Buddhism should reflect on these everyday practices as well as the contradictions inherent within popular Buddhism (Swearer 2010, 2). Popular "does not mean less serious, less worthy, or further removed from the ideal; rather, it refers to Theravāda Buddhism as it is commonly perceived, understood, and practiced by the average traditional Sri Lankan, Burmese, Thai, Cambodian, and Laotian" (Swearer 2010, 3). In the same way that the popular tradition of Buddhism is worthy of study, newcomers to meditation and Buddhism are as well. A significant aspect of religious studies takes into account lived, modern religiosity, of which popular forms of Buddhism as well as international meditators play a part. International meditators demonstrate how Buddhism is lived, adapted, embodied, and translated in contemporary Thailand.

Chapter summaries

In order to foreground the historical context of international meditation centers in Thailand, I first turn to the circumstances that led to the popular practice of *vipassanā* meditation in 'Theravāda meditation and the history of modern *vipassanā*.' At the outset, this chapter describes the path to *nibbāna* from a Theravāda perspective in order to demonstrate the complexity of Theravāda thought. Second, this chapter offers an overview of the mass lay meditation movement in Burma and Thailand. The creation of the institution of the lay meditation center is given explicit attention, illustrating the trajectories through which international meditation centers became popular. Chapter 3, "The field of international

20 *Imagining Buddhism*

engagement with Thai meditation centers" offers an overview of the popular sites and practices of international meditators in order to orient the reader into this world. Highlighting centers, teachers, and methods in Central, Northern, and Southern Thailand, I discuss the history of engagement for international meditators. In addition to delineating the social roles of the actors involved in these centers, the international meditators, and their teachers, this chapter also offers a snapshot of the various features and components of the international meditation center. Furthermore, Thai Buddhist understandings of *vipassanā* meditation are contrasted with those of the international meditators, highlighting the decontextualized nature of international meditators' conceptions of the practice.

The next chapter, "Narratives of international meditators' experiences" takes a look at the diversity of this group as well as offering portraits of long-term international meditators. This chapter highlights prominent discourses relating to meditation for international meditators, especially nature, tourism, therapy, and health. Long-term meditators are those ordained and lay teachers and volunteers who act as intermediaries between international meditators and Buddhist meditation practice. They represent a possible trajectory for some international meditators to become deeply engaged and committed to specific centers, teachers and meditation methods. The last part of this chapter takes a close look at international meditators' typical experiences and daily practices within two retreat centers with different programs.

After this background of the motivations and experiences of international meditators, Chapter 5, "Meditation for tourists in Thailand: Commodifying a universal and national symbol," explores the representations of meditation in tourism brochures, meditation guidebooks, and meditation retreat pamphlets in Thailand. Investigating these materials through a postcolonial lens, I argue that Romantic, ancient, authentic, and scientific discourses of meditation serve to reinforce Orientalist ideas of an Other, as well as consumer values, constituting a commodification of meditation for tourists. Described as both modern, with its rational and scientific approach, as well as rooted within the traditional Thai monastic setting, meditation provides the best of all possible worlds for advertising a spiritual vacation. Although much has been said about consumerism within modern Thai Buddhism, the methods by which Thai Buddhists have tried to communicate meditation teachings and practices to a foreign audience have not been explored. I demonstrate that this commodification is an example of the creative adaptations possible for reaching a wide variety of audiences.

Advertisements represent the initial encounter and assumptions about Thai Buddhism and meditation. However, international meditation center teachers provide specific teachings and adaptations for their students based on imaginaries of meditation. Chapter 6, "Pedagogical techniques for translating *vipassanā* meditation" gives voice to the international meditation center teachers and their various pedagogical strategies. I discuss their translation of the Thai Buddhist retreat model into practices concerning individual choice and preference, psychological understandings of the self, and secular, universal interpretations of meditation.

Imagining Buddhism   21

Sometimes this translation is ineffective however, and this chapter lastly investigates the subversion and dissent of the retreat model by international meditators. Obeying the Buddhist codes of behavior in the temple, limited sleep and conversation, as well as restrictions on leaving the temple are all difficult rules to follow. I examine some of these transgressions and the reasons why translation and intercultural dialogue was unsuccessful. Overall this chapter describes the varying ways international meditation center teachers utilize, to varying extents, the discourses of modern Buddhism and imaginaries of meditation, and how this has emerged from a history of international engagement.

Next I turn back to the international meditators with a closer analysis of their bodily performance during the retreat in Chapter 7, "Embodying meditation." I argue that contrasted with the practices of the self seen in historical and ethnographic accounts of Christian and Buddhist monastic as well as Muslim practitioners' lives, international meditators are not participating in the retreat with tradition-specific goals. Because of the increased importance of self-authority and one's inner life in modernity, many international meditators exhibit discomfort with outward, external devotional practices within the retreat. I describe the ways their teachers make these external practices optional, allowing for the decontextualization of the retreat for international meditators. The chapter next turns to questions of conversion and religious identity. I argue that the project of the international meditation center lies in contrast with the scholarly literature discussing conversion and that religious identity is becoming less significant within the study of modern religion. The conclusion, "The future of Thailand's international meditation centers," describes the future of the institution of the international meditation center in Thailand and how missionizing practices of meditation abroad have resulted from connections made between international meditation center teachers and their students, creating new communities of practice in Thailand and throughout the world.

Conclusion

It is difficult to locate 'Buddhism' today as it has changed dramatically throughout the religions' history. Buddhism has been reformulated as it engages with each new time period and culture. Justin McDaniel writes about how the "lack of consensus of where Buddhism begins and ends remains today" (McDaniel 2011, 228). Buddhism has most recently been imagined through modernity, colonialism, encounters with other religions, secularism, and tourism. These various imaginaries are enacted in the reactions, assumptions, and reflections of international meditators as they engage with Buddhism in Thaiand. This book investigates this recent reimagining of Buddhism and the consequences of this including translation and commodification.

Throughout this book, I use McDaniel's (2011) helpful term, repertoire, to discuss the nature of religion for international meditators. He writes: "A repertoire is a constantly shifting collection of gestures, objects, texts, plots, tropes, ethical maxims, precepts, ritual movements, and expectations that any individual agent

22 *Imagining Buddhism*

employs and draws upon when acting and explaining action" (McDaniel 2011, 225). This repertoire can be inconsistent and contradictory. International meditators draw from the repertoires that are available to them through their cultural backgrounds, travel experiences, and through the discourses in modern Buddhism. Henrietta Moore finds that individuals do not have singular identities or even two or three different ones that can be parsed out and labeled modern, traditional, or hybrid. These identifications coexist and intersect but are not synchronized (Moore 2013, 81). International meditators add meditation to their religious and cultural repertoires without subtracting their own previous religious beliefs, practices and affiliations.

Because of the numerous well-known international meditation centers and opportunities to join retreat programs, many questions arise that will be explored throughout this book. How is this particular group of travelers learning about Buddhism? How do international meditation center teachers present meditation to non-Buddhists? What are the consequences of treating meditation as a decontextualized practice; what happens to ritual and devotional activities in this context? What kinds of new social spaces are being created through international meditation centers? What are the motivations and goals of international meditators? What are the significant discourses surrounding the promotion of meditation? How do these discourses in turn affect the ways meditation is taught? How are international meditators affecting Thai Buddhism, if at all? These are the questions that arose most prominently during fieldwork. Moreover, these questions connect with important discussions within the study of modern religion. Issues of religious identity, conversion, embodiment, commodification, and interreligious dialogue are all topics related to the people and spaces of Thailand's international meditation centers.

Notes

1 I use 'international' to indicate that international meditators are from countries other than Thailand. This is the term the centers use themselves, so international meditation centers are places where non-Thai people regularly participate. 'Meditator' here refers to a person who is currently taking part in a meditation retreat.
2 Although solid foods are not allowed after noon when participating in a meditation retreat, substances such as juice and some dairy products are allowed in the afternoon and evening as are medicines and tonics during times of sickness, hunger, or cold.
3 McMahan notes that this phenomenon is possible because of the construction of Buddhism as a 'way of life' that has no belief in a god-like figure, rendering it compatible with other traditions (McMahan 2008, 243). There are dozens of handbooks and memoirs of Jewish—Buddhist or Christian—Buddhist practice that demonstrate this. See for example MacInnes 2003; Knitter 2009; Johnston 1971; Boorstein 1996.
4 Wandering Dhamma Website existed on the Internet from 2009–2015.
5 I will use the former name, Burma, when referring to Myanmar's history before 1989, when the name was officially changed.
6 *Mae chii* are white-robed Thai Buddhist nuns. Because females cannot be fully ordained within the Thai sangha, the status of *mae chii* creates for the female renunciant a lifestyle that is more disciplined than that of a lay person, but does not adhere to as many behavioral rules as that of a fully ordained monastic.

7 Theravāda Buddhist countries include Sri Lanka, Mayanmar, Cambodia, and Laos. Sri Lanka and Myanmar were colonized by the British and Laos and Cambodia by the French. Thailand was never formally colonized; however, it still displays some of the attributes of a colonized nation.

8 Roughly, this colonial period can be taken to begin during the reign of King Mongkut (Rama V) in 1851 and last through the reign of King Vajiravudh (Rama VII) in 1925. During this time period Siam faced Western colonial powers in a substantial way for the first time. Siam's name was changed to Thailand in 1939.

9 For a critique of this view see Winichakul (1994).

10 Desire for religious tourism and the commodification of this experience was possible due to the role of print capitalism (Anderson 2006). According to Anderson, print-capitalism, or the expansion of printed materials, contributed to the historical rise of nationalism and the sense of imagined nations. People who spoke and read one vernacular became aware of the many others like them who spoke and read the same vernacular. This contributed to a sense of an "imagined community" (Anderson 2006, 44–46). In a similar way, people who have access to printed materials about meditation are able to imagine themselves as part of a larger community, practicing meditation in an exotic setting in the mountains of Asia.

11 An earlier version of this section was published in *Explorations, A Graduate Student Journal of Southeast Asian Studies*. See Schedneck (2010).

12 In this section I use the former name of Thailand, Siam when referring to the country's history before 1939, when the name was officially changed.

13 King Mongkut (Rama IV; 1851–1868), King Chulalongkorn (Rama V; 1868–1910), and King Vajiravudh (Rama VI; 1910–1925).

14 I am not arguing that the monarchy was solely responsible for modernizing Siam but that their collective reigns mark a period of challenge and negotiation with modernity.

15 The Kalama Sutta in the Anguttara Nikaya (AN 3.65) is often cited by modern Buddhists as evidence of the Buddha's positive evaluation of self-authority. For a critique of this interpretation see Bhikkhu Bodhi (2010).

16 Justin McDaniel questions the significance of the Sangha Act of 1902 for the centralization of the Thai Sangha (2006, 69). He investigates education systems within Northern Thailand and finds that this law did not establish a definitive break between modern and premodern. McDaniel argues that little in the way of standards or systems from Sangha Act of 1902 are in place within Northern Thai manuscript libraries (McDaniel 2008, 85).

17 Very few international meditation centers track the nationalities of their international meditators. This information is based on interviews with international meditation center teachers. When discussing teaching international meditators with them, their generalizations of the population encompassed Westerners from English-speaking countries and other parts of Europe. However, two research sites under consideration here, Wat Rampoeng and Wat Prathat Doi Suthep, have calculated the countries of international meditators since 2006. At Wat Rampoeng from 2006 to 2010 Americans were the most numerous group, with German and other European countries, Canadian, British, and Australian populations making the top ten groups. At this same temple, there seemed to be a shift beginning in 2011, as Chinese meditators began to visit Wat Rampoeng in large numbers. At Wat Doi Suthep the statistics reveal similar trends in terms of the highest populations of international visitors arriving from North America, Europe, and Australia. However here the number of Chinese meditators has not risen significantly.

2 Theravāda Buddhism and the history of modern *vipassanā*

Vipassanā meditation, through the discourses of modern Buddhism, has become one of the most significant pathways to communicate Buddhist teachings to an international audience. Traditionally, *vipassanā* meditation had been taught almost exclusively within monastic institutions through close teacher-disciple relationships. Within its modern history, the practice has spread to Buddhist laity with the relatively new institution of the lay meditation center, where replicable methods of meditation allow for a large number of students to practice at once. Most recently this global religious practice further expanded to reach an international audience of non-Buddhists. These trajectories of *vipassanā* meditation highlight the reimaginings of the practice.

This chapter first demonstrates the complexity of *vipassanā* meditation, providing information on the practices, sources, and path to liberation of Theravāda Buddhism. This is not meant to be comprehensive but instead introduces for the reader the intricacy of *vipassanā* meditation as it is embedded within the Theravāda Buddhist world. The Buddhist path to the end of suffering contrasts with the decontextualized nature of the practice for international meditators, which is highlighted in later chapters. The next section describes the history of modern *vipassanā* in Burma and Thailand. Particular contexts in each country created distinct formations of *vipassanā* meditation centers. Colonialism, Buddhist sectarian rivalry, politics, and the rise of the urban middle class affected the ways meditation became a lay Buddhist practice and then a practice an international, non-Buddhist audience could participate. This modern history of *vipassanā* meditation illustrates the processes through which this practice has produced new spaces for international travelers to engage with Thai Buddhist culture and participate in this global religious practice. In order to understand the goals of *vipassanā* meditation I turn first to the Buddhist path to *nibbāna*.

The path to *nibbāna*

The Eightfold Path is recognized by Theravāda Buddhists as articulating aspects along the path to *nibbāna*.[1] These eight features can be divided into three main parts: morality (*sīla*), concentration (*samādhi*), and wisdom (*paññā*).[2] According to this path, morality must be cultivated first as the basis for the other practices (Cousins 1973, 117).[3] In meditation retreat settings, morality is cultivated by

The history of modern vipassanā   25

taking a series of precepts as a framework for the development of a pure mind.[4] *Samatha* (concentration) meditation is part of the second aspect of the path, which is concerned also with correct effort and mindfulness. In the modern interpretation of this path, these two aspects of the practice are performed in preparation for the cultivation of wisdom, which is to be achieved through *vipassanā* (insight) meditation. Therefore both *samatha* and *vipassanā* are widely seen to be a significant part of the path to *nibbāna* (Cousins 1973, 116).

The two main meditation techniques used in Theravāda Buddhism[5] are *samatha* and *vipassanā*. These two types of meditation are not separate but complementary and must be in balance in order to progress along the Buddhist path of practice (Thanissaro 2011, no page). Within modern *vipassanā* meditation methods, the relationship between *samatha* and *vipassanā* is complex and is debated among different lineages and teachers, which I discuss later in this chapter. However, although lineages and traditions throughout the Theravāda world have articulated techniques and methods for these two types of meditation, in general the meditator must calm the mind and then apply this to investigation and insight (Gethin 1998, 176). *Samatha* is usually translated as 'calm' and has synonyms such as tranquility, one-pointedness of mind, unification of the mind, and a state of undistractedness, but I will refer to it here as concentration meditation. *Samatha* is often regarded as a state of mind, which either focuses exclusively on one object or consists of a state of awareness where the mind is steady and one-pointed (Shankman 2008, 4). The purpose of *samatha* meditation is to train the mind to remain focused rather than distracted. This training allows meditators to pay close attention to one object by continually bringing awareness back to that object when the mind wavers. This functions to bring the mind to a state of clarity, which can temporarily block mental defilements of the five hindrances (*nivāran a*), including sensual desire, ill-will, tiredness and sleepiness, restlessness and remorse, and doubt (Gethin 1998, 175). The experiences of *samatha* meditation are considered pleasant and important attainments that can also allow access to supernatural abilities (Crosby 2013, 141). Varying degrees of this practice are seen as necessary for perceiving reality directly through the practices of *vipassanā* meditation.

One can develop extremely deep states of concentration, called *jhānas*, by focusing the mind on one object for an extended period of time. When a *jhāna* state is reached, the mind is not in its ordinary condition but is temporarily outside of disturbances of the five senses (Gethin 1998, 176). The *jhānas* are eight states of mental absorption that the Buddha learned from his teachers before attaining *nibbāna*.[6] After mastering these states, the Buddha found that the *jhānas* alone could not alleviate his suffering. Indeed, *jhāna* practice is intended as a stage of preparation, not a goal in itself (Cousins 1973, 117). Instead he perceived the *jhānas* as stepping-stones to liberation,[7] and they have been a pillar of Buddhist practice since the tradition's inception. The first *jhāna* state arises as a result of the mental factors or limbs of applied (*vitakka*) and sustained (*vicāra*) attention. After this, joy (*pīti*)[8] and bliss (*sukha*) arise. Finally the fifth limb of the one-pointed mind (*ekaggatā)* arises, allowing the mind to become unified and rest on one object of consciousness (Gethin 1998, 181). If the meditator continues this

26   *The history of modern* vipassanā

practice, one can continue to attain further *jhānas* until reaching the fourth *jhāna*, which is accompanied only by the mental factor of equanimity (*upekkhā*). After one attains the fourth *jhāna*, one has a choice to continue to practice further the next four formless (*arūpa*) *jhānas*, try to attain supernormal powers (*abhiññās*),[9] or pursue insight meditation (Gethin 1998, 185). The goal of insight meditation is the attainment of the four stages of *nibbāna*.[10]

The *ariya-puggala*, or the Noble Ones is the supermundane (*lokuttara*) path of training that leads to *nibbāna*. Each attainment is achieved in succession and is accompanied by distinct transformations. The first path is the stream-enterer (*sotāpanna*), who will take a maximum of seven lifetimes to attain *nibbāna*. The second path is known as the once-returner (*sakadāgāmin*), who will be reborn only one more time before reaching liberation. The non-returner (*anāgāmin*) is on the third stage of the noble path. This term refers to one who will not be reborn as a human but will either attain *nibbāna* in this lifetime or be reborn in one of the highest heavens and attain *arhatship* there.[11] The fourth noble person is the *arhat* who has reached *nibbāna*. Along this path of the *ariya-puggala*, defilements[12] are continually destroyed until one has completely eradicated them as an *arhat* (Nyanatiloka 2004, 23–25). This is the culminating experience of the Buddhist path that includes cultivation of morality, concentration, and wisdom.

Vipassanā meditation, Buddhists hold, leads to *nibbāna* and the disappearance of defilements, through understanding the nature of suffering (*dukkha*), imperma-nence (*anicca*), and non-self (*anattā*) (Gethin 1998, 187). One first understands the existence of suffering, impermanence, and non-self within oneself and then extends to other people to understand it as a general principle of reality. Burmese Buddhist monk and meditation teacher, U Silananda calls contemplating your own body 'direct *vipassanā*' and contemplating the experiences of others 'inferential *vipassanā*' (Silananda 2002, 39). When a meditator contemplates clearly into the nature of the mind, this meditator is using the methods of *vipassanā* meditation (Gethin 1998, 175). This contemplation is not an abstract concept but beyond con-ceptual, intellectual thinking and directed toward understanding the Four Noble Truths: seeing suffering, its cause, its cessation, and the path leading to its cessa-tion (Gethin 1998, 188). In *vipassanā* one moves from object to object, staying with what is most dominant (Shankman 2008, 56). This is accomplished through awareness of one's reality and applications of mindfulness to bodily sensations, feelings or emotions, actions of the mind, and mind objects, where one comes to perceive directly the characteristics of reality.[13]

There is a range of practices and methods aimed at understanding the nature of the mind and suffering. In both modern practice and ancient manuals, the point during meditation practice where one turns to contemplate the three characteristics of real-ity is not fixed (Gethin 1998, 188). Therefore there are competing claims regarding the amount of concentration necessary before proceeding to *vipassanā* meditation, ranging from developing a high level of concentration to a minimum basis of calm (Cousins 1996, 38). Modern teachers demonstrate both of these extremes. At one end is Burmese monk Pau Auk Sayadaw,[14] who advocates attaining all eight *jhānas* before moving to *vipassanā* practices. At the other is Mahasi Sayadaw, who asserts that lesser forms of concentration such as momentary concentration (*khanika-samādhi*)

The history of modern vipassanā   27

and access concentration (*upacara-samādhi*) provide a sufficient basis for *vipassanā*. Teachers who favor cultivating the *jhānas* before insight, therefore, sometimes debate with teachers who begin straightaway with *vipassanā* practices. Because *vipassanā* is agreed to be the only practice that can lead to *nibbāna*, teachers often claim that their method is true *vipassanā* and other methods rely too much on *samatha*. Another common disparagement critiques methods advocating low levels of *samatha* as '*sotāpanna*' factories because after a beginning course many students are told they attained stream-entry.[15] The existence of these very real debates was apparent to me even before I began my research. In talking to a Thai Buddhist in Arizona about my project and my previous experiences meditating in Chiangmai, she observed that I practice focusing on the rise and fall of the abdomen while she practices watching the breath move in and out of the nostril. She said this with an attitude that the nostril was a much superior point of attention. At the time I did not realize the implications of these distinct points of focus. After research on the various meditative techniques popular in contemporary Thailand, it is clear that this is a major point of contention surrounding Theravāda meditation. The significant feature here is that all the meditation methods within this study claim to derive from the authoritative canonical and commentarial texts of the Theravāda tradition. As well meditation methods are created within the context of this path and goal. The point of noting this is to compare this with the nature of foreign engagement with meditation, which is contextualized with different paths and goals.

Sources of Theravāda meditation

Meditation teachers often state that their meditation technique is reproduced directly from canonical Buddhist meditation texts. It is not within the purview of this book to judge whether these attempts are successful but to point out that there can be no direct reproduction as interpretation is always involved. Additionally, the proliferation of diverse meditation methods that purport to be based on Buddhist texts attests to the great possibilities of variable readings. Within modern Theravāda Buddhism, meditation teachers and their didactic methods draw mainly from three authoritative texts along with their teachers, lineages, and traditions. These are two suttas of the Pāli Canon, called the Satipaṭṭhāna Sutta and the Ānāpānasati Sutta, which are treated by Buddhists as direct teachings of the Buddha, and the commentary by Buddhaghosa from the eighth century called the Visuddhimagga.[16]

The most significant meditation teaching for the modern revival of *vipassanā* meditation is the Satipaṭṭhāna (The Four Foundations of Mindfulness) Sutta.[17] Many *vipassanā* meditation teachers assert that all instructions and practices necessary for *vipassanā* meditation are contained in this sutta.[18] The Satipaṭṭhāna Sutta gives instruction on meditation by describing these Four Foundations of Mindfulness: body (*kāya*), feelings (*vedanā*), mind (*citta*), and mind objects (*dhamma*). Each of these foundations delineates a set of practices to follow with the aim of *nibbāna*. For some of the meditation practices described within this sutta it is unclear whether they should be performed as *samatha* or *vipassanā* meditation, therefore the interpretation varies depending on the meditation teacher and method of practice (Shankman 2008, 54).

28 *The history of modern* vipassanā

With each of these applications of mindfulness the meditator progresses toward increased sensitivity and awareness; however, each foundation of mindfulness continues to be relevant on the path towards *nibbāna* (Anālayo 2008, 21). The first practice delineated in this text is mindfulness of the body, where one contemplates one's own body through fourteen different applications. These include awareness of one's breath (whether its quality is long or short), the four postures of the body (sitting, lying, standing, walking), reflection on the repulsiveness of the body,[19] the four material elements in the body (earth, water, fire, and air),[20] and nine cemetery contemplations.[21] These basic practices form the basis for contemplations of more abstract qualities such as feelings and states of the mind (Anālayo 2008, 19). Furthermore, different meditation methods within the contemporary Theravāda world utilize different practices regarding contemplation of the body.[22] Since the sutta provides a variety of options instead of one standard program for all meditators, meditation teachers have selected the practices they find most suitable for their students.

The next two applications of mindfulness are associated with fewer practices. For mindfulness of feelings one notes three types—pleasant, unpleasant, and neutral—that comprise one's experiences in the present moment. These practices emphasize the changing nature of one's feelings in order to understand them as impersonal and impermanent states. Practices associated with mindfulness of the mind include being aware of the state of the mind, if it is concentrated or distracted, and whether the qualities of greed, hatred, and delusion are present or absent. Similar to mindfulness of feelings, the practice of mindfulness of the mind facilitates the perception of mind states as impermanent and not belonging to a self (Shankman 2008, 22).

The fourth application of mindfulness, mind objects or *dhammas*, entails contemplating five sets of mental and material objects including the five hindrances, the five objects of clinging, the six internal and external sense-bases, the seven factors of enlightenment, and the Four Noble Truths (Shankman 2008, 21–22). Each of these contemplations is meant to remove attachment, craving, and wrong view. The Satipaṭṭhāna Sutta concludes with an assurance that through these practices successful meditators can expect to reach the level of non-returner or *arhat*. These practices associated with the Satipaṭṭhāna Sutta have developed into various meditation methods throughout the Buddhist world (Anālayo 2008, 22). There are many applications of mindfulness within these four foundations, and different teachers emphasize certain practices while removing or deemphasizing others. For example, within contemporary Theravāda meditation methods, practices for the contemplation of the body occur much more frequently than those utilizing the last three foundations of mindfulness.

The Ānāpānasati (Mindfulness of Breathing) Sutta is the other important teaching in the Pāli Canon regarding meditation.[23] The instructions in this sutta have been used as preparatory practices in developing Satipaṭṭhāna practices, although the sutta itself claims that mindfulness of breathing alone can encompass all four foundations (Shankman 2008, 28). Here mindfulness of breathing is detailed in sixteen steps that follow a similar program to that of the Satipaṭṭhāna

The history of modern vipassanā   29

Sutta. Each of the Four Foundations of Mindfulness in the Ānāpānasati Sutta is practiced through the awareness of breath. It begins with understanding that the duration of breath can vary. The next steps describe how, as one deepens in concentration, one trains the mind in experiencing the pleasant feelings that accompany this. In the final steps, the meditator directs this level of purification of the mind toward insight practice (Shankman 2008, 30). Therefore the first twelve steps can be considered *samatha* practices and the last four contemplate *vipassanā* knowledges such as impermanence, fading away, cessation, and letting go. The Ānāpānasati Sutta shows how *vipassanā* practices build upon the foundation of *samatha* (Buddhadasa Bhikkhu 2001, 83). This sutta offers a number of practices associated with the breath out of which meditation teachers have been able to establish a variety of methods. Within one interpretation of the Ānāpānasati Sutta, Buddhadasa Bhikkhu offers a number of practices, shortcuts, and tricks to progress.[24]

Both of these meditation suttas in the Pāli Canon[25] are open to a range of interpretations by contemporary teachers. These suttas were recited orally and contain many repeated phrases in order to aid in memorization. Since they were not intended as meditation manuals, the suttas do not impart the full practice and provide little descriptive detail.[26] As a result, all meditation methods contain both *vipassanā* and *samatha*, but differ in the amount of each component (Shankman 2008, 101). In contrast to the Pāli Canon suttas, the Visuddhimagga is a systematic presentation of the stages leading to *nibbāna*, with detailed instructions on how to reach liberation (Shankman 2008, 54). Buddhaghosa, an Indian monk who lived in Sri Lanka, wrote the Visuddhimagga (Path of Purification) in the fifth century (Ñāṇamoli 2010, xxxiii). This work is another authoritative source that Theravāda Buddhists use to understand the practice of meditation and remains one of the most influential postcanonical texts (Ñāṇamoli 2010, xlviii). Although an independent composition and an explication of the Buddha's teachings, the Visuddhimagga uses as a framework two verses from the Samyutta Nikāya (Heim 2013, 8).[27] Buddhaghosa structured the text by using the tripartite path that leads to morality, concentration, and wisdom.[28]

Instead of using *samatha* and *vipassanā* practices within one discourse as in the Pāli suttas, the Visuddhimagga envisions two distinct paths in the form of a meditation handbook (Griffiths 1981, 606). The first path uses *samatha* to a high degree without *vipassanā* and the second focuses almost exclusively on *vipassanā*. For the *samatha* path, Buddhaghosa introduces forty meditation objects that relate to the meditator's temperament in order to cultivate *jhāna* states. Once one emerges from the *jhāna* state, one begins practicing insight. On the insight path, the first *jhāna* or lower levels of concentration may be attained, as one practices awareness of the changing nature of experience. Buddhaghosa discussed *vipassanā* practice without *jhāna* called 'dry insight' because there is no 'moisture' from the *jhānas* on this path (Shankman 2008, 55–56). The Visuddhimagga has significantly influenced the way *samatha* and *vipassanā* practices are taught and understood within Theravāda Buddhism and specifically in Thailand (Tambiah 1984, 28). This text has informed and influenced the ways recent *vipassanā* meditation teachers

30   *The history of modern* vipassanā

interpret the Pāli suttas, as contemporary methods often underscore a distinct separation between *samatha* and *vipassanā* practices (Cousins 1996, 42).[29]

Within the path of morality, concentration and wisdom, Buddhaghosa describes the development of stages of insight knowledge (*ñana*) (Buddhaghosa 2011, 609–744). This is meant to be a descriptive account of what occurs naturally when following the Buddhist path. The sixteen stages of *vipassanā* knowledge[30] unfold as one reaches higher and more advanced insight through directly perceiving reality during *vipassanā* practice. These stages are expected to progress in the same order for every practitioner. However, meditators will remain at one level for varying amounts of time. This list of stages is meant for advanced practitioners and for teachers to evaluate their students.

The Pāli suttas and the Visuddhimagga have been interpreted in various ways among contemporary *vipassanā* teachers, creating a multiplicity of methods. These methods include a range of *samatha* practices from minimal to experiencing *jhāna* states and *vipassanā* techniques using traditional objects such as the breath but also daily activities such as eating, or other daily activities. To greater and lesser degrees modern *vipassanā* movements emphasize this distinction between *samatha* and *vipassanā* types of meditation. Both *samatha* and *vipassanā* practices are used within Thailand's international meditation centers, and all centers claim to use the same authoritative meditation sources described earlier. Before describing the *vipassanā* techniques that international meditators encounter in contemporary Thailand, one must first understand the modern reimagining of *vipassanā* meditation. This reimagining of the practice has eventually led to the meditation retreat being practiced with goals decontextualized from the Theravāda path outlined above. Only recently, with the rise of lay meditation for Theravāda Buddhists, have spaces been created for international meditators.

The history of modern *vipassanā* meditation

In order to understand meditation's recent appeal to foreigners it is important to recognize the history and discourses surrounding the practice. The trajectory of *vipassanā* meditation begins primarily as a monastic practice, becomes a mass lay movement in Burma and then Thailand, and finally opens to international meditators. Each trajectory produces reimaginings of the practice. Although there are two main forms of meditation, *samatha* and *vipassanā*, *vipassanā* meditation has become especially dominant in the revival of interest in meditation in Theravāda Buddhist countries. This rhetoric of meditation within modern Buddhism can be traced to twentieth century Asian Buddhist reforms, which were at least partly influenced by developments in the West. The idea that meditation is the central practice of Buddhism can be found in the collaborations and dialogues between Asian religious leaders[31] and interested intellectual Westerners (Sharf 1998, 99). *Vipassanā* meditation techniques became portable, standardized, repeatable techniques developed along with lay urban meditation centers.[32] In this way *vipassanā* meditation became a global religious practice. As part of the discourses of modern Buddhism and ideals of modernity, it has been presented as a universal and scientific tool for the mind, rather than as a component of a religion or even part of the path to *nibbāna*.

The history of modern vipassanā   31

Historically, meditation has been the preserve of a few specialized meditation monks. These individuals studied meditation but did not practice or facilitate the institutionalized methods and centers for monastics or laity (Braun 2013, 2). There became a divide between monks whose primary practice was learning (*pariyatti*) or those whose 'burden is the book' (*ganthadhura*) and the practice of meditation (*paṭipatti*) or those whose 'burden is meditation' (*vipassanādhura*). The number of scholar-monks grew, as preserving knowledge of the textual tradition was deemed more critical. This rise in scholarship and division of labor was gradual, developing along with village temples (Carrithers 1983, 231). In this way town monks became more involved with scholarship and a separate category developed for meditation monks who often wandered throughout forests (Ray 1994; Tambiah 1984). However, these two types are not mutually exclusive so that village monks have been known to be meditation masters and forest monk communities contain noted scholar-monks as well (Tambiah 1984, 53).

Meditation monks were also scarce because it was believed that over time the Buddha's teaching will decline and the chances for liberation will be so rare that *nibbāna* will not be a reasonable goal even for monks.[33] Because *nibbāna* was seen as an almost impossible goal, meditation manuals such as the Visuddhimagga were not only used as guidebooks along the path but also as amulets (Sharf 1995, 241). One gained merit from interacting with the books themselves through copying, memorizing, chanting, or conducting various devotional activities.[34] In fact, Robert Sharf states that "the actual practice of what we would call meditation rarely played a major role in Buddhist monastic life" (Sharf 1995, 241). The closer ideal therefore, was a preferable rebirth attained through practices of merit making and studying scriptures. Meditation practices that scholars have found in premodern Buddhist societies were not *vipassanā* but *samatha* techniques of chanting Pāli texts which list the qualities of the Buddha or the thirty-two parts of the body (Sharf 1995, 242).

Meditation in Theravāda Buddhism uses the Pāli and Sanskrit word *bhavana*, meaning development or cultivation. This includes a range of practices such as performing rituals, studying, chanting, and keeping the precepts (Braun 2013, 5). Together with chanting meditation practices, devotion also played a role in meditation. Kate Crosby finds that in premodern Theravāda Buddhism, devotion and meditation are not located on opposite poles but "Devotion is advocated specifically for the religious specialist, the monk or layperson undertaking the more rigorous path of meditation practice aimed at Buddhahood" (Crosby 2005, 272). Using a survey of medieval meditation manuals, Crosby demonstrates that Buddha worship is advocated as preparation to meditation. Traditionally meditation began with these types of worship and that practice without these features is a modern phenomenon (Swearer 1995; Crosby 2005). It was not *vipassanā*, therefore, but the first two stages of the path, *samatha* practices of chanting and devotion, along with the cultivation of proper morality through generosity and maintaining the Five Precepts, that were thought to be more appropriate Buddhist practices.

In addition to the emphasis on study, devotion, and chanting, when meditation was practiced in premodern times, it was taught individually between a teacher

32   *The history of modern* vipassanā

and student, usually both monks with an established relationship. Following the Visuddhimagga, which lists forty meditation objects, a 'Good Friend' (*kalyana-mitta*) or meditation teacher who knows the student well, would be asked to assign one of these objects[35] to combat the defilements of that particular person (Shankman 2008, 59). Each meditation student needed to search for a teacher who could select the correct method for that student's character, considering the student's past experiences with meditation and his temperament (Kornfield 2010, 276). For example, meditation that concentrates on repeating statements of loving-kindness to all beings is prescribed for people with a propensity toward anger, and contemplation on dead bodies aids in combating excessive lust (Carrithers 1983, 225). This highlights the importance of the teacher for Buddhist practice. The meditator should have faith in the Buddha's teachings just as one should trust their meditation teacher. Therefore paying respect to one's teacher helps cultivate this faith (Gethin 1998, 179).

Buddhists traditionally believed that meditation, because of its powerful mental techniques, should only be undertaken under the supervision of a monastic teacher whom one knows well. Kamala Tiyavanich finds that occasionally in the North and Northeast of Thailand during the first half of the twentieth century, wandering monks would teach laypeople *samatha* meditation as well as expound the *dhamma* during their travels (Tiyavanich 1997, 37). This kind of individual instruction still exists in some Buddhist communities within Thailand, Cambodia, and Myanmar today. However, this personalized relationship contrasts greatly with the rationalized, one-size-fits-all approach of large urban lay meditation centers meant for the masses.

This focus on Buddhist scholarship and individual instruction for monastics changed through *vipassanā* reform movements that repositioned meditation in the forefront of Buddhist practice. *Vipassanā* meditation underwent a process of laicization that ultimately opened the cultural sphere so that the practice became accessible to Buddhist laity as well as 'spiritual travelers' from abroad. Offering *vipassanā* meditation to laity on a large scale transformed the relationship of monastics to their lay students. Through these transfigurations, laity undertake steps toward liberation without taking up the vocation of a renouncer (Jordt 2007, 18). Monks are still teachers of the *dhamma* but the laity has become more monasticized. This term refers to how laity are now undertaking practices previously reserved for monastics. Within a meditation retreat, the laity come to act more like monastics, thus blurring the distinction between the two groups (Braun 2013, 99). This has reconfigured Buddhist practice in Burma and Thailand, as well as created openings for international meditators.

Famous monks in Burma, such as Mahasi Sayadaw (1904–1982), U Ba Khin (1899–1971), and their successors, made meditation a primary focus. Theravāda *vipassanā* reform movements, above all, emphasized the importance of meditation and offered this practice and its goal of *nibbāna* as a possibility for both laity and monastics. These reform movements, it must be remembered, took place amidst the backdrop of modernization and colonialism. Through these processes a new elite class emerged with Western-style education and a need to align

The history of modern vipassanā   33

themselves with their national culture and religion. Because of these societal changes, Theravāda Buddhism resembled less the traditional village practices and more the ideals of modernity such as individualism, rationality, and universalism (Bond 1988; Gombrich & Obeyesekere 1988). These reform movements, especially the one propagated by Mahasi Sayadaw, stress the speed and accessibility of *nibbāna*. Remembering that *nibbāna* was seen as an almost impossible ideal traditionally, even for monks, and that scholarship was deemed more appropriate, it is remarkable that Mahasi Sayadaw's courses, which typically last over one month, are aimed at attaining the first stage of enlightenment (*sotāpanna*).

The ability for laity to undertake meditation practice on a mass level could not occur without the new institution of the urban lay meditation center. The meditation center is different from any other Buddhist institution in history (Jordt 2007, 15) because the center is not a monastery but a place where both monks and laity practice meditation together.[36] This is a new type of institution in that it is preoccupied with a universalizing ideal about the possibility of *nibbāna* for anyone, Buddhist or not. This institution is designed for temporary meditation practice usually for large numbers of people. In addition to the core buildings of any monastery, the meditation center has ample facilities for the temporary resident meditators including accommodation, assembly halls, dining halls, kitchens, administrative offices, etc.[37] This administrative complex is needed to coordinate the large turnover of meditators on a regular basis that is not normally necessary for routine monastic life.[38] The daily routine of the meditation center is extremely regimented and revolves almost exclusively around the practice of meditation.[39]

This new institution began in Burma, transforming the laity's relationship with Buddhist practice (Houtman 1990, 18). The Burmese meditation center model and meditation methods spread to Thailand and beyond. This institution constitutes a reinterpretation of *vipassanā* meditation, which not only led to lay Buddhist practice, but also to opportunities for international meditators to engage with meditation. In what follows I describe the history and main actors of this transformation in Burma and Thailand.

Vipassanā meditation in Burma

The lay meditation movement began in Burma within the context of modernizing reforms of Theravāda Buddhism, influenced by the changes during colonial rule (1824–1948). The British colonial administration dismantled the kingship in 1885 and sought to create a rational, bureaucratized state. Because the monarchical state, which had protected Buddhism, no longer existed, Burmese teachers sought to lessen this degeneration through purifying the laity (Jordt 2007, 25). To this end, the well-known teacher, Ledi Sayadaw (1846–1923), expanded Buddhist learning opportunities beyond the monastic tradition during the colonial period. He was known for his ability and interest in writing commentaries of the Buddhist scriptures, especially the philosophical section of the Pāli Canon called the Abhidhamma, that were comprehensible to the laity. By allowing laity access to Buddhism in new ways he created the trajectories necessary to establish

34   *The history of modern* vipassanā

the institution of the meditation center. Although he did not begin the mass lay meditation movement and emphasized scripture study for laity, he argued that meditation could benefit anyone without needing to cultivate a large amount of calm and concentration first (Braun 2013, 6). He advocated this inclusive meditation practice, opening the practice more widely, thereby influencing the mass lay meditation methods in Burma. Erik Braun writes, "Ledi was one of the first teachers in the modern era to offer this approach of pure insight practice as a viable—even preferred option" (Braun 2013, 139). But for Ledi Sayadaw meditation was one factor and not the most important.

The simplified methods of influential Burmese meditation masters Mahasi Sayadaw and U Ba Khin enabled the laity to participate in *vipassanā* meditation, without having to attain the high levels of concentration associated with *samatha* meditation, and thus endorsed practitioners to strive for the goal of *nibbāna*. Mahasi Sayadaw, the most well-known student of the Mingun Jetavana Sayadaw (1870–1955), or U Narada, took these new possibilities for the laity further than previous lay teachers. U Narada developed his method through study of the Satipaṭṭhāna Sutta,[40] which Mahasi Sayadaw popularized. Mahasi Sayadaw studied the Mahā Satipaṭṭhāna Sutta thoroughly as well as practiced intensely under his teacher's guidance. Mahasi's method is also based on his own subcommentary of Bhuddhaghosa's Visuddhimagga, where he elaborated on the sixteen stages of *vipassanā* knowledge that lead to liberation, creating a more simplified and practical system (Jordt 2007, 65). His reputation spread within Burma because of his authoritative combination of study and practice. It was during the era of U Nu (1907–1995), the country's first democratic prime minister who led from 1948–1962, that meditation became a popular movement for laity. U Nu actively promoted mass meditation as a basis for nation-building and as part of a multifaceted program to revitalize Buddhism in Burma (Mendelson 1975, 263).

U Nu and Mahasi Sayadaw worked together to establish the first meditation center called the Mahasi Thathana Yeiktha, and subsequently a network of meditation centers for laity within Burma. These branch centers soon extended to Sri Lanka and Thailand. Beginning in the late 1950s, there were also visitors from the West coming to practice at the Mahasi Thathana Yeiktha so that *vipassanā* meditation linked Burma with the international community, and meditation was famously hailed as the country's leading export (Jordt 2007, 55). Ingrid Jordt relates that often an invitation for a monk teacher to visit international meditators' home countries ultimately generated construction of new branch centers abroad (Jordt 2007, 37). Through these connections, the method circulated further so that there are now centers throughout the world.[41] Therefore Mahasi Sayadaw not only spread this replicable method of meditation, he also disseminated a model for an urban lay meditation center.[42]

Mahasi Sayadaw's technique does not rely on the charisma of the teacher but can be replicated and expanded through a prescribed rationalized method (Jordt 2007, 32). His method is also unique within Theravāda Buddhism because the object of concentration is the rise and fall of the abdomen, as Mahasi argued it is easier to detect the physical experience of rising and falling than the breath

The history of modern vipassanā 35

coming in and out of the nostril or more abstract mental states (Jordt 2007, 65). Meditation teachers who promote the tip of the nostril as the focal point of the breath have questioned Mahasi's focus on this part of the body, as the abdomen is not listed as one of the Satipaṭṭhāna practices of the body. Mahasi justifies his choice in his *Practical Insight Meditation* by stating that the rise and fall of the breath in the abdomen constitutes wind element, which is part of the four elements meditation recommended in the Satipaṭṭhāna Sutta (Mahasi 1972, 59). Mahasi Sayadaw based his method on the idea that it would take the average person two months to achieve the first stage of enlightenment, a timeframe that he determined by observing many thousands of practitioners (Jordt 2007, 33). He describes his method in detail in *The Progress of Insight*. The practice begins with contemplation of the body that ultimately leads to the direct experience of impermanence, suffering, and non-self. Mahasi Sayadaw expanded on the contemplation of the postures of the body by including other small movements such as bending, stretching, or moving the foot (Silananda 2002, 31). The technique remains the same as the meditator reaches new stages of insight and even the first paths of *nibbāna*. Meditators only deepen their understanding of impermanence, non-self, and suffering through increasing recognition of previously held wrong views.

The Mahasi Thathana Yeiktha and each branch meditation center uses the same technique developed by Mahasi Sayadaw. The method starts as a 'dry' *vipassanā* practice without *samatha* meditation as preparation. The *vipassanā* practice is facilitated through periods of sitting and walking throughout the day while noting one's present experience in detail. The constant noting practice is meant to remind the meditator to maintain awareness but not to become interested in the content of one's experiences. The main practice in formal sitting meditation is to be aware of the rise and fall of the abdomen as one's central meditation object. Between the rise and fall of the breath, other thoughts will enter, each of which should be noted as well. One should be aware, or note, each activity one performs during the day from the moment one wakes up. As the beginning meditator progresses, the noting of concepts drops as physical experience becomes primary and the meditator is aware of the four elements such as heat (fire), breath (wind), etc. (Jordt 2007, 65). This method spread throughout the Theravādin world as *vipassanā* revitalization movements unfolded throughout South and Southeast Asia, along with a proliferation of other methods for lay practitioners. Consequently, it is common for lay meditators to dedicate themselves to a particular meditation teacher and a particular practice.

Besides Mahasi Sayadaw, another influential Burmese teacher for the *vipassanā* revitalization movement is U Ba Khin. U Ba Khin, a lay government official under Prime Minister U Nu, whose interest in *vipassanā* meditation began late in life, founded the International Meditation Centre in Rangoon in 1952. His primary teacher was Saya Thetgyi (1873–1945), who taught meditation during the first half of the twentieth century and was a direct disciple of Ledi Sayadaw (Braun 2013, 156–157). U Ba Khin developed his technique based on his own experience as well as the Satipaṭṭhāna Sutta. Instead of the rising and falling of the abdomen and the practice of noting, U Ba Khin's method involves sweeping the mind

36 *The history of modern* vipassanā

through the body, noticing every sensation in order to realize impermanence. The sweeping method is performed by paying attention to the body, part by part, noticing impermanence of all sensations. As one progresses, the sweeping becomes more rapid because energy flows in the body become unblocked. This develops until one experiences one's mind, body, and the world as a series of vibrations (Kornfield 2010, 251). According to U Ba Khin, one should practice this particular *vipassanā* technique after developing a certain level of concentration by focusing on the upper lip and feeling the in and out breath at this point. U Ba Khin chose to focus mainly on the body because this is the most accessible for beginning students (Kornfield 2010, 235). With his international meditation center and his international students, the influence of U Ba Khin constitutes another lineage of *vipassanā* meditation that has spread globally.

U Ba Khin himself was important because he developed a distinct, replicable method, but it was his student, S.N. Goenka (1924–2013), who more significantly propagated U Ba Khin's technique worldwide. Goenka was authorized to teach *vipassanā* by U Ba Khin in 1969, when he left Burma to bring the teaching to his homeland of India. From here the Goenka method has become a worldwide phenomenon with centers in North America, Europe, Australia, the Middle East, Africa, Latin America, and Asia. Goenka centers have had widespread popularity in Thailand, with nine centers often reaching capacity within a few days of announcing an upcoming meditation retreat.[43] As well, a center has opened in Battambang, Cambodia, where meditation is being used to relieve trauma in this postconflict society. Like the Mahasi method, Goenka's courses are replicable and portable, with authorized teachers and volunteers facilitating and playing videotapes of Goenka's instructions each evening. Through these tapes, Goenka's courses are enacted in almost exactly the same ways in each retreat facility.

Both U Ba Khin and Mahasi Sayadaw propagated meditation within Burma and abroad, initiating new trajectories and lineages[44] of *vipassanā* meditation. In addition to Goenka, another one of U Ba Khin's students was Ruth Denison who became an American *vipassanā* teacher.[45] Mahasi Sayadaw as well influenced the *vipassanā* movement in North America. This movement began in 1975 when meditation teachers Jack Kornfield, Joseph Goldstein, and Sharon Salzberg returned from their study of meditation in India, Burma, and Thailand, and purchased land for the construction of the Insight Meditation Society (IMS) in Barre, Massachusetts. Each of these American *vipassanā* teachers studied under Mahasi Sayadaw in Burma. For this reason, IMS still traces its lineage directly to Mahasi (Cheah 2004, 91).[46] Many international meditators have learned about *vipassanā* through the teachings and writings of these teachers.[47]

The presentation of Buddhism initiated by Ledi Sayadaw, Mahasi Sayadaw, and U Ba Khin facilitated adaptations to *vipassanā* meditation for their international students who became teachers in their countries. The openness and transcendence of any local or national Buddhist sect offered new international teachers a significant amount of flexibility to define *vipassanā* and its practices in their own ways (Cheah 2011, 58). Joseph Cheah argues that simplifying and rationalizing Buddhist practices to a single method of meditation and removing

The history of modern vipassanā   37

devotional practices created the context for reinterpretation, utilizing individualistic and secular ideologies (Cheah 2011, 48). The history of *vipassanā* meditation in Burma led to new reinterpretations in Thailand for both Thai Buddhist lay meditators and international meditators. The history of *vipassanā* in Thailand, as we will see, is linked to its emergence in Burma as a popular mass movement among urban and rural laypeople.

Vipassanā meditation in Thailand

In Thailand, newly formed Thai Buddhist sects propagated *vipassanā* meditation. The two trajectories of *vipassanā* meditation that formed in Thailand are characterized by their relationships with two distinct sects, Mahanikai and Thammayut. The Mahanikai sect borrowed the Mahasi method from Burma, while the Thammayut branch utilized the charisma of the wandering, meditating, forest monks, in what has come to be called the Thai forest tradition. These two trajectories shaped the understanding and practice of *vipassanā* in Thailand and had implications for international meditators.

The history of the creation of the reform sect Thammayut and the division of Thai Buddhism into two sects, the Mahanikai and Thammayut, has been covered by a number of scholars (McDaniel 2006; Tiyavanich 1997; Taylor 1993; Tambiah 1984; Reynolds 1972). What I want to highlight is how the creation of these sects contributed to the mass lay meditation movement in Thailand. In the nineteenth and early twentieth centuries, King Mongkut (1804–1868) and King Chulalongkorn (1853–1910) of the Chakri dynasty sought to centralize and purify the *sangha,* the community of Buddhist practitioners. As discussed briefly in Chapter 1, when he was a monk and before he ascended the throne, Prince Mongkut created a new sect in 1829 in response to what he thought were lax practices in order to protect an ideal of 'pure' Buddhism (Reynolds 1972, 63).[48] King Chulalongkorn furthered these reforms with his half-brother, Wachirayan, also a monk who later became abbot of Wat Bovonniwet, the head temple of the Thammayut sect, and eventually Supreme Patriarch of the *sangha.* King Chulalongkorn and Wachirayan sought to educate the nation and centralize the *sangha* by creating a national *sangha* hierarchy (McDaniel 2006, 104). What had once been characterized by variation and decentralization became a rationalized order with its distinctive system of monastic education and ecclesiastical rank (Tiyavanich 1997, 9). Because of this centralization, the leaders of both Mahanikai and Thammayut sects sought to be elected to the highest ranks by sponsoring and promoting meditation through different avenues and sources of legitimacy.

Phra Phimolatham (1903–1989), of Wat Mahathat,[49] a Mahanikai royal temple of the highest class, was the first to be successful in propagating meditation. Phra Phimolatham established *vipassanā* meditation branch centers in Mahanikai temples based on the method of Mahasi Sayadaw (Cook 2010, 30). He brought teachers from outlying regions of Thailand to Bangkok to train as meditation teachers and sent monks from Bangkok to Burma in order to learn the Mahasi method. After one of his students, Maha Chodok Yanasithi, returned with two

38   *The history of modern* vipassanā

Burmese teachers, Phra Phimolatham introduced and further developed Mahasi Sayadaw's *vipassanā* technique for the laity at Wat Mahathat and founded many other meditation centers throughout Thailand (Tiyavanich 1997, 228).

The selection of Mahasi Sayadaw's method was intentional for a number of reasons. Phra Phimolatham chose this method because it claimed to have roots in the Satipaṭṭhāna Sutta (Cook 2010, 27). He also preferred a generalized approach that didn't require a method specific to particular personality types, as was the traditional practice. Mahasi Sayadaw's one-size-fits-all method also had the advantage of being a 'dry' *vipassanā* technique, which meant that there was no preparatory *samatha* practice. Phra Phimolatham thought *vipassanā* especially appropriate for laity because they could practice at home without supervision, unlike *samatha*. Practicing *samatha* without supervision, within Theravāda Buddhism, is thought to be dangerous because it is considered possible to attain supernatural powers through the deep absorption states. The status of *samatha* has been denigrated because of this and is still deemed suspicious today (Cook 2010, 32–33). In this way *vipassanā* meditation, and not *samatha*, fit the image of a rational religious practice.

In the 1970s, increased standards of literacy, education, the development of an urban middle class, and new media such as cassette tapes allowed for the reproduction of popular teachings for a mass market. Before this time, meditation teaching was available only at monasteries with well-known meditation teachers in residence. When those teachers passed away, so did the opportunity to learn meditation (Tambiah 1984, 168). This changed through the widespread dissemination program of Phra Phimolatham and his successor, Phra Thepsiddhimuni, which trained monks from all regions of the country to teach meditation.[50] At Mahachulalongkornrajavidyalaya Buddhist University, within the grounds of Wat Mahathat, courses in meditation and Abhidhamma added to the available options (Van Esterik 1977, 56). At this time, the Abhidhamma, the section of the Pāli Canon that presents a scholastic and detailed analysis of physical and mental processes, was linked with meditation. Both studying the Abhidhamma and practicing meditation were seen as endeavors cohering with Western science for educated middle class urbanites. Through these transformations, once considered the preserve of specialized monks, meditation became a practice appropriate for a much larger audience that coincided with the newly rising urban middle class.

The popularity of *vipassanā* propagated by the Mahanikai sect affected the perception of the wandering *thudong* forest monks of the Thammayut sect.[51] Luangbu Man Phurithatto (1870–1949) initiated a revival of the forest tradition beginning in the 1920s.[52] In their rivalry, the Thammayut leaders co-opted the charisma of the forest meditation masters led by Luangpu Man, who were also a part of this sect, in order to continue to legitimate their reform movement and identity of this sect.[53] Before the *vipassanā* movement, forest monk practices were viewed as peripheral and strange. Luangpu Man had informal links with ecclesiastical elite in the capital that eventually led to his lineage's incorporation within the Thammayut order (Taylor 1993, 37). James Taylor writes that Luangpu Man and his disciples "remained on the rim of the establishment for much of their lives—yet constituted the mystical core of orthodoxy, eventually recognized at the centre" (Taylor 1993, 1).

The history of modern vipassanā   39

Relatively few laypeople or monks took up the practices of the forest tradition. These masters were symbolically important in their limited teaching of meditation to laypeople but did not formulate a method or institution. Therefore the most popular methods in Thailand remain those from Burma (Braun 2013, 123).

Luangpu Man's meditation teachings did not reach the level of a mass lay meditation movement in Thailand as compared to the Mahasi method imported from Burma. Tambiah argues that amulets blessed by forest monks were the major source of the forest monks' charisma and lay following,[54] rather than the actual propagation of meditation. Strict ascetic practices established the forest monks as a great field of merit but their austere *thudong* practice did not encourage the formation of lay meditation centers. Therefore, the forest tradition's meditation practices do not have as much bearing on the rise of the lay modern mass meditation movement in Thailand as those shaped through Mahanikai schools and the teachings they adopted from Burma (Van Esterik 1977, 52).[55] Through the expansion of *vipassanā* within the Thai religious landscape, Thai meditation teachers developed traditions following the Mahasi method and their own local contexts. The establishment of lay meditation centers in locations throughout the country created spaces for international meditators to practice in meditation retreat programs.

Conclusion

This history of modern *vipassanā* illustrates the trajectory that led to foreign engagement with meditation in Thailand. The path to *nibbāna*, authoritative sources used for meditation, and the various methods that arose demonstrate the complexity and controversy of *vipassanā* meditation as it is embedded within the Theravāda Buddhist world. In the next chapters we will see how the meditation retreat is embedded within different contexts for international meditators. Replicable meditation methods propagated by Mahasi Sayadaw and U Ba Khin in Burma created and spread a model for the meditation center and retreat format. Once the institution of the meditation center became easily transmissible and was not dependent on the knowledge or charisma of a particular teacher, branch centers could proliferate nationally and even internationally. Urban, lay, middle class Buddhists were drawn to the rational and scientific *vipassanā* practice and Abhidhamma classes. These particular historical trajectories of *vipassanā* meditation reveal the openings created for international meditators. Through modern Buddhist discourses of meditation's universalism, not only Buddhist laity but also foreign non-Buddhists could be included in the meditation retreat program. Because the practice was available for Thai laity, foreign visitors also sought to be included. When meditation teachers saw this interest from abroad, international meditation centers developed where English-speaking teachers and translators were available. Therefore in this chapter we have explored both the Theravāda path to liberation as a contrast to foreign engagement with meditation as well as the socio-historical circumstances that led to their involvement in Thai Buddhist meditation retreats. In the next chapter we will look at this more recent aspect of the formation of international meditation retreats in Thailand and the ways international meditators' engage with these new possibilities.

40   *The history of modern* vipassanā

Notes

1 The Four Noble Truths are the basic teachings of the Buddha that establish the basis for a path leading out of suffering. These truths state that suffering in life is unavoidable, there is a cause to this suffering, this cause is attachment, and finally, there is a way to end this suffering. This way is described further in the Noble Eightfold Path: Right Understanding, Right Thought, Right Speech, Right Action, Right Livelihood, Right Effort, Right Mindfulness, and Right Concentration. These are further classified within three groups: morality (speech, action, and livelihood), concentration (effort, mindfulness, and concentration), and wisdom (understanding and thought).

2 *Samatha* and *vipassanā* are two approaches to meditation found in the Pāli Canon. They became more distinct in Buddhaghosa's *Visuddhimagga*, an authoritative commentary discussed later in this chapter. These two types of meditation are differentiated more starkly in the modern period (Crosby 2013, 141).

3 In my fieldwork in Thailand, meditation teachers have emphasized that if one has lied or committed some other ethical misbehavior, it will be difficult to focus the mind in meditation as one's mind will continuously revert back to those transgressions.

4 Buddhist laity often receive the Five Precepts when visiting a temple. For retreats and holy days, three extra precepts are added. The Five Precepts include refraining from killing, stealing, sexual activity, lying, and intoxicants. In addition to these, the Eight Precepts include refraining from eating after noon each day, entertainment and beautification of the body, and sleeping in a luxurious bed.

5 Other branches of Buddhism use other systems such as Tibetan visualization, for example.

6 I am using here the standard system consisting of eight *jhānas*; however, in the Pāli sources there are other systems describing four, five, or nine *jhānas* (Griffiths 1981, 609).

7 The *jhānas* were a part of the Buddha's path to enlightenment throughout his life. Buddhist texts record that the Buddha first experienced a *jhāna* state spontaneously as a young boy while sitting under a tree. During his search for *nibbāna* the Buddha entered the ascetic life and began a systematic training in the *jhānas* (Mahasaccaka Sutta, MN 36). The night of the Buddha's enlightenment he entered the fourth *jhāna* before investigating the characteristics of reality (Ariyapariyesana Sutta, MN 26). It is also recorded that the Buddha's final act before death was to enter each of the *jhānas*, rising from the first to eighth, and back down to the first, settling back again and remaining at the fourth *jhāna* (Mahaparinibbāna Sutta, DN 16).

8 Cousins demonstrates that *pīti*, the bodily experience of joy, is central to understanding early Buddhism. The Visuddhimagga describes five different kinds of *pīti* from minor and momentary to more powerful and pervasive (Cousins 1973, 120).

9 These powers are described in the suttas as psychic powers, the divine ear, the ability to read minds, the ability to remember past lives, the divine eye, and the destruction of corruptions (Shankman 2008, 50).

10 Cousins describes two types of practitioners: one whose vehicle of practice is calm and one whose vehicle is insight. Both vehicles lead to *nibbāna*; however, the vehicle of calm allows one to develop the four *jhānas* and optionally the higher *jhānas* or psychic powers, before moving on to insight meditation. One whose vehicle is insight does not cultivate the *jhānas* before practicing insight. Therefore a range of possibilities is accounted for within Theravādin literature (Cousins 1973, 116).

11 Within Buddhist cosmology there are thirty-one realms of existence wherein beings can be reborn. These include realms of hell, ghosts, animals, humans, and gods.

12 Defilements, known as *kilesas*, are the negative habits of the mind that hinder liberation from suffering. The three main defilements are greed (*lobha*), hatred (*dosa*), and delusion (*moha*).

13 I am describing *vipassanā* meditation in general here; however, there are many methods of this kind of meditation depending on the teacher and lineage. See

The history of modern vipassanā 41

Kornfield (2010) for a sense of the variety. In the next chapter I describe the methods used most among international meditators in Thailand.

14 Pau Auk Sayadaw is the abbot of the Pau Auk Forest Monastery in Mawlamyine, Myanmar. His method of meditation is described in Snyder and Rasmussen (2009).

15 These critics often conclude that the practitioner fell asleep or entered a *jhānic* state, and this experience of blackout or unconsciousness is confused with the experience of the first glimpse of *nibbāna* in stream-entry.

16 These are the main sources that modern Theravāda meditation teachers in Thailand utilize that I have found from ethnographic research in meditation centers. However, other sources from the Pāli Canon also discuss meditation. The Karanīyametta Sutta (SN 1.8) discusses the benefits of *mettā* or loving-kindness meditation, where one extends feelings of love to oneself and all beings in the world (Crosby 2013, 144). Shaw (2006) presents an anthology of meditation texts such as the Samaññaphala Sutta (DN 2) (see Shaw, 59–75). Other suttas describing meditation include the Kayagata-sati Sutta (MN 119) and the Bhikkhunupassaya Sutta (SN 47.10), among others.

17 This sutta is located in the Majjhima Nikāya, or Middle Length Discourses of the Sutta Pitaka of the Pāli Canon (MN 10). The Mahā Satipaṭṭhāna Sutta in the Digha Nikāya, or Collection of Long Discourses (DN 22), is identical except it contains a more detailed elucidation of the Four Noble Truths.

18 Because of the relatively recent significance of the Satipaṭṭhāna Sutta within the modern *vipassanā* revitalization movement, a number of scholars and teachers have written both academic and more accessible commentaries of this text. See Anālayo (2008); Silananda (2002), Soma Thera (1967), Nyanaponika Thera (1996 [1954]).

19 According to the Satipaṭṭhāna Sutta there are thirty-two parts of the body upon which to reflect. Within this reflection, meditators are asked to see one's hair, flesh, bones, organs, blood, sweat, etc. as repulsive in order to lessen attachment to oneself and one's body.

20 The purpose of this contemplation is to understand oneself not as a solid being with which to identify but as a process of four elements moving through space (Silananda 2002, 68).

21 Similar to the reflection on the repulsiveness of the body, the nine cemetery contemplations are meant to develop detachment from the body. These contemplations include a swollen corpse, a blue corpse, a festering corpse, for example (Soma Thera 2013).

22 Many techniques, such as Mahasi Sayadaw's, stress the contemplation of breathing, while some others, such as the forest tradition of Thailand, focus on the repulsiveness of the body and cemetery contemplations.

23 This sutta is located within the Majjhima Nikāya (MN 118).

24 For more information, see the section on Buddhadasa Bhikkhu's meditation method in Chapter 3.

25 By Pāli Canon (following Collins 1990) I am referring to the historical collection of texts of Theravāda Buddhism rather than a religious conception of the 'origins' of an already defined Theravāda school. Collins argues that scholars should see the Pāli Canon from a historical perspective. This body of texts was meant as a strategy to legitimate the particular Buddhist communities in the first centuries of the Common Era.

26 The suttas are presented as records of the Buddha's teachings. Often the Buddha is teaching to a particular audience. Because of the contextual nature of the presentation, it is difficult to take the Ānāpānasati Sutta and the Satipaṭṭhāna Sutta as detailed instructions for all meditators without allowing for further commentaries, teachings, or interpretations by meditation teachers.

27 The verses Buddhaghosa specifically refers to are: "When a wise man, established well in virtue, develops consciousness and understanding, then as a bhikkhu ardent and sagacious he succeeds in disentangling this tangle. The inner tangle and the outer

42 *The history of modern* vipassanā

tangle—this generation is entangled in a tangle. And so I ask of Gotama this question: Who succeeds in disentangling this tangle?" (SN 1:13).

28 This is communicated through a series of seven purifications: purification of virtue, purification of mind, purification of view, purification of overcoming doubt, purification by knowledge and vision of what is the path and what is not the path, purification by knowledge and vision of the way, and purification by directly experiencing knowledge and vision.

29 See the Mahasi Sayadaw and Ajan Tong methods discussed in Chapter 3.

30 These sixteen stages fit within the larger scheme of the seven purifications. The sixteen stages are: 1) knowledge to distinguish mental and physical states (*namarupa pariccheda ñana*); 2) knowledge of the cause-and-effect relationship between mental and physical states (*paccaya pariggaha ñana*); 3) knowledge of mental and physical processes as impermanent, unsatisfactory and nonself (*sammasana ñana*); 4) knowledge of arising and passing away (*udayabbaya ñana*); 5) knowledge of the dissolution of formations (*bhanga ñana*); 6) knowledge of the fearful nature of mental and physical states (*bhaya ñana*); 7) knowledge of mental and physical states as unsatisfactory (*adinava ñana*); 8) knowledge of disenchantment (*nibbida ñana*); 9) knowledge of the desire to abandon the worldly state (*muncitukamayata ñana*); 10) knowledge which investigates the path to deliverance and instills a decision to practice further (*patisankha ñana*); 11) knowledge which regards mental and physical states with equanimity (*sankharupekha ñana*); 12) knowledge which conforms to the Four Noble Truths (*anuloma ñana*); 13) knowledge of deliverance from the worldly condition (*gotrabhu ñana*); 14) knowledge by which defilements are abandoned and are overcome by destruction (*magga ñana*); 15) knowledge which realizes the fruit of the path and has *nibbāna* as object (*phala ñana*); 16) knowledge which reviews the defilements still remaining (*paccavekkhana ñana*). Mahasi Sayadaw describes these stages in detail in his *Progress of Insight* (1994). As well, Kornfield's *A Path with Heart* (2009), Sayadaw U Pandita's *In This Very Life* (2012), Bhante Gunaratana's *The Path of Serenity and Insight* (1995), Daniel Ingram's *Mastering the Core Teachings of the Buddha* (2008), Sri Nanarama Mahathera's *The Seven Stages of Purification and the Insight Knowledges* (2010), and Mathew Flickstein's *The Meditator's Workbook* (2012) contain descriptions of this cycle.

31 Sharf (1998) gives an example from Zen Buddhism of the well-known teacher and writer, D.T. Suzuki (1870–1996), and his apprenticeship under American academic Paul Carus (1852–1919). Sharf argues that their relationship helped to establish meditative experience as a significant aspect of Japanese religiosity. In Theravāda Buddhism, the collaboration of Anagarika Dharmapala in Sri Lanka with Henry Steel Olcott and Helena Blavatsky of the Theosophical Society is also well documented (Prothero 1996).

32 Two of the most well-known *vipassanā* meditation techniques are the Mahasi Sayadaw method (Jordt 2007) and S.N. Goenka's method (Hart 1987). Both of these methods consist of a precise retreat format that is replicated almost identically in centers throughout the world. They are discussed in detail in the next section of this chapter.

33 This decline in the availability of the Buddha's teachings is asserted in one of the Pāli suttas (Cakkavatti-Sihanada Sutta, DN 26). This sutta declares that there will be a future where the dhamma is so degenerate that *nibbāna* will no longer be possible.

34 For more information on Buddhist manuscript cultures see Berkwitz et al. (2009).

35 Some examples of these forty objects are: the four elements of earth, water, fire, and air, the four colors of blue, yellow, red, and white, ten kinds of bodily decay such as different kinds of corpses, the ten recollections including the Buddha, Dharma, Sangha, virtue, generosity, mindfulness of death, mindfulness of the body, mindfulness of breathing.

36 Separation of monastics and laity is not as strict in meditation centers as in temple environments. Temples are places for monastics to study and observe the *Vinaya* while

The history of modern vipassanā   43

living with other monastics. The modern institution of the meditation center is meant primarily for lay people.

37 This is in contrast to solitary meditation locations within huts and caves.

38 The meditation center can be contrasted with the typical monastery in many ways. Monasteries provide for the residence of a limited number of monks. Some have spare accommodation available but few possess the same type of facilities as meditation centers. The monastery serves many functions and so there is more freedom within the daily schedule. Besides the morning almsround, morning and evening chanting, and meals, monastics' schedules vary. Novices carry out duties like sweeping the floors, cleaning, and preparing offerings for the Buddha statue. More senior monks often conduct ceremonies away from the temple or for visitors to the monastery and have other administrative duties.

39 For descriptions of meditation centers in Myanmar see Houtman (1990) and Jordt (2007). For Thailand see Cook (2010) as well as Chapter 3 of this book.

40 U Narada is reported to have discovered the importance of the Satipaṭṭhāna Sutta from discussions with a meditating monk in a cave in the Sagaing Hills (Van Esterik 1977, 53; Nyanaponika 1996 [1954], 85).

41 There are centers using the Mahasi method in the USA, United Kingdom, France, Switzerland, Sweden, Thailand, Sri Lanka, Nepal, and Korea. Mahasi Sayadaw chose his disciple, Sayadaw U Silananda (1927–2005), to teach in America and be responsible for spreading the dhamma in the West. He arrived in America in 1979.

42 Mahasi also developed a program certifying the attainments of meditators as well as public lists where one can view the names of people who have attained *nibbāna* in the Mahasi Thathana Yeiktha.

43 In Thailand Goenka centers are located in Bangkok, Kanchanaburi, and Phitsanulok in Central Thailand, Khon Kaen and Udon Thani in Northeast Thailand, Lampun in Northern Thailand, Nakhon Si Thammarat in Southern Thailand, and Chanthanaburi and Prachinburi in Eastern Thailand.

44 Within Theravāda Buddhist monasticism, lineage is an important concept. It is the duty of Theravāda lineages to preserve the teachings of the Buddha through proper monastic ordination. Theravāda ordination lineages historically relate to political power and royal alliances, reform movements, orthodoxy, and a concern for pure, unbroken lines. These lineages attempt to create the belief that the teachings have been preserved since the time of the Buddha, which legitimates contemporary Buddhist communities. Lineages based on the teachings of particular meditation masters link teachers, students, meditation, and disciplinary practices over successive generations. Meditation teachers authorize particular students to teach in their lineage, ensuring continuity into the future. Within modern Buddhism, however, meditation lineages become less clear as teachers authorize both laity and monastics. As well increased value placed on Buddhist ecumenism creates more fluid affiliations.

45 For a biography of Ruth Denison, which includes her period of study under U Ba Khin, see Boucher (2005).

46 IMS also traces their lineage to the Thai forest tradition in Thailand (Cadge 2005, 32).

47 Popular books by the founders and leading teachers of this *vipassanā* movement attest to its popularity and significance among English-readers. Kornfield's *A Path with Heart* (1993) and *After the Ecstasy, The Laundry* (2001) both describe how one can bring spiritual insights into one's life and relationships. Goldstein's *One Dharma* (2003) envisions a way to unite all Buddhist traditions. Salzberg's books, such as *Lovingkindness: The Revolutionary Art of Happiness* (2002) and *A Heart as Wide as the World* (1999), focus on *mettā* or loving-kindness meditation.

48 It is not uncommon for Thai kings to be ordained for short periods of time. However, having a monastic career before ascending the throne is unusual. Due to royal politics and claims to the throne by his half-brother, King Mongkut remained a monk until the time was right for his ascension. For full information on this see Reynolds (1972, 66–80).

44 *The history of modern* vipassanā

49 The full name of this temple is Wat Mahathat Yuwarajarangsarit Rajaworamahavihara.

50 The meditation program of Phra Phimolatham encountered an obstacle when he was arrested, prosecuted, and incarcerated in 1963. Tambiah argues that his widespread meditation networks were thought to constitute political power by the prime minister of this time Marshal Sarit Thanarat. The monks of this program amassed religious power, which was inaccessible to the lay military leaders (Tambiah 1976, 260).

51 *Thudong* (Pāli, *dhutanga*) refers to thirteen austere practices fully described in the Visuddhimagga. In Thailand the word refers to those forest monks who leave the monastery and walk, often covering vast distances, dwelling in forests and other secluded places for the purpose of practicing meditation.

52 Because of the popularity of this lineage, forest monks today are treated as exemplary followers of the Buddha's path and have become famous nationally and internationally for their teachings. Originally comprised of individual wandering monks, the forest tradition eventually became institutionalized. This process is detailed in Taylor (1993).

53 The forest monks' location in North and Northeastern Thailand also gave Thammayut administrators bases for the spread of their reforms.

54 Amulets function to remind the practitioner of the Buddha and the charismatic monks depicted on them. Tambiah (1984) argues that in modern Thailand, amulets are used to increase one's power in worldly activities. For more information on the commodification of amulets, see Chapter 5.

55 As will be described in Chapter 3, forest teachings have been popular with Western international guests. The focus of this engagement mostly concerns monasticism, though, not exclusively meditation.

3 The field of international engagement with Thai meditation centers

The field[1] of engagement for international meditators in Thailand is complex. There are many meditation centers in Thailand with varying meditation methods and modes of instruction. It is difficult to estimate the exact number but there are thought to be close to 200 centers (Fuengfusakul 2012, 221). Only a small percentage of these centers are able to host international meditators with consistent instruction in English. This chapter describes this diversity by offering a map of the most popular and well-known international meditation centers in Thailand. I have compiled and created this map through research using meditation guidebooks (discussed in Chapter 5), Internet resources, international meditation centers' statistics, and discussions with international meditators and international meditation center teachers. Before I began fieldwork I contacted these popular sites listed online and in guidebooks and asked about conducting research. From here I developed a research plan to visit these initial places. But as I continued interviewing meditators and teachers, I found more popular sites to visit. Word of mouth functioned for me as it does for international meditators when they are locating centers to practice. Throughout this chapter I describe these findings and how each international meditation center contributes to the diverse field of international engagement in Thailand.

The first part of the chapter describes the main meditation methods and places of meditation for international meditators. In this section I follow tourism patterns as I have found these were significant in forming and developing the most popular international meditation centers. After describing the people and settings of the various popular international meditation centers, I then discuss the social roles in each center including the roles of teachers, volunteers, and Thai and international meditators. In the second section I pay special attention to the ways many Thai Buddhists understand *vipassanā* meditation and contrast this with the decontextualized understanding of meditation from Thai Buddhism held by international meditators. This map of Thailand's international meditation centers not only provides background for further chapters but also highlights the diversity, accessibility, openness, inclusivity, and flexibility of international engagement with Buddhism in Thailand. I now turn to the meditation center itself—its project, main features, and aims.

Figure 3.1 Map of Thailand

The meditation center

This field of engagement is only possible for foreigners through the mass meditation movement that began in Burma, described in the previous chapter. The word 'mass' is significant because it connotes the way meditation courses are organized and managed based on an 'urban cultural logic' (Fuengfusakul 2012, 221). Meditation centers themselves are diverse, with different sizes, types of accommodation, number of people, techniques, teachers, styles of management, course lengths, and environments. Therefore it would be difficult to describe a typical international meditation center, but I will list some of the possibilities

Engagement with Thai meditation centers 47

Table 3.1 Temple regions

International meditation center	Location
Middle Way Retreat Wat Dhammakaya	Pathum Thani, Central Thailand
Wat Luang Por Sot Buddhist Meditation Institute	Ratburi, Central Thailand
Wat Mahathat Section 5	Bangkok, Central Thailand
Wat Prayong Gittivararam	Bangkok, Central Thailand
Diphavan Meditation center	Koh Samui, Southern Thailand
International Dhamma Hermitage	Surat Thani, Southern Thailand
Wat Kow Tahm International Meditation Center	Koh Phangnan, Southern Thailand
Wat Pah Tam Wua	MaeHongSon, Northern Thailand
Wat Prathat Doi Suthep International Meditation Center	Chiangmai, Northern Thailand
Wat Prathat Sri Chom Tong International Meditation Center	Chiangmai, Northern Thailand
Wat Rampoeng Tapotaram	Chiangmai, Northern Thailand
Wat Tam Doi Tohn	Chiangmai, Northern Thailand
Wat Umong	Chiangmai, Northern Thailand

Table 3.2 Statistics

Research site	Number per year	Total	Program
International Dhamma Hermitage	On average 1000	20,000 since 1989	Once per month
The Middle Way Meditation Retreat Wat Dhammakaya	Not calculated	Participants since February 2006 to end of 2009 = 536	7 days almost every month
Northern Insight Meditation Center Wat Rampoeng	On average 450	Participants from 2006–2009 = 1,759	Length of stay and timing dependent on retreatant
Wat Kow Tahm International Meditation Center	Not calculated	7,000 since 1988	Dependent on the teachers' schedule
Wat Luang Por Sot Buddhist Meditation Institute	80 in 2009	320 since 2005	Length of stay and timing dependent on retreatant
Wat Mahathat Section 5	On average 750	Participants from 1998–2009 = 9070	Length of stay and timing dependent on retreatant
Wat Prathat Doi Suthep	On average 417	Participants from 2004–2009 = 2504	Length of stay and timing dependent on retreatant

* These statistics contain information only on those sites that calculated the number of foreign meditators. Many smaller sites do not calculate these statistics and are not listed here.

I encountered while participating as an international meditator myself. Some meditation centers house hundreds of lay meditators who sleep on mats on the floor in a large, open room. Others accept only a limited number of thirty to forty participants per retreat, who sleep in their own little houses with a bed and

48 *Engagement with Thai meditation centers*

other furniture. Meditation centers are sometimes easily accessible within a city, while others comprise a large sprawling area located in a more rural environment. Courses are usually run by meditation teachers, ordained or lay, while some enlist the help of lay volunteers to manage and orient the participants. Some centers follow a clearly defined group schedule where retreatants arrive, practice, and depart on the same dates, while others allow participants to practice for a set number of days according to each individual's personal schedule, with meditators coming and going continually. Some meditation centers are set within temple grounds, while others are adjacent to the temple or are affiliated with a temple but not physically close to one. Most centers require students to wear white clothing and to keep the standard Eight Precepts[2] while living in a temple; however, some will allow their international guests to don modest multi-colored outfits and follow the Five Precepts, the basic code of conduct for all lay Buddhists.

There are many criteria to consider when locating a retreat and there is much to research beforehand to understand the retreat program of a particular center. No two centers are exactly alike in all of these characteristics, even if they are related branch centers of the same teacher. But all of them are based on a systematized, formalized retreat program. In all retreat programs, meditators are required to conform to particular rules and daily schedule, wear certain clothing, and try to maintain continual mindfulness. I describe here thirteen sites where I participated in meditation retreats, interviewing all teachers and as many international meditators as possible. I visited more sites than these thirteen and spoke with more teachers and facilitators of other retreat sites, but these primary thirteen sites detailed below are the most illuminating for reflecting on the diversity of international meditation centers. Of these thirteen sites, smaller centers usually have between five to eight international meditators at any time while the larger centers host up to 100 each month. Other centers I visited did not have this frequency of international meditator participation so did not face the same issues as the more established and well-known ones described below.

Thailand's international meditation centers: history, sites, and meditation methods

The popular appeal of meditation leads many travelers to explore opportunities to practice in Asian Buddhist countries. With the rise of lay meditation among Thai Buddhists and many meditation centers already catering to Thais, some temples and meditation centers have sought to accommodate an international audience by providing English instruction. This shift has created a need for separate English-speaking teachers to manage the international groups while physically separating international meditators from the Thai meditators in many cases. The language barrier is not the only reason to separate international meditators. Since their cultural frameworks are different from Thai meditators, international meditators receive separate, decontextualized teachings from the Thai Buddhist worldview, which is instead embedded within modern discourses I explore throughout the remaining chapters.

Engagement with Thai meditation centers 49

In order to understand the field of international meditators' engagement, I highlight the main actors, meditative practices, and sites that have contributed to Thai Buddhism's international status. Meditation methods such as those of particular teacher such as Buddhadasa Bhikkhu, Ajan Tong Srimangalo, Dhammakaya, and the more general techniques of the Four Foundations of Mindfulness are the most influential within Thailand's international meditation centers. Through a mix of charismatic teachers, tourist locations, English instruction, and accessibility to information about these sites, particular meditation methods have emerged as the most well-known among international travelers. These methods and actors have gained popularity through various modes such as international disciples teaching abroad, translations of *dhamma* talks and meditation method manuals, English websites, and word of mouth of particular teachers' willingness and effectiveness in teaching meditation.

The history of these centers is best told by following tourism patterns of the regions of Thailand. I take this approach because each region developed international meditation centers in different ways that follow both tourist patterns and lineages of charismatic teachers with international disciples. International meditation teachings began in Central Thailand because Bangkok was the first hub for international travel. As tourists arrived in large numbers to Southern Thailand in the 1970s and 1980s, group retreats developed in that region. And when tourists discovered the 'Lanna' culture of Northern Thailand via tourism promotion for Thai tourists in the 1980s (Evrard & Leepreecha 2009a, 244), meditation centers for Thais using the method of Ajan Tong transformed into international centers soon afterward, starting in the 1990s. Erik Cohen (2001, 7) has identified the three main areas in Thailand where tourism is located: Bangkok in Central Thailand, Chiangmai in Northern Thailand, and Phukhet in Southern Thailand (tourism in these regions also includes areas beyond Chiangmai in Northern Thailand such as Pai and Mae Hong Son as well as southern islands on the Gulf of Thailand such as Ko Samui and Ko Phangan).

The Thai Forest Tradition of Northeast Thailand is known among international travelers through two of the famous disciples of Luangpu Mun Bhuridatta— Ajan Chah (Venerable Phra Bodhiñāna Thera) (1918–1992) and Luangta Mahabua Ñāṇasampaṇṇo (1914–2011)—who founded large forest monasteries in Northeast Thailand. International networks of Ajan Chah's branch temples[3] as well as translated books of Ajan Chah's and Luangta Mahabua's teachings,[4] represent another trajectory of foreign engagement with Thai Buddhism, one based partly on meditation but mostly on monasticism. However, these forest tradition teachers are not included here because they do not have retreat programs for lay meditators and their methods are not taught in the systematic, regimented way of guided retreats at international meditation centers.[5] When I visited both Wat Pah Nanachat founded by Ajan Chah, and Wat Pah Baan That, the temple of Luangta Mahabua, during my fieldwork, I was struck by how different these temples are from the mass lay meditation retreat model. Therefore it would be difficult to compare and include them in my study. Other teachers such as Ajan Naeb[6] Mahaniranonda and Luangpor Theean[7] Jittasubho also have distinct methods; however, these are not widely available in English with fewer international disciples or English-language materials. Therefore,

50 *Engagement with Thai meditation centers*

my discussion does not provide a comprehensive list of international meditation in Thailand, but instead focuses on those practices international meditators are most likely to encounter at international meditation centers. Because there is no one comprehensive list of Thailand's international meditation centers, I have determined which were most populous through their consistent hosting of international meditators each month. By analyzing the available statistics, following internet and printed guides, and speaking with international meditators about how they had selected each meditation center, I have labeled the following thirteen sites as the most well-known among international meditators. Next, I discuss these sites within the history of international meditation centers and methods used.

Central Thailand

Most travelers first arrive in Bangkok, the country's capital for the last 200 plus years. It was here that the first engagements of foreigners with Buddhism and meditation occurred. In 1954, Wat Paknam held the famous ordination of the first foreign monk, Kapilavaddho, which was followed by another ordination of three more British monks two years later.[8] Wat Mahathat was another important temple for foreign engagement. Section 5 of Wat Mahathat has a long history of offering a practice space and instruction to both Thai and foreign meditators that begins with Phra Phimolatham's propagation of meditation in the 1950s. At Section 5 currently there is a program titled 'The Insight Meditation Practice Program for a Good Life,'[9] which utilizes *vipassanā* meditation based on the Four Foundations of Mindfulness. The goals of the program as stated in the brochure are to lead life according to Buddha's teachings, cultivate the mind, be familiar with roles of Thai Buddhist monks in society, and lead one's life toward the cessation of suffering. The schedule consists of three practice times of three hours in the morning (7–10am), afternoon (1–4pm), and two hours in the evening (6–8pm). Attending one of these sessions, one will hear an opening instruction conducted in Thai. After this, each meditator sits silently until a closing chanting of spreading loving-kindness and sharing the merit of the meditation with others. The small meditation hall remains empty until the next period. International meditators receive separate instruction from the English-speaking person designated to take care of the foreigners, usually Ajan Suputh Kosalo, who has been instrumental in teaching international meditators for over twenty years. He estimates that most days there are usually three to five international meditators; however, if it is not the hot season, there might be more.[10] Meditators enter and depart this center as they wish, staying for one or several nights or practicing for just a day.[11]

Some international meditation centers teach a variety of methods, leaving it up to the students to choose which one works for them. Many international meditators practicing in sites within Central Thailand engage with some form of meditation method that is based on the Four Foundations of Mindfulness, as outlined in the Satipatthāna Sutta. International meditators find this method at centers which typically cater to a small number of international meditators and a larger number of Thai meditators, through friends, websites, or by chance when passing by. These centers do not trace their lineages to a specific teacher like Ajan Tong or Buddhadasa Bhikkhu nor do they have charismatic meditation teachers. Instead these centers utilize teaching practices from the Satipatthāna Sutta. From my experience at these sites, this usually means instruction on some form of contemplation of the body, most commonly the breath as one's main concentration point.

A site utilizing this method is Wat Prayong Gittivararam. Mae Chii Brigitte from Austria established the international meditation center at Wat Prayong in April of 2009. Mae Chii Brigitte[12] first discovered Wat Prayong through the advice of a taxi driver.[13] Upon her first visit the abbot impressed her because he could tell her about her past without having met before. She was so moved that she came for a personal retreat and later moved here to establish the lay center, where she teaches both Thais and foreigners in Thai, English, and German. Almost half of her students are German and Austrian meditators because they can receive instruction in their native language. At this temple Mae Chii Brigitte offers group meditation in the morning and meditation instruction and discussion in the evening from the first to the seventh of every month. Usually she has between twenty and thirty students but her New Years retreat has attracted over 100 students. Mae Chii Brigitte has practiced in many styles but usually teaches a method based on the Four Foundations of Mindfulness. This is a center with developing facilities that offers opportunities for both guided and group practice as well as individual periods of meditation. Additionally, it is a place where Thai and international meditators can learn about each other and practice together. This is one of the only centers that allows for this kind of retreat experience.

Dhammakaya meditation is a unique method and the temples that use this technique owe their existence to the famous monk known by both his monastic name Luang Por Sot Chandassaro (1885–1959), and Luang Por Wat Paknam, after the temple he came to be most closely associated with. This meditation technique contains many levels and becomes increasingly complex as one progresses, but the beginning stages are meant for everyone. There are three main temples that offer instruction in Dhammakaya meditation: Wat Dhammakaya, Wat Luang Por Sot, and Wat Paknam. Wat Dhammakaya, located outside of Bangkok, is the largest temple in Thailand and was founded in 1970. Other disciples who felt that they could represent the legacy of Luangpor Sot more accurately founded Wat Luang Por Sot, another temple teaching Dhammakaya meditation in Ratburi province (Newell 2008,118). In Thonburi, across the river from Bangkok, lies Wat Paknam, the temple where Luang Por Sot was abbot, and where many people still come to pay respects to him.[14] Only the first two have the possibility for international engagement with Dhammakaya forms of meditation.

Sources for the unique visualization method known as Dhammakaya meditation include scholars (Newell 2008; Bowers 1996) as well as teachers of the Dhammakaya meditation method (Rajyanvisith 2009). Although its meditation teachers claim this method is based on the same Satipatthāna Sutta, this technique differs from other meditation methods, which utilize the Four Foundations of Mindfulness.[15] This exemplifies the variety of ways the practices of the

52 *Engagement with Thai meditation centers*

Satipatthāna Sutta have been interpreted. Dhammakaya meditation, unlike other Thai meditation practices, is usually conducted in groups and utilizes visualization. When one begins this practice, one first uses three techniques: concentration on the breath, the repetition of a mantra (*samma araham*), and concentration on a bright object. As the meditator repeats the mantra, she/he will also visualize a sphere of light or crystal ball that moves through seven bases within the body, starting at the nostril and moving down to the center of the body.

The meditator takes these steps before initiating concentration on the bright object in the center of the body, which is considered to be about two finger-widths above the navel. Focusing on this sphere (*pathama-magga*) will eventually produce the first image in a series of spheres. For intermediate and advanced meditators there is a series of further spheres and bodies that arise as one's concentration deepens (Rajyanvisith 2009, 72–84). On most beginner retreats though, this high-level meditation is not discussed. For most people, Dhammakaya meditation is promoted as simple and effective, and something that can easily transform one's life. Another point of difference between Dhammakaya meditation and other Thai forms is the focal point of the concentration. Instead of at the nostril or abdomen, Dhammakaya meditation focuses on the center of the body. And instead of focusing solely on the breath, the meditator concentrates on the imagined bright object.

The Middle Way Retreat, the international program of Wat Dhammakaya, began in Thailand in 2004, making it one of the newer international meditation centers. Unlike the individual meditation retreats discussed earlier, this is a retreat where a group practices meditation and all activities together for a predetermined length of time. The retreats take place at centers in Loei,[16] Northeast Thailand from May to December, and in Phukhet, Southern Thailand from April to September. The retreat participants gather at Wat Dhammakaya in Bangkok and are transported together to the retreat site. About thirty to forty participants attend each monthly retreat. This retreat began as a way to introduce the meditation techniques of Dhammakaya to a foreign audience and is unique because the participants are encouraged to get to know one another. Indeed, when I took part in the retreat in Loei, I was surprised at the expectation that the group members talk to one another and share experiences, which differs significantly from the structure at most retreats. This demonstrates that there are different models for a meditation retreat besides Goenka or Mahasi Sayadaw available in Thailand. There is also time for formal group discussions, yoga sessions, and teachings about how to incorporate Wat Dhammakaya teachings into one's life. Participants learn about Buddhism and the history of Wat Dhammakaya during afternoon and evening lectures. After the seven-day retreat, participants are provided with transportation back to Wat Dhammakaya and are offered opportunities to tour the temple and to stay overnight at hotels nearby. International meditators usually discover this retreat from the Middle Way's extensive English website.[17]

Wat Luang Por Sot's Buddhist Meditation Institute (BMI)[18] in Ratburi, Central Thailand, was created through the efforts of the late Khru Baitika Dr. Barton Yanathiro,[19] or Phra Bart, and the abbot of the temple, Dr. Phra Rajanvisith in

2006. Instruction of Dhammakaya meditation takes place mainly through guided meditations, three to four times a day for one hour. International meditators can stay at BMI for any length of time, but Phra Bart recommended two weeks. BMI also hosts two-week intensive retreats, three times a year, for foreigners and Thais together. At these retreats foreigners can have more access to instruction from the abbot, Dr. Phra Rajanvisith. There is slightly more intensive training during this time as well in the form of group meditation and activities. Many participants used to come to BMI through volunteer exchange programs such as Global Service Corps, and in addition to learning meditation they also taught English to the many monks and novices residing at this temple. With the passing of Phra Bart there is no longer a volunteer program here but English meditation instruction remains available.

Southern Thailand

In the South of Thailand, most international meditators attend one of two large group retreats. The first international retreat site in this region was Buddhadasa Bhikkhu's Wat Suan Mokhh, which began in 1985. Starting in 1990, through the enthusiasm and encouragement of the present abbot, Venerable Ajan Bodhi Buddhadhammo, or Ajan Pho as he is called, the International Dhamma Hermitage was built across the highway from the temple.[20] In addition, Ajan Pho also established a similar retreat on the island of Koh Samui. The large numbers of travelers interested in meditation in the touristy beach region led to a second group retreat in the south, Wat Kow Tahm International Meditation Center on Koh Phangan.

Buddhadasa Bhikkhu (1906–1993) was a famous Buddhist scholar whose English writings cover many shelves on subjects such as comparative religion and Buddhist teachings for daily life.[21] He has many more publications available in Thai, and he is well-known among this audience for his interpretation of Buddhist teachings. Swearer (1989), Jackson (2003), and Ito (2012) have written separate volumes on Buddhadasa Bhikkhu and his thought. They are interested in his innovative ideas regarding Buddhist teachings in the modern world.[22] Buddhadasa Bhikkhu's interests not only related to meditation, but to the whole of the Buddhist tradition and religious thought in general. He believed all are fundamentally similar, pointing to the same essential nature of self and reality and teaching an ethic of selflessness (Swearer 1989, 11). His original ideas, which can be contrasted with normative, orthodox Theravāda thought, and are in opposition to popular lay practices such as merit-making, demonstrate his continued creative engagement with the teachings of the Buddha and his attempts to make them relevant to Thai society (Swearer 1989, 3–5).[23]

The temple Buddhadasa Bhikkhu founded, Wat Suan Mokkhabalarama, or Suan Mokkh (Garden of Liberation), in Chaiya, Southern Thailand, still bears his legacy. This is a meditation temple for the monks and *mae chii* in residence as well as lay meditators. Each area of Wat Suan Mokkh is meant to teach its visitors about *nibbāna*. For example, the 'spiritual theater' inside the temple expresses Buddhist truths through art and sculpture from around the world. His legacy also includes the International

54   Engagement with Thai meditation centers

Dhamma Hermitage, a meditation center he established.[24] Interest in Buddhadasa continues with another project in Bangkok called the Buddhadasa Indapanno Archives,[25] which has been created to preserve his teachings.

In addition to his teachings at these sites, he imparted a meditation method that is practiced today at his temple and meditation center. Similar to the mass lay meditation movement methods, Buddhadasa's is a general method that can be used by all meditators. However, Buddhadasa Bhikkhu bases his meditation technique on the Ānāpānasati Sutta instead of the more popular Satipatthāna Sutta, with its delineation of the Four Foundations of Mindfulness. He asserts that out of the many meditation methods and systems of *samatha* and *vipassanā* created by various teachers—*ānāpānasati*, or mindfulness of breathing, is the closest one to the Buddha's teachings. Although the Satipatthāna Sutta has received much attention in scholarship and within meditation centers, Buddhadasa finds the text meandering, confusing, and vague. He asserts that there is no explanation of how to practice the Four Foundations of Mindfulness as the sutta only lists the names of practices and fails to expand on how the meditator should progress (Santikaro 2001b, 126). Instead Buddhadasa recommends using the Ānāpānasati Sutta as a framework that offers complete and clear guidance. In his meditation instructions, Buddhadasa recommends following this sutta from beginning to end as one progresses on the path (Buddhadasa 2001, 18). He believes that this system "is simply the correct way as recommended by the Buddha" (Buddhadasa 2001, 17).

The meditation instruction of Ajan Buddhadasa Bhikkhu (2001) can be read in full in his *Mindfulness with Breathing* translated by Santikaro.[26] In this book Buddhadasa writes that the correct and complete practice of *ānāpānasati* is to take one truth or reality of nature and then observe, investigate, and scrutinize it in the mind with every inhalation and every exhalation (Buddhadasa 2001, 5). In order to begin on this journey, Buddhadasa writes that we need *sati* or awareness, and we can cultivate this by being mindful of each breath. Ajan Buddhadasa Bhikkhu makes clear what this system of *ānāpānasati* is not in his *Mindfulness with Breathing*:

> [T]his system is not the Burmese or Chinese or Sri Lankan style that some people are clinging to these days. Likewise, it is not the system of 'achan this,' 'master that,' 'guru this,' or 'teacher that' as others are so caught up in nowadays. Nor is it the style of Suan Mokh or any other wat. Instead, this system is simply the correct way as recommended by the Buddha.
>
> (Buddhadasa 2001, 17)

Thus he argues that these meditation instructions are the fundamentals of the practice without any national or lineage distinction. Buddhadasa Bhikkhu continues to detail practices for all of the sixteen stages of the Ānāpānasati Sutta, which he considers to be the complete path toward liberation. The retreat program for English-speakers based on this method that began in 1989 is still a significant aspect of foreign engagement with meditation in Thailand today.

Since 1990[27] the International Dhamma Hermitage has received foreigners each month and has averaged 1,000 participants yearly for nearly twenty-five years.[28] Through its accessible website and history of offering retreats, this is one of the most well-known international meditation centers. The ten-day retreat program for foreigners is conducted in English in a large group beginning on the first of every month. All meditation here is done as a group, and everyone follows the same schedule, with periods for meditation, chores, meals, and visiting the hot springs on site. Instead of mandatory daily interviews with a teacher, there are optional ones toward the middle of the retreat. One can sign up to meet with one of the volunteers, or dhamma friends, who help to run the retreat. Replacing daily interviews are dhamma talks throughout the day by volunteer dhamma friends as well as teachings about basic Buddhist concepts and the thought of Buddhadasa Bhikkhu by British monk, Than Dhammavidu. Meditators also have the option to participate in a daily one-hour chanting session, which is another opportunity to learn about Buddhism. Foreigners chant in both Pāli and English and are given explanations about the meanings of each chant. Besides chanting, this retreat experience is secular with no Buddha statues, ceremonies, or bowing to the monk teacher while sitting in a meditation interview. Even with this more familiar environment and explanations in English, this retreat is still difficult and challenging for many participants, with a rigorous schedule and few comforts.

Dipabhavan Meditation Center was founded by Ajan Pho,[29] current abbot of Wat Suan Mokhh. He was born on the island of Koh Samui and had a long-time wish to start a retreat center there. He had seen the arrival of tourism on the island and felt that Thailand had more to offer than sun and sand. Thirty years ago he attempted to establish a group retreat on Koh Samui with limited success. The retreat at Wat Suan Mokhh became popular because the well-known teacher Ajan Buddhadasa Bhikkhu was able to teach the foreigners at that time. Only in 2006, through the donation of land by a Thai lay female follower, Ajan Pho was able to realize his dream of a meditation center on his homeland, with separate retreats each month for English-speaking and Thai meditators. The Dipabhavan Meditation Center program is based on the twenty plus years of retreat experience at the International Dhamma Hermitage. The retreat schedule is less strict with more sleep, fewer meditation hours, and a seven-day retreat program instead of ten.[30]

Wat Kow Tahm International Meditation Center began in the late 1980s and early 1990s, when tourists hiked from Baan Thai Beach up the hill to the temple called Wat Kow Tahm and asked the head nun there, Mae Chii Ahmon, how they could learn meditation. She discovered a way to share the practice of meditation in the forms of two experienced meditators who sought out this unique temple. Married couple Rosemary and Steve Weissman arrived in 1987 when they were soon asked to lead retreats.[31] Wat Kow Tahm has monks in residence but Mae Chii Ahmon is the leader of the meditation center.[32] This center[33] was established based on location rather than affiliation with a particular Thai lineage, a unique situation for Buddhism in Thailand. Most of the foreign international meditation center teachers in Thailand are affiliated with a Thai meditation master and lineage. Although Rosemary and Steve have studied with several Thai and non-Thai teachers, they do not place their teachings within any one lineage. A majority of international meditation center teachers thus carry on a Thai lineage but adapt it

Figure 3.2 Meditation hall, Diphabavan

for English-speakers and bring this particular lineage to other countries. Steve and Rosemary represent a possible future for the transmission of the Dhamma; one which follows no particular teacher or lineage but that begins anew from a mixed lineage, spurred by and expanded through tourism, with methods developed and adapted from many years of teaching retreats to international meditators.

Each day of this retreat is filled with sitting, walking, and standing meditation periods, meditation exercises, mindful chores, mindfulness activities, teachings by Rosemary and/or Steve, three vegetarian meals (with a smaller evening meal) and postmeal breaks. There are also three interview opportunities scheduled for each international meditator throughout the retreat, the only allowances for speech. The retreat is interspersed with guided meditations in order to learn how to practice compassion/loving-kindness meditation, as well as meditation on sympathetic joy and wise-reflection meditation.[34]

Northern Thailand

While these group retreats were starting in the South, in the North of Thailand individual retreats for Thai Buddhists turned into international centers, as curious

Figure 3.3 Rules and regulations at Wat Kow Tahm

Figure 3.4 Accommodation at Wat Kow Tahm

58   *Engagement with Thai meditation centers*

travelers showed an interest in the practice. An early example of foreign participation is a memoir called *A Meditator's Diary* by Hamilton-Merrit (1986), about her retreat experience in Northern Thailand. In the 1970s, an international meditator was a rare sight, especially a woman. The situation transformed over the next twenty years as international interest in meditation coupled with increased tourism helped develop several international meditation centers. Phrakhru Phiphat Khanaphiban, or Ajan Tong Srimangalo (1923–present), is known for promoting an adapted version of the *vipassanā* technique of Burmese teacher Mahasi Sayadaw.[35] Many Thai and international meditators have participated in Ajan Tong's twenty-plus-day meditation courses in the numerous temples that utilize his method, mostly in Northern Thailand. Kathryn Chindaporn translated into English Ajan Tong's (2004) most extensive book on his meditation method, *The Only Way: An Introduction to Vipassanā Meditation. The Only Way* describes the precise method of meditation Ajan Tong created. It lists the exercises of prostration, standing, walking, sitting, lying, and minor positions. These exercises are all explicitly connected to the Four Foundations of Mindfulness.

Ajan Tong was able to spread *vipassanā* meditation throughout Northern Thailand because of opportunities to study in Bangkok and Burma. The abbot of Wat Phra Singh Voravihara in Chiangmai selected Ajan Tong as the Northern Thailand representative to study *vipassanā* meditation at Wat Mahathat in 1952. He also researched *vipassanā* meditation for over two years in Yangon through the connections already made in Bangkok by Phra Phimolatham (Tambiah 1984, 172). Upon Ajan Tong's return to Chiangmai, he established one of the first satellite monasteries, Wat Mueang Mang, to adopt the meditation program propagated at Wat Mahathat. He continued to institute a number of meditation centers throughout the region. Through increased foreign tourism and interest in meditation as well as granting authorization to foreign, English-speaking teachers, three of these Ajan Tong meditation centers in the Chiangmai area are now international meditation centers.

These three popular international centers are housed at Wat Rampoeng Tapotaram,[36] Wat Prathat Sri Chom Tong,[37] and Wat Prathat Doi Suthep.[38] Wat Chom Tong and Wat Rampoeng opened their doors to foreigners in the early 1990s and Wat Doi Suthep did the same in 2006.[39] These three international meditation centers are among the most popular meditation retreat sites in the region for foreigners given their consistent teaching in English, and web presence.[40] They are all easily accessible from the city of Chiangmai and have a large amount of space to accommodate many meditators. Especially Wat Doi Suthep is one of the largest tourist attractions in Chiangmai,[41] one of the reasons this temple established their international meditation center. These are intense retreats with a minimum commitment of ten days as a review or advanced course for those who have already completed the basic course of twenty-one to twenty-six days (depending on the center) culminating in a 'determination' period when one meditates for seventy-two straight hours. This basic course is the period of time Ajan Tong determined it takes to reach the first path of Enlightenment and complete one cycle of insight. These centers operate on a system of rolling enrollments with students beginning and ending retreats on any given day, depending on availability and the meditator's schedules.

When one enters this retreat program, he or she immediately begins a difficult schedule consisting of increasing amounts of meditation starting at seven to eight hours per day and ending at twenty-four. Nightly sleep is minimal and decreases as one progresses in order to create space for more meditation. Aside from the daily individual interview with the meditation teacher, silence is mandatory. No one monitors the individual meditation practice so meditators are free to practice in their rooms or anywhere else within the temple compound. At the daily interview, one reports to the teacher the number of hours spent in meditation and one's meditative experiences. At Wat Rampoeng, there is minimal instruction about Buddhism except a few key meditation terms presented by the abbot in the opening ceremony; at Wat Chom Tong there is usually one dhamma talk concerning the Five Hindrances; and at Wat Prathat Doi Suthep the daily dhamma talk usually deals with the monastic life and aspects of Thai Buddhist culture.

Wat Umong is another individual retreat site similar to the temples using the Ajan Tong method, where the meditators come and go according to their own schedules. However, unlike the temples that teach the Ajan Tong method, at Wat Umong there is no set program of ten or twenty plus days, meaning international meditators may stay for as few as three days or as long as several months. There are usually a small number of both Thai and foreign meditators at this temple. Usually there are between three and seven international meditators, depending on the season. This temple, with its natural setting in the forest, caves and tunnels to explore, and rich history is popular with tourists as most Thailand guidebooks mention it. Therefore the international meditators I spoke with there told me they found out about the mediation center through visiting as a tourist first. This international meditation center opened in 2007 and continues to expand with new meditation halls, dormitories, and a meditation office for the monk teachers. There are several teachers for the Thai meditators and the head of the center assigns a monk dedicated to teach in English for the foreigners. The meditation method usually taught here is one based on the Four Foundations of Mindfulness and consists of periods of sitting and walking meditation, adapted from the Mahasi Sayadaw method. However since the meditation teachings are separate for international meditators at this center, the method can be different for this group, depending on the method the international meditation center teacher offers. Therefore there is not always one predetermined method that international meditation center teachers exclusively follow.

Ajan Nawi Piyadassi offers seven-day courses in Wat Tam Doi Tohn within the natural setting of Mae Wang, Chiangmai.[42] Thai and international meditators must apply for spots in these retreats offered about once a month for thirty to forty participants. This is a serious course with time for group sitting and walking meditation and separate optional interview times for Thai and international meditators. There is a focus here on meditating, as there are no ceremonies, evening or morning chanting, or chanting before meals. Tapes of Phra Ajan Nawi's speeches or a live dhamma talk are played for about twenty minutes in almost every sitting session. Under the name Piyadassi Bhikkhu, Ajan Nawi has written *Vimuttidhamma: From Chakra to Dhammachakra*,[43] which has been translated by his international disciples. In this book Ajan Nawi follows the path of the meditator through the three-fold training of morality, concentration, and wisdom. It was not Ajan Nawi's intention to start an international center and he is reluctant to accept foreigners who have not practiced before. However, at every retreat at Wat Tam Doi Tohn, there are usually five to eight international meditators, and a local professor who translates for Ajan Nawi. International meditators know about this retreat through connections made in the USA during Phra Ajan Nawi's teaching abroad.[44] Otherwise international meditators chanced upon the accessible website with beautiful pictures of this scenic temple. Indeed Ajan Nawi told me that he welcomes foreigners, although he is surprised at the number who continually find their way to his temple.

Wat Pah Tam Wua is a forest temple located about an hour's drive from Mae Hong Son, and represents another small retreat center where Thai and international meditators practice together. Phra Ajan Saayut Pannatharo, or Ajan Luangta, as he is known to his students, comes from the Thai forest tradition but his temple focuses on lay practice and has a retreat program, unlike most other temples within this tradition. He guides beginning meditators through the four meditative postures of sitting, standing, walking, and lying down. Using the breath as the main object of concentration, meditators are encouraged to observe their bodies and their environment. This temple is located in a beautiful forest setting and the schedule allows time for visitors to explore and enjoy the surroundings. There are periods of both group and individual practice with a mandatory chore period. Meditators can arrive

Figure 3.5 Buddha cave, Wat Tam Doi Tohn

Figure 3.6 Sign outside Wat Pah Tam Wua

at any time and stay for as long as they would like, with a week recommended as the minimum duration. International meditators usually find this temple while traveling from Pai to Mae Hong Son in Northern Thailand or through word of mouth. When I spoke with Ajan Luangta, he estimated there are usually between six and ten international meditators in residence each month since he posted an English sign at the temple gates welcoming all to try meditation in 2004.

Central, Southern, and Northern Thailand are the three regions where popular international meditation centers have developed mostly through following these tourism patterns, teaching lineages that are accessible and open to foreigners, word of mouth, as well as information available in guides and through Internet searches. Interested tourists fueled the establishment and development of these international meditation centers. The rest of this chapter explores further this diverse field of international engagement in terms of environment, practices, and people that international meditators are likely to encounter in Thailand.

Thailand's international meditation center teachers

Lay and ordained, female and male, Thai and foreign—all of these characterize international meditation center teachers who share a role in the processes of teaching and dialogue within Thailand's international meditation centers. Equally as diverse as the meditation center itself, international meditators encounter a variety of teachers from different social backgrounds. Nationality, gender, and religious status of teachers directly shape international meditators' experiences and provide structures through which international meditators encounter Thai Buddhism.

62 Engagement with Thai meditation centers

These teachers' roles are significant as they establish the flexibility necessary for participation of international meditators and in some cases attempt to provide continuity with modern imaginaries of meditation. Some meditators prefer a Thai monk teacher, who may be considered more 'authentic' by some international meditators, while others feel uncomfortable with the rituals surrounding a monastic and would prefer a more secular experience led by a lay international teacher.

Thai monk meditation teachers, who teach at the majority of international meditation centers, fall into two categories—those who cater to both Thai and international communities and those who only teach international meditators. The first group must differentiate their teachings depending on their students. Since these monks assume different roles when teaching separate groups, there is not a shared worldview that emerges from the intersection of Thai and international meditators. These Thai monk teachers acknowledge and accommodate for international, non-Buddhist meditators' religious and cultural backgrounds, constantly shifting teaching practices and languages while weaving between the worlds of Thai Buddhists and international meditators. This group therefore is most articulate about their strategies of translation and adaptation of the Thai retreat model. Those who instruct both Thai and international meditators can be temple abbots who have recently opened their temples for foreign guests. They typically have no formal training in English but learn through their interactions with the first international meditators they host, such as the example of abbot Ajan Luangta at Wat Pah Tam Wua. The second group of Thai monk teachers is usually appointed by the head of the international meditation center to dedicate their time exclusively to international meditators. These monks are nearly fluent in English and are often younger than the monks who teach Thai meditators. In fact in Chiangmai, there are two Buddhist universities[45] with monk students from Vietnam, Cambodia, Laos, Myanmar, Nepal, and Bangladesh who are learning about meditation in English. These monks are sometimes tasked with teaching international meditators, as is the case at Wat Umong.

Many Thai monk meditation teachers don't have enough fluency in English to be an international meditation center teacher. In part because of this lack of proficiency in English among Thai monastic meditation teachers, the increasing presence of international meditators has created opportunities for English-speaking lay teachers. This small group of meditation teachers consists of both Thai and foreign laity. The need for different skills, such as knowledge of English and a multicultural perspective, creates new social spaces and roles. International meditators respond differently to lay teachers who do not require practices such as bowing and making offerings. Teacher and student can interact on a more familiar and informal level, especially if the lay teacher is also a non-Thai and native English speaker. Lay foreign teachers, the smallest group with only two sites exclusively utilizing lay foreigners, usually only instruct international meditators and have likely achieved their status through their meditation experience and authorization from their Thai monk teacher or other lay, foreign teachers. Another group of international meditation center teachers consists of foreign monastics, utilized at four sites. These teachers occupy a unique position, as they are able to teach with the authority of an ordained

Engagement with Thai meditation centers 63

person and without a language barrier. However international meditators often feel awkward bowing to and maintaining monastic protocol with someone of their cultural background where these practices are not the norm.

In a similar way as foreign and lay spaces have been opened through the mass meditation center movement, alternative roles for female teachers are also created. Joanna Cook (2010) has observed this in her study of *mae chiis* in a Northern Thai meditation temple. She argues that with the rise of lay *vipassanā* meditation, a significant way *mae chiis* can embody the monastic ideal is through teaching meditation. International meditation centers follow this trend by creating roles for women such as Thai *mae chii* and foreign and Thai female retreat facilitators and teachers at the International Dhamma Hermitage, an international female monastic at Wat Prayong, and lay female meditation teachers at Wat Chom Tong and Wat Kow Tahm. The rise in popularity of meditation practice and the international meditation center is therefore opening new spaces and alternative forms of authority for women, foreigners, and laity within Thai Buddhism (Schedneck 2013).

Other roles for those interested in helping international meditators include volunteers who manage international group retreats at the International Dhamma Hermitage, Dipabhavan, and Wat Kow Tahm. These roles exist for both monastic and laypeople, foreign and Thai and can include giving a dhamma talk of one's personal experiences and conducting interviews for those international meditators with questions about their practices. These different roles open new spaces for a diversity of teachers and teachings. But regardless of their status each teacher faces similar issues of how to adapt the retreat program. Even though international meditation center teachers, especially those who are Thai monks, find it hard to envision the worldview of their international students, many of them have

Figure 3.7 Mae Chii chanting, Wat Chom Tong

64 *Engagement with Thai meditation centers*

had enough interaction and feedback from this group in order to be aware of the need to decontextualize the teachings and practices of Thai Buddhism for this audience. I discuss this in detail in Chapter 6. Another group that international meditators encounter as part of the world of the international meditation center but often do not interact with is the Thai laity meditating beside them. These distinct groups demonstrate the extent to which international meditators are separate from and have little affect on the Thai Buddhist retreat model.

Thai and international meditators

Although the majority of foreign participants as reflected by interviews with international meditation center teachers are Euro-American with little to no experience with Buddhism, there is diversity among international meditators. Some international meditators have lived in Thailand for many years and have deep knowledge of Thai Buddhism. Interesting members of this group will be discussed in the next chapter. Some international meditators whom I encountered at Wat Kow Tahm and Wat Mahathat had investigated Tibetan and East Asian forms of Buddhist meditation, attended retreats in India and China, and wanted to see how Thailand would compare. In addition, a minority of Japanese, Chinese, Korean, Malaysian, Singaporean, and other international meditators from Buddhist backgrounds have knowledge of other types of Buddhism. Thai meditators are for the most part Buddhist; however, a small number of Thai Christians partake in meditation retreats as well. Their role as non-Buddhists places them in similar positions to the international meditators who also do not attend devotional activities of the Thai Buddhist group. Many Thai Buddhists arrive in groups of family members, friends, colleagues, and fellow students. They remain embedded within social relationships of family, community, and society. In this way they are not autonomous from their social roles as international meditators are, who usually attend retreats with one or two traveling partners or alone.[46] Since it is impossible to capture the full range of international and Thai meditators, the picture I paint is one that international meditation center teachers use to characterize their students, based on broad knowledge cultivated over many years or, in some cases, decades of teaching both groups. My observations of and interviews with international meditators at all sites and Thai meditators at four sites during fieldwork also contribute to this picture.

International meditators encounter and engage to a limited extent with Thai Buddhists. Therefore the presence of international meditators does not penetrate into the ways Thai Buddhists conduct their meditation retreats. This is because the Thai Buddhist retreat model is explicitly adapted for international meditators' understanding of meditation as decontextualized from Thai Buddhism. Through the establishment of lay meditation centers for Thai Buddhists, many meditation teachers have created a standard retreat format, which they use as a base for their international retreat programs. The Young Buddhists Association of Thailand (YBAT), with a number of centers within Central Thailand, is an explicit example

Engagement with Thai meditation centers 65

of this. Administrator Khun Tom discussed with me that YBAT's aim is to create a routine English-speaking program at their centers. In order to implement this, international teachers are encouraged to modify the standard Thai retreat format as they deem suitable, and they do so in a number of ways.[47] Because Thai and international meditators attend these kinds of retreats at separate times, it is difficult for the groups to interact. However, in some retreats there are opportunities to practice together.

As described earlier, there are two types of retreat programs for international meditators within Thailand. One is a group retreat that completely separates Thai and English-speaking participants, with one group practicing at the beginning of the month and the other at the end of the month. Examples of this occur at the International Dhamma Hermitage and Dipabhavan in Southern Thailand, where there is little chance of interaction between Thai and international meditators. The second type is an individual retreat where participants arrive according to their own schedules so Thai and international meditators attend at the same time, such as the Ajan Tong retreats in Chiangmai. Within centers where international and Thai meditators are integrated, of course, the language is a major dividing factor. So even though retreatants attend the centers at the same time, the two groups are separated for most activities. Thai meditators have daily interviews with different instructors at different times of the day, they attend separate dhamma talks and orientations, and they may have separate meditation areas. This is what I wrote in my fieldnotes from my discussion on this topic with one of the foreign lay meditation teachers at Wat Chom Tong International Meditation Center:

> [S]ome of the Thai meditators at Wat Chom Tong meditate for only 3 or 4 hours a day and meet the monk teacher in a group. The teacher heard one woman complain about being instructed to meditate for 25 minutes. These Thai Buddhists come to the temple to make merit and participate in the ritual activities. In contrast, international meditators have the teacher available to them individually, whenever they need and for as long as they need. They are challenged to do intense meditation.

Of course this is one observation and there are many Thai meditators who practice meditation seriously.

There is a range of devotional activity that is part of the retreat for Thai meditators. Especially, the practice of making merit is a significant component of the retreat experience for Thai meditators in a way that it is not for international meditators. Not being familiar with Thai Buddhist practices, some international meditators do not understand the concept of merit. Particularly they observe the stray, starving cats and dogs within the meditation center and wonder why they don't have any food while the monks receive abundant amounts of food each morning. Caroline, in her late 20s from Ireland, took one of the new-born kittens from Wat Chom Tong back to a yoga studio in Chiangmai where she worked

66 *Engagement with Thai meditation centers*

because she felt it would be better cared for there. For many Thai Buddhists, giving to monks offers greater merit than giving to animals. This is because monks, unlike cats and dogs, are considered sources of merit on account of their observance of the monastic rules as delineated in the *Vinaya*.[48]

Many Thai Buddhists attend meditation retreats in order to gain merit. Within Theravāda Buddhism, one can make merit (*tam bun*) in a number of ways by following the Buddhist path of morality, concentration, and wisdom.[49] One of the main functions of merit is to cultivate generosity, one of the Ten Perfections one must practice on the path to becoming a Buddha.[50] One cultivates giving so that it becomes a natural intention to have less attachment to one's possessions. Activities of merit-making are enacted in daily rituals of Thai Buddhism as well as special holidays and events. Buddhists create good *kamma*[51] for themselves and others by participating in these activities, such as offering food, money, or other necessary items to monks and temples. From the almost weekly *wan phra* ritual activities to *Visakha Bucha*, the celebration of the Buddha's birthday, Enlightenment, and death, special events mark an auspicious and appropriate time to make merit. On major Buddhist holidays, many meditation centers are packed beyond capacity with meditators who believe that their actions on these important days within the Buddhist calendar will gain much merit. Other ways of making merit include individual practice and study of Buddhism, listening to the dhamma, or helping to publish or write a dhamma book. Thai Buddhists often make merit on their birthdays, before a big event such as an exam or business venture, during a festival (*ngaan*) at an individual temple, and, as mentioned, during special days on the Thai Buddhist calendar. Therefore contributing in any way to the livelihood of monastics, any persons with a field of merit,[52] to the institution of Buddhism, or bettering oneself through meditation and learning about Buddhism creates merit for the individual.

Lavish merit-making donations by individuals have been documented in the Southeast Asian Theravāda region demonstrating the societal function of merit (Cate 2003; Schober 1995). Wealthier members of a community are obliged to act as hosts (*chao phap*) for temple functions (Cate 2003, 27). Wealthy people make merit, giving large amounts, as evidence that they are deserving of their status in this life and are wealthy because of their generosity in previous lives. For instance, at many international meditation centers a wealthy family will sponsor a meal or evening drink for the meditators. This is especially common during the rainy season (*phansa*) as the heightened religious practice of monks and meditators during this time marks them as a greater field of merit. Through keeping the Eight Precepts even meditators can be considered a field of merit, however, not as great as that of monastics. Therefore merit-making is part of one's social and ontological status.

Merit-making is also done for fun (*sanuk*). Day or weekend trips to a number of temples in regions throughout Thailand are organized as merit-making tours. Individuals, temples, or companies organize these tours, which are popular activities among lay Buddhists. The distance and effort one makes to seek out temples adds to the supposed amount of merit to be accrued. Thai Buddhists on these tours

Engagement with Thai meditation centers   67

also get a chance to see their friends and new places while learning more about Buddhism. Therefore merit-making not only supports Buddhism but is also a social activity creating meaning and relationships between individuals and institutions.[53]

Many international meditators do not recognize or are not familiar with these wider dimensions of religious practice outside of meditation. Because of the location of many international meditation centers within Buddhist temples in a Buddhist country, there is a heightened atmosphere of religious practices that some international meditators find confusing and disconcerting. For international meditators, adaptations of the retreat format and dialogue with their teachers create an intensification of meditation while deemphasizing and separating out ritual and devotional practices. Because of this, the retreat for international meditators consists of many optional activities, discussed more in Chapters 6 and 7. Within various centers, English-speaking meditators are able to chant with Thai monks, ask to speak with a Thai monk about meditation practice, listen to a dhamma talk in Thai, and attend any ritual or celebration that is occurring at the temple if they wish. However, it is not expected and sometimes not encouraged that international meditators attend these extra activities. Therefore only those who are comfortable, interested, and familiar with Buddhism in Thailand take advantage of special activities beyond meditation. International meditation center teachers expect the main activity for their international students on retreat to be meditation and may see other activities as a way to avoid another hour of meditation and not be truly devotional. If a meditator were observed to be less than serious, they would not be encouraged to attend any extra temple activities. Therefore, international meditation center teachers find that there are different responses to temple activities, including curiosity, disingenuousness, and disinterest. In contrast, it is natural for Thai Buddhists to attend all temple functions. For Thai meditators the meditation center exposes a religiosity where meditation is one part of a larger experience of living in a Buddhist temple that includes maintaining ascetic precepts, listening to dhamma talks by monks, chanting, and devotional activities. In this way, learning and engagement with Thai meditators by international meditators can take place in some situations, but this is limited and in some cases restricted.

Although most devotional practices are optional for international meditators, some new practices are added for them. At Wat Umong I was able to participate in both groups' activities since they were at different times. In the mornings at this temple, Phra Viriya, a monk from Vietnam, taught some yoga poses that he learned from former students. This is not a typical procedure at meditation retreats led by Thai monks and is idiosyncratic to this temple. For international meditators there is a flexibility of practices. Yoga is an ambiguous activity to conduct within temple grounds, often frowned upon by conservative monks and laypeople. However, for this international meditation center teacher, yoga is seen to be especially important for foreigners who are not used to sitting cross-legged on the floor for several hours a day. The Thai meditators, in contrast, during their group practice time, have a much longer chanting session, dhamma talk, and no yoga. This flexibility for international meditators allows space for them to imagine the retreat in new ways. In this way, international meditators do not interact with or affect the Thai meditators or their standard retreat format.

68   *Engagement with Thai meditation centers*

Thai meditators often do not notice that the practices and teachings are being adapted and reimagined for their international counterparts, as evidenced by my conversations with Thai meditators.[54] I asked one Thai meditator at Wat Umong if she participated in an opening ceremony. She responded that she had and asked about my experience. I told her that international meditators do not participate in an opening ceremony. This statement confused her, and I had to repeat the information. She assumed that international meditators would go through the same process as Thai meditators. Thai meditators are often happy to see international meditators and assume similar motivations or that international meditators have more discipline than Thais. Two Thai Buddhists at Wat Chom Tong, seeing my white clothing, commented to me that they admire foreign meditators because they take meditation seriously. International meditators generally are regarded highly without much knowledge about their motivations or experiences. Because of these new and adapted practices for international meditators along with the different imaginaries of meditation and the retreat program from Thai Buddhists, a shared worldview does not emerge between the two groups.

Thai Buddhist understandings of *vipassanā*

International and Thai meditators not only have separate and distinct groups, they also have different aims within the meditation retreat program and understand meditation in different ways. These differences can be encapsulated by the perception of *vipassanā* meditation as a means to construct perceptions of reality and gain merit within an embedded social and ethical context versus that of *vipassanā* as a decontextualized practice from Thai Buddhism.[55] Both of these views are contextualized in different ways. International meditators' imaginaries are decontextualized from the Thai Buddhist worldview but embedded within modern discourses of Romanticism, psychology, and secularism. Here I want to contrast this with a Thai Buddhist understanding of *vipassanā*, which is embedded within the wider cultural understanding and public sphere of Thai Buddhism. Of course it is an impossible task to describe a general view of Thai Buddhist understandings of meditation. I do not conceive of all Thai Buddhists as regarding meditation in the same ways nor do I seek to create an oversimplified dichotomy between them and international meditators. Like any group, some Thai Buddhists have a more complex understanding of Thai Buddhism, while others relate more closely with the modern discourses of international meditators. However there are explicit assumptions via cultural backgrounds that many Thai Buddhists bring to a meditation retreat. Striving for *nibbāna* or realization of the three characteristics of *anatta* (non-self), *anicca*, (impermanence), and *dukkha* (suffering) is limited to advanced practitioners. Earlier stages of practice hope to generate an embodied awareness or increased ability to remain mindful or concentrated, along with other more practical goals. Thai meditators, therefore, understand the practice of *vipassanā* both conceptually and practically. This section focuses on both the advanced and beginner meditation goals, describing the various aims of *vipassanā* meditation.

Meditation is embedded in specific social, ethical, and cosmological frameworks, involving ritual, social, and magical dimensions. Therefore Thai Buddhist piety needs to be placed within this context. Pattana Kitiarsa (2012) describes popular Thai Buddhist practice as consisting significantly of a distinction between a monastic or religious layperson belonging to the *lokkutara* (world-transcending) sphere with the goal of *nibbāna*, and the lay householder in the *lokiya* (worldly) sphere, with material goals of wealth, love, and beauty. Within this latter sphere piety is expressed outwardly though merit-making in the form of offerings, chanting, wearing amulets, and making vows. These acts have helped to produce "a significantly new Buddhist personhood and sensibility, with greater emphasis on this-worldly benefits and practical morality" (Kitiarsa 2012, 120). Thai Buddhists can attend a meditation retreat focused on the *lokiya* sphere by hoping to gain merit from keeping the Eight Precepts and staying in the temple. I encountered many examples of this during the course of my fieldwork. A Thai lay female meditator commented to me that she was attending a retreat for one week at Wat Prayong because her husband's business was starting a new venture. Her meditative performance therefore was not exclusively directed towards understanding reality but toward gaining merit that could be transferred to her husband for a specific purpose. Similarly I encountered a young woman at Wat Rampoeng who was attending the retreat for a week in order to fulfill a vow. She had vowed that if she got into Chiangmai University she would practice meditation. In this way her practice is enacted as gratitude for her worldly success. Therefore, along with the ultimate goal of *nibbāna* within the *lokuttara* sphere, meditation can be used to generate pragmatic goals and accomplishments in school and business, as well as good *kamma*, and better rebirths as rich humans or in heaven realms.[56] Supernatural powers can also be a goal within the *lokiya* sphere. People who gain these powers are important in Buddhist communities, providing knowledge about the future or even healing illnesses.

In addition to accessing the retreat through the *lokiya* sphere, the *lokuttara* sphere remains operational due to the mass lay meditation movement. In this movement both monastics and laity practice together under the prevailing idea of the mission of the meditation center, that *nibbāna* is possible for both groups. Joanna Cook's fieldwork in a meditation center in Northern Thailand is concerned with the deep and long-term effects of meditation for monastics, and therefore represents the ideal or *lokuttara* goals of *vipassanā* practice. She argues that the practice of *vipassanā* is intended to bring about a change in perception in the meditator consistent with Buddhist ethical principles (Cook 2010, 95). As a result of the dedicated practice of meditation, each mental and physical movement becomes evidence of religious principles. Meditators engage in specific practices in order to change their experiences in relation to religious concepts, so that religious tenets become real. Practitioners are encouraged to interpret the everyday flow of their own awareness in terms of impermanence, suffering, and non-self and to see in it evidence of these religious truths (Cook 2010, 2). Doctrines are transformed into experience through the practice of complete awareness of one's present moment and changing mental formations. However, this does not mean that monastics cannot be concerned with protection, power, and other *lokiya* goals of meditation.

70 *Engagement with Thai meditation centers*

It is possible to enter into a meditation retreat with both *lokiya* and *lokuttara* goals, as they are not contradictory but rather modes and processes through which Thai Buddhists use to think about and access the meditation retreat. Each action of the meditation retreat, taking the Three Refuges, keeping the Eight Precepts, and practicing meditation not only displays one's discipline and helps one to accrue merit but can also imbue one with power and protection (Cook 2012, 37).

Considering both the *lokuttara* and *lokiya*, *nibbānic*, and merit-making orientations of Thai Buddhist understandings of meditation, the practice is in both cases embedded within Buddhist ethical and doctrinal frameworks. Whether one intends to gain merit, attain a worldly goal, or perceive directly the truth of suffering, non-self, and impermanence, Buddhist teachings and cosmological worldview provide the context for these various goals. Because of the different cultural backgrounds of international meditators, their practice is not embedded in these Thai Buddhist contexts but imaginaries of meditation and how it can be connected to their individual, cultural, and religious repertoires.

Conclusion

Although during the course of my research I visited more sites, the ones described above are the international meditation centers I will refer to throughout the remaining chapters. These are also the sites which host the largest numbers of international meditators and are the most well-known among travelers. Most of these centers have websites and other promotional materials to welcome international meditators. Word of mouth and Internet discussion forums spread information concerning international meditators' opinions of each retreat center.

To provide more context for understanding the world of the international meditation center, this chapter discussed the contemporary Thai history of this phenomenon, the social roles of teachers and students, and the most popular methods and sites for international meditators. All of this can be characterized by diversity. There is a diversity of teachers, lay and ordained, Thai and foreign, as well as a diversity of international meditators in terms of national origin and orientation toward Thailand and Buddhism. In addition there is a range of centers and methods to choose from. The limited interactions between Thai and international meditators and their varying understandings of the meditation retreat informed by their cultural backgrounds helps to explain that a shared worldview does not emerge from their communal practice. Although there are international meditators more informed by Thai Buddhism and Thai Buddhists who view meditation as a decontextualized practice, the differences mainly lie in the embededness of the retreat for Thai Buddhists in social and ethical contexts and the decontextualized nature of the practice for international meditators from the Thai Buddhist world that is inserted within secular, modern discourses instead.

It is important to note that international meditators do not have the whole of Thai Buddhism available to them as only the most popular, well-established methods, lineages, and sites offer opportunities to learn and practice in English. Although international meditators are limited they can choose between a number

Engagement with Thai meditation centers 71

of sites in Central, Southern, and Northern Thailand. These three areas are the most important for tourism in Thailand. The Forest Tradition of the Northeast is popular for international visitors and monastics but does not follow the mass lay meditation center model. Most international meditators choose a center based on location but some are more thoughtful about lineage, teacher and method they want to practice. The next chapters continue to discuss the imaginaries of international meditators, focusing closely on their experiences.

Notes

1 A field (Bourdieu 1993, 349) is a social organization that offers specific social roles and structures. Within international meditation centers the major roles of meditation teacher and meditation student are enacted during interviews, orientation, and any time when the teacher observes the student's progress and understanding of the meditation technique.

2 These are the training rules undertaken during meditation retreats or when a person is living at a temple for a short period, usually during a Buddhist holy day. The first five are the same as the Five Precepts, while the three additional rules help to facilitate meditation practice and temple living. These eight precepts begin with "I undertake the precept to refrain from . . ." 1) destroying living creatures; 2) taking that which is not given; 3) sexual activity; 4) incorrect speech; 5) intoxicating drinks and drugs which lead to carelessness; 6) eating at the forbidden time (i.e., after noon); 7) dancing, singing, listening to music, going to see entertainments, wearing garlands, using perfumes, and beautifying the body with cosmetics; 8) lying on a high or luxurious sleeping place.

3 Important international monasteries of the Ajan Chah lineage are located in the USA, United Kingdom, New Zealand, Australia, Switzerland, and Italy. For a complete list of monasteries see forestsangha.org.

4 For a list of books by and about Luangta Mahabua see forestdhamma.org. Books relating to the Ajan Chah tradition can be found at forestsanghapublications.org. Although both Luangta Mahabua and Ajan Chah consider themselves disciples of Ajan Man Luangpu Mun, they have different groups of disciples who manage the memory of each teacher and disseminate their teachings in English through separate venues.

5 Current abbot of Wat Pah Nanachat, Ven. Ajan Kevali, the international forest monastery founded by Ajan Chah, recommends that visitors participate in a meditation retreat based on the Four Foundations of Mindfulness, or the Goenka method, before arriving for a stay at Wat Pah Nanachat. Because this temple offers no meditation instruction, a retreat experience will give the meditator a method to follow independently.

6 Ajan Naeb Mahaniranonda (1897–1983) studied meditation under Ajan Pathunta U Visala, a Burmese teacher at Wat Prog in Bangkok. She then studied the Abhidhamma and taught meditation and Buddhist philosophy in Thailand for many years. Naeb's (1982) book *The Development of Insight* deals with awareness of the body in the four major postures: walking, sitting, standing, and lying down as they relate to the characteristics of suffering, impermanence, and non-self. Through this focus, she wants students to see the inevitable suffering that comes with having a body.

7 Luangpor Theean Jittasubho's (1911–1988) method of meditation is characterized as dynamic rather than static sitting meditation. The system is based on the mindful action of the hands in a set pattern. This method is popular with monks and laypeople and has no direct connection with canonical texts. He identified it as new and it became popular because it was perceived as effective.

8 For more information on this ordination see Skilton (2013).

9 I collected this brochure during my stay at Wat Mahathat, Section 5, from June 13th–June 15th, 2010.

72 Engagement with Thai meditation centers

10 Interview with Venerable Phra Suputh Kosalo (Ajan Suphat), Section 5, Wat Mahathat, June 18th, 2010.
11 More information can be found here: www.centermeditation.com/english_version_mainpage.php
12 Interview with Mae Chii Brigitte, Wat Prayong Gittivararam, March 10th, 2010.
13 More information about Mae Chii Brigitte's life can be found in the next chapter and on her website: www.meditationthailand.com/maechee_index.htm.
14 See Newell (2008) for more information on Dhammakaya temple networks.
15 Some scholars have argued (Crosby 2000; Newell 2008) that Dhammakaya meditation takes as its origin *yogāvacara* (known as a form of Tantric Theravāda) meditation techniques. This is one of the reasons why Dhammakaya meditation has many features that are different from other forms of Theravāda meditation.
16 When I participated in their retreat in June 2010, it took place in Loei.
17 For more information see: www.mdwmeditation.org/meditationthai.php.
18 See BMI's website: www.dhammacenter.org/retreat/monastery/buddhist_meditation_institute.
19 Interviews with Phra Bart took place at Wat Luang Por Sot on March 7th, 2010, and June 28th, 2010.
20 For information on Wat Suan Mokkh see: www.suanmokkh.org/.
21 Swearer notes that Buddhadasa's writings constitute "the largest corpus of thought ever published by a single Theravāda thinker in the entire history of the tradition" (Swearer 1989, 2).
22 Buddhadasa Bhikkhu's important reinterpretations of dhamma include creating categories of everyday language (*phasaa khon*) and Dhamma language (*phasaa tham*) and envisioning *nibbāna* within everyday experience. Through these theoretical understandings, Buddhadasa built a framework for socially active Buddhist practices directed towards politics and socioeconomic development.
23 Swearer specifically contrasts Buddhadasa with Buddhaghosa, author of the Visuddhimagga, and Wachirayan, the reformer of Thai Buddhism in the early twentieth century (Swearer 1989, 3).
24 See website: www.suanmokkh-idh.org/.
25 In August of 2010, the Buddhadasa Bhikkhu Indapanno Archives (BIA) opened in Bangkok. The BIA's mission is to uphold the three wishes of Buddhadasa Bhikkhu: for people to understand their own religion, have mutual understanding for other religions, and to be able to remove themselves from the grips of consumerism and materialism. The BIA was set up as a new and separate foundation to maintain Buddhadasa Bhikkhu's writings and recordings. They have support and cooperation from Buddhadasa Bhikkhu's monastery, Wat Suan Mokkh, and the Dhammadana foundation. See website: www.bia.or.th/.
26 Santikaro, known formerly as Santikaro Bhikkhu, was Buddhadasa Bhikkhu's main translator, helping to bring many of Buddhadasa's works to an English-speaking audience. He has since disrobed and established a retreat center in Wisconsin, USA, called Liberation Park (www.liberationpark.org). I discuss this transnational link further in Chapter 8.
27 Interviews conducted at the International Dhamma Hermitage include Mae Chii Aree February 3rd, 2010; Than Medhi, February 6th 2010; Ajan Pho, February 10th, 2010; Than Dhammavidu, February 10th, 2010. Additionally I interviewed lay volunteer Reinhard, of the International Dhamma Hermitage, via email on February 22nd, 2010.
28 See the website for more information: www.suanmokkh-idh.org/suanmokkh-idh.html.
29 I attended the retreat at Dipabhavan Meditation Center from June 20th–June 27th, 2010.
30 For more information see: www.dipabhavan.org/.
31 For more information see: www.watkowtahm.org/data/watmain.htm.
32 Since my research at this meditation center, Rosemary and Steve Weissman have moved to Australia and currently teach there and Europe, New Zealand, and Asia.

Mae Chii Ahmon remains head of the meditation center and experienced teachers continue to lead seven and ten day retreats for international meditators.

33 I attended the retreat at Wat Kow Tahm from January 9th–January 18th, 2010, and conducted an interview with Steve Weissman on January 19th, 2010.

34 See Weissman and Weissman (1999) for more details on the content of their retreat program. And Weissman (2006) for details on this specific practice of wise reflection.

35 The two techniques use the same basic practices of sitting and walking meditation with a focus on the rise and fall of one's abdomen. However, international meditation center teachers at Wat Chom Tong explained to me that Ajan Tong's basic retreat course is over a month shorter than Mahasi Sayadaw's recommended basic course. As well Ajan Tong's recommended speed for walking meditation and daily activities while in retreat is relatively quicker than Mahasi Sayadaw's method.

36 For Wat Rampoeng's meditation center website see: www.palikanon.com/vipassana/tapotaram/tapotaram.htm.

37 For Wat Chom Tong's meditation center website see: www.northernvipassana.org.

38 For Wat Prathat Doi Suthep's meditation retreat information see: www.fivethousandyears.org.

39 Ajan Tong is currently abbot of Wat Chom Tong and former abbot of Wat Rampoeng and the two centers remain connected; however Wat Prathat Doi Suthep uses the Ajan Tong method but is not a branch temple.

40 Statistical data is available for Wat Rampoeng and Wat Doi Suthep. However, Wat Chom Tong's International Meditation Center does not record their numbers of meditators nor do they have any available statistics. This information was told to me during interviews and more recently confirmed again through email correspondence with an assistant to the international meditation center on March 25th, 2014.

41 Evrard and Prasit (2009b, 301) call Doi Suthep one of the main destinations for tourists in Northern Thailand, both Thai and foreign. It is estimated that 120,000 tourists visit Wat Doi Suthep per month.

42 Wat Tam Doi Tohn's website is: vimuttidhamma.org.

43 This book can be found online: http://vimuttidhamma.org/Vimuttidhamma%20From%20Chakra%20to%20Dhammachakra%20by%20Piyadhassi%20Bhikkhu.pdf.

44 I discuss the transnational networks Ajan Nawi and others create through their teaching abroad in Chapter 8.

45 The two universities are the Mahachulalongkornrajavidyalaya Buddhist University, Chiangmai Campus located at Wat Suan Dok, part of the Mahanikai Sect, and the Mahamakut Buddhist University, Chiangmai Campus, at Wat Jedi Luang, part of the Thammayut Sect.

46 Hori (1994, 49) has found similarly in his comparison of Asian and Western Buddhists in America.

47 Interview conducted at YBAT Headquarters, Thonburi, on December 12th, 2010. I discuss these ways most clearly in Chapter 6. Specifically at YBAT the format for international meditators changes to include less strict silence, natural airflow instead of air-conditioned meditation halls, and vegetarian food. For more information on YBAT see: http://www.ybat.org/eng/.

48 Campbell finds similar circumstances concerning convert Canadian Buddhists in Toronto's Zen Buddhist Temple. This group felt that practices of merit-making were not a means of spiritual attainment. She writes, "Respondents aspired to be their own source of spiritual merit and the agents of their own spiritual growth and were less willing to rely upon external powers or authorities" (Campbell 2010, 198).

49 See Chapter 2 for a discussion of these terms.

50 The Ten Perfections are: generosity (*dana*), morality (*sila*), renunciation (*nekhamma*), wisdom (*pañña*), effort, (*viriya*), patience (*khanti*), truthfulness (*sacca*), determination (*adhitthana*), loving-kindness (*metta*), equanimity (*upekkha*).

51 *Kamma* in Pāli or *karma* in Sanskrit is the complex Buddhist law or theory of moral causation. This is an impersonal force, which determines one's realm of birth based on

74 *Engagement with Thai meditation centers*

one's past actions. However, this is not a fatalistic doctrine as individuals continue to make new choices and new *kamma*. For a clear introduction, see Thanissaro (2000).

52 It is considered that a person keeping Buddhist precepts has a field of merit. Depending on the person and amount of precepts they keep, this field of merit can be large or relatively small. Donating or offering to a person with a large field of merit allows the giver to receive a larger amount of merit than if they donated to a person with a small field of merit. Thai Buddhists judge a field of merit to be large or small based on the person's lifestyle and discipline. Monastics generally have a large field of merit because of the strict rules they keep.

53 Modern Buddhist leaders such as Buddhadasa Bhikkhu, Sulak Sivarakasa, and Samana Bodhirak critique merit-making and ritualism in mainstream Thai Buddhism. Buddhadasa Bhikkhu, the internationally known scholar monk, did not condone merit-making in his writings and instead stressed the importance of insight into the state of all beings. He told his followers that instead of making merit as a way to go to heaven or have a better life one should practice dhamma by doing one's duty selflessly in the current moment. Buddhadasa Bhikkhu saw the preoccupation with merit-making in mainstream Thai Buddhism as a refutation of the central Buddhist teaching of non-attachment, as it is often performed in order to gain material benefits (Swearer 1989). Sulak Sivaraksa, lay Buddhist intellectual, creates a distinction between Buddhism with a capital B and Buddhism with a small b. The former he recognizes as mainstream Buddhism including culture and customs such as ritual and merit-making but small b Buddhism is oriented toward the message of the Buddha (Sivaraksa 1992, 68). Samana Bodhirak veered from mainstream Thai Buddhism with his movement called Asoke. This movement critiques all ritual and commercial aspects of Thai Buddhism, stating that merit-making in contemporary society has become based on capitalism (Scott 2009, 171). Instead he promotes merit-making as sacrifices one makes for oneself, one's community, and society. These consist of work activities that are free from attachment to material riches and personal desires (Essen 2005, 61). These thinkers' ideas align with modern Buddhist imaginaries and sensibilities of international meditators. Although its value is contested within the Thai Buddhist public sphere, merit-making remains an important feature of Thai Buddhist practice.

54 For my fieldwork in centers with mixed Thai and international meditators, I was able to participate in both groups' activities, joining the chanting and dhamma talks of the Thai meditators and the English meditation instruction with the international meditators. Although I focused on discussions with international meditators, the interactions with Thai meditators were quite useful. Interviews with Thai meditators and Thai international meditation center teachers were conducted in Thai while I used English with international meditators and foreign international meditation center teachers.

55 I will discuss in detail in later chapters how *vipassanā* is decontextualized for international meditators. As well some international meditators have a deep knowledge of Thai Buddhist and meditation practices that I will discuss in Chapter 4.

56 Within Buddhism there is a complex cosmology consisting of thirty-one realms of existence to which a being can be reborn. The realm of rebirth is temporary and based on one's *kamma*. Wholesome *kamma* leads to a pleasant birth in a heaven realm, while unwholesome *kamma* leads to a hell realm. These realms are usually divided into three parts: the immaterial world (*arupa-loka*), the fine-material world (*rupa-loka*), and the sensuous world (*kama-loka*). See Access to Insight Website for more detailed information: www.accesstoinsight.org/ptf/dhamma/sagga/loka.html.

4 Narratives of international meditators' experiences

Narratives of international meditators' experiences illustrate the extent to which meditation has become divorced from the Thai Buddhist context, as well as the diversity and dynamism of this group. International meditators' imaginaries of meditation include a Romantic, natural setting and a practice that can be used as therapy, healing, and overall well-being, representing the different ways to enter into and access the meditation retreat. Placing meditation within these various frameworks may involve the removal of the practice from its ethical, social, and cultural contexts within Buddhism. Buddhist meditation has become extremely successful as a practice that can be reproduced in a variety of contexts. From travelers who mix meditation with a beach vacation to serious practitioners with hopes of becoming ordained, from accidental religious tourists to people who set out to change their lives, the experiences and responses to the meditation practice and lifestyle in the international meditation centers can have many faces. This chapter introduces the reader to international meditators—their motivations, narratives, experiences, reflections, and imaginaries of meditation, including most significantly Romanticism, health, and well-being. This group appropriates aspects of the meditation retreat selectively according to their motivations and goals. Some seek conversion via rejection of their own culture while others select aspects most familiar to their ways of life. Experiences of the exotic, a connection with nature, a way to recover from addiction, and therapeutic practices are all discourses that international meditators engage with when deciding to attend a meditation retreat. For some meditators, a deep connection to and understanding of Thai Buddhism can be launched through the initial engagement at a meditation retreat. I discuss these various points on the spectrum of engagement with Thai Buddhism in this chapter.

Along with different motivations, interpretations of the meditation experience can also be varied. Some meditators interpret the experience as cathartic, relaxing, an interesting encounter with a foreign culture, a religious experience, or a once in a lifetime opportunity. Some meditators discuss their experiences at meditation retreats in Thailand in terms of a tourist and cultural experience, others a secular practice for therapeutic purposes, representing manifestations of both Rational and Romantic Orientalism, but with many variations in between. In addition to international meditators who participated in a retreat, I also conducted more lengthy biographical interviews with foreign ordained and lay teachers who had once

76   *Narratives of international meditators' experiences*

been international meditators. Their stories, recounted later in the chapter, demonstrate the possible outcome of this engagement with Thai Buddhism. I introduce their stories in more detail because they simply have richer stories to tell about longer engagements with Thai Buddhism. Using semi-structured interviews with the international meditators I encountered at each site during fieldwork, correspondence with former international meditators and the ordained and lay teachers mentioned earlier, participant observation, and writings from international meditators' travel blogs, this chapter looks at the variety of these experiences toward understanding the imaginaries of meditation and Thailand that international meditators bring to international meditation centers.

Many travelers have posted their experiences in blog format or on websites dedicated to their travels. It is clear from these sources that meditation is one part of a larger cultural experience of Thailand. Meditators often participate in meditation retreats in addition to elephant training camps, massage courses, cooking classes, or even events that are not related to Thai culture such as the all-night full moon party on Koh Phangan, the southern island home to Wat Kow Tahm. Despite or even because of these various tourist activities, travel blogs document the experiences of modern international meditators and help to augment the participant observation and semi-structured interviews I conducted with international meditators at each site.[1] It would be quite difficult to obtain a comprehensive or exhaustive account of international meditators through my individual research efforts as there is such a variety of sites, large numbers and diversity of participants, and a long history of participation; however, the information presented here meaningfully speaks to the common discourses, imaginaries, and experiences of international meditators.

Through speaking with international meditators, searching discussion forums and travel blogs, I have found that some people attend retreats because a friend recommended it or they have recently experienced something difficult like a relationship breakup or the death of a loved one and believe this practice will help. Others have no particular reason other than the practice is part of the cultural zeitgeist. For others still it seems a good way to begin or end a travel tour of Asia. Learning about meditation can be part of any tourist experience that searches for difference and the 'exotic.' Many international meditators begin the practice this way, and for some it is transformative. The popular imaginaries of meditation and Buddhism motivated this trend of experimentation. In her memoir of a mid-life existential crisis called *Devotion*, Dani Shapiro writes about her experimentation with meditation and defines her religious identity as a meditating, Jewish yogi. She writes, "For years, I had wanted to be someone who regularly meditates. I had a sense that sitting quietly—for five or two minutes every day—was key to a sense of inner peace" (Shapiro 2010, 9). Her words demonstrate how far meditation has penetrated into the popular imagination and become a global religious practice.

Romanticism, nature, and tourism

The depth and difficulty of a meditation retreat is often not reflected in the stock images and narrative tropes of meditation. In the modern popular imaginary of

Buddhism, its meditative practices are equated with nature and, for some, this is the primary impetus for attending a retreat. These Romantic ideas of meditation move to the forefront as Buddhist teachings and rituals become less prominent. In this context, the feeling of being at peace in nature is the goal of the practice. Natural settings within a forest along with ancient temple structures are part of the fascination and desirability surrounding meditation. These signs emerge when discussing with international meditators their initial motivations and choices to participate in a meditation retreat in a particular temple. Meditation and nature are intertwined and semiotically linked for many international meditators, as they seek out centers located in forests and mountains and avoid busy city meditation temples. In response to my research website, I have received over forty emails inquiring about which meditation retreat in Thailand to attend. The criteria given almost always include a center in a quiet, natural setting.

Tourism has fueled much of the development of international meditation centers. International meditators are attracted to those temples situated within tourist destinations, ranging from the beautiful beaches of the south to the scenic mountains of the north. My recordings of the histories of international meditation centers reveal that through visiting a temple, often by chance, travelers become interested in staying and learning about meditation. The creation of international meditation centers often began with frequent inquiries about meditation from travelers inspired to practice in natural settings. This helped pave the way for international meditators today who are able to plan their retreats in advance. The idea of practicing in nature is an important discourse that connects meditation with tourism and highlights the selective appropriation of international meditators. In fact, as is often the case, international meditators are disappointed when their chosen retreat setting does not match that of their imagination. Matt, a young college graduate from America and one of the ten international meditators I interviewed at the International Dhamma Hermitage, understood this but many of the foreigners he was surrounded by did not. He stayed at Wat Suan Mokkh before attending a monthly retreat at the International Dhamma Hermitage. His email to me illustrates what he describes as a typical reaction of international meditators' disappointment when faced with reality of temple life:

> [I]n Thai temples there can be a muted hub-bub of commotion. Parades of devotees are coming and going—making pilgrimages . . . A foreigner loaded with preconceptions about the peace and serenity often toted about Asian mysticism and meditation would be discouraged by the obviously very mundane foot traffic near the temple gate and the lack of zen gardens or whatever!

For many foreigners this juxtaposition of loud devotional activities with contemplative meditation seems inauthentic and incorrect. Wat Chom Tong also disappointed Tom, a thirty-year-old professional from the USA and one of the five international meditators I was able to communicate with there. Wat Chom Tong is a busy temple located along the main road in a small town. He writes:

78 *Narratives of international meditators' experiences*

> [M]y motivation in going to the retreat was to clear and rest my mind. I was expecting a quiet place surrounded by nature. Things that I found disheartening about the retreat was there was construction going on during our meditation sessions and a sound of loud music coming in from the town until 12AM in the morning. . . . I believe a meditation center should provide an environment of serenity where we can improve our meditation experience with as minimum distractions as possible.

Therefore, a temple situated within a city without natural views is not ideal for many international meditators seeking a separation between society and the meditation retreat.

The connection with nature that meditation is commonly thought to provide is a noted theme in the appropriation of Buddhism by Euro-Americans, as well as a characteristic of modern Buddhism and Romantic Orientalism. David McMahan argues that:

> many staples of Buddhist modernist literature – the exaltitude of nature, the idea of spiritual experience as identifying with the natural world or a universal spirit . . . owe much to the intertwining of Buddhism and Romanticist-Transcendentalist stream of thought.
>
> (McMahan 2008, 76)

McMahan goes on to assert that Romanticism caused an opposition between society and nature. In this discourse, the West becomes identified with consumerist city life and the East offers hope for a more natural lifestyle. Therefore, some modern Buddhists look to the East for a less artificial way of life, corresponding with Romantic thought. Michael Carrithers (1983, 39) argues that Romanticism influenced the well-known German forest-monk in Sri Lanka, Nyanatiloka Mahathera.[2] He finds that Nyanatiloka, along with other European monks in Sri Lanka in the early 1900s, originally had an interest in German Romanticism, which later developed into an interest in Buddhism. The tropes of Romanticism and being 'at one' with nature continue into the present and can be seen especially when international meditators in Thailand decide to undertake a meditation retreat. In this context, Buddhist teachings and meditation practices are placed within a framework of affection for nature, as well as cultural exploration. Modern tourists often display this romantic interest. A common trope I discovered in conversations with international meditators was that they characterized their motivation to visit Thailand as 'a fascination with Asia in general.' In this way Orientalist projections of Buddhism continue in the popular imagination. In the modern tourist imaginary of Thailand, the country is a place where modern ills of consumerism and capitalism have not intruded. Buddhism and its meditative practices become equated with nature and for some this is the primary impetus for attending a retreat. These Romantic ideas of meditation move to the forefront as Buddhist teachings and rituals are not as prominent when a feeling of being at peace in nature is the goal of the practice.

When embedded in this Romantic mode, a visit to the scenic temples of Thailand, often situated on mountaintops with dramatic views, is not enough for some international meditators. They set out to find a way to stay longer and admire the beauty over an extended period. Some examples of this orientation I highlight in the rest of this section serve as examples and representatives of this Romantic imaginary of the meditation retreat. This concern for nature and the importance of tourism is exemplified at the International Meditation Center at Wat Prathat Doi Suthep, one of the most famous and frequented temples in Chiangmai, Northern Thailand.[3] Some meditators attend the retreat here just for the experience of living in this temple set on a mountaintop with stunning views of Chiangmai city. These tourists locate the International Meditation Office and make an appointment to return for a ten-day retreat. Heather, a young Canadian female tourist exemplifies this mode. She told me that she chose to visit Thailand because the country, especially its Buddhist traditions, inexplicably fascinated her. She chose to attend this retreat because the setting captivated her when she first arrived as a tourist and wanted to learn more about meditation practice and the monks' lifestyles. Her imaginary of Thailand as a tourist destination included learning about Buddhism, monasticism, and meditation. Donald, a mid-twenties Irishman had had enough of late nights drinking with his buddies and took this meditation retreat as a further symbol of his renunciation of that lifestyle. These motivations and responses convey a discourse of looking to the East for answers in the face of modernity. In this way meditation offers the possibility of an interesting alternative lifestyle divorced from modernity and its temptations, consumerism, and busy schedules. For some, the experience of living in a temple environment can inspire ordination, as one annual visitor, a 50-year-old Brazilian woman, Maria, told me she would like to take steps to be a *mae chii* at Wat Doi Suthep. The natural setting of this temple and desire for cultural exploration, despite the different motivations and levels of engagement, attracted these travelers to meditate in this location.

Another temple known for its scenic location along a popular tourist route is Wat Pah Tam Wua. Many visitors stumble upon this temple while visiting the touristy spots along the beautiful and windy scenic drive of Highway 1095 in Northern Thailand, the route that runs from Chiangmai to Pai, and through to Mae Hong Son. Shimmering limestone karsts encircle the temple, which lies in a lush green valley. The main *sala* and *kutis*, dwelling places of monks, are constructed with wood and stone, allowing the architecture to blend in with the natural setting. After some of these interested tourists stopped by, the abbot, Ajan Luang Ta, put up signs in English welcoming foreign tourists. Tom, a middle-aged professional from America, found the temple through exploring this tourist route and now comes back every year for a retreat and to teach English to the monastic community. What started as an attraction to the beauty of this temple became a more lasting interest in meditation and relationships with monks. Now many hear about this temple through word of mouth, attracted by its picturesque scenery, as well as the charismatic Ajan Luang Ta, who has learned English from many of the tourists he has taught. Since 2004, international meditators from over 100 countries have come to practice here. The tourist path along Highway 1095 created a trail for

80 *Narratives of international meditators' experiences*

Figure 4.1 Scenic view, Wat Pah Tam Wua

international meditators looking to spend time in a scenic spot and converse with a Thai monk meditation teacher.

Moving south of Chiangmai, the area around Wat Tam Doi Tohn in Mae Wang is also beautiful, as Phra Ajan Nawi told me that many international meditators who come to the temple remark that the pictures on their website inspired their journey. Mountains lying in the distance, beautiful wooden architecture, open-air meditation halls, and a large cave provide international meditators with much to be enchanted by. A golden Buddha statue and stupa sit in the nook of a rocky cave with a newly constructed wooden platform for sitting meditation in this calm, placid setting. There are nearby natural green spaces and walkways surrounding the cave for break time or walking meditation. A two-storied teakwood *sala* built in the Lanna style is open for meditation, adjacent to a small pond. For international meditators, these beautiful backdrops constitute the essence of the Romantic imaginary of meditation. Indeed one of the reasons a young professional in his late twenties ordained as a novice in this temple temporarily was because he wanted to live in this beautiful setting before returning to his responsibilities in America.

Aside from the mountains of the North, beaches of the South provide international meditators with equally beautiful settings, where ocean views stand in for the mountains. International meditators often mix beach holidays with spiritual travel so that meditation is part of a broader context of the tourist experience. In the large group retreats in Southern Thailand, international meditators discuss and relate travel plans before and after the retreat. They compare guidebook information on which beach on the island has the cheapest hotels or best food and ask advice from others who have stayed there before the retreat. Some meditators relate that at the beginning of their retreats they felt they were missing out on more stimulating activities, such as recreation by the beach. However, those more interested in mental development stated that they wanted to attend the retreat precisely because the beach and other tourist activities were ultimately unsatisfying. Other experienced meditators come to Thailand every year specifically for the retreat and are not concerned about coupling their meditation with an island vacation. The International Meditation Center at Wat Kow Tahm on Koh Phangan is another interesting example of tourism that leads to a spiritual vacation. Koh Phangan has been known as a destination for backpacking with a reputation for social recreation and heavy partying, especially on full moon nights. Situated on a hill overlooking Baan Thai Beach, Wat Kow Tahm has attracted curious tourists since the 1980s. The particular groups of meditators that travel to Koh Phangan are often used to bungalows, partying, and traveling, but not necessarily living in a temple. After more than twenty years of running these retreats, the Weissmans know their audience well and have many warnings in the form of notices that must be read before attending the retreat. Signs posted on the notice boards declare, "This is not a bungalow" and, "You must be willing to work hard." Steve Weissman likens the creation of the many rules for this center to the creation of the monastic rules by the Buddha. As situations arose, more rules were added. Because they are so close to the beach and parties they choose to be strict and make sure all the participants are committed. Steve and Rosemary find that, as they continue teaching, the number of tourists arriving from the beach has gotten smaller and the majority comes just for the retreat. Therefore, tourism created particular adaptations for this international meditation center where participants learn how to behave in a temple along with meditation.

Dipabhavan Meditation Center on the island of Samui is another meditation center borne out of tourism. When Ajan Pho was a young monk, foreigners did not know about Samui, as tourism had not yet developed there. However, once tourists arrived, Ajan Pho wanted to show them Thailand's best offering, as he told me, its meditation practice.[4] He found that many tourists only were interested in material things or lying on the beach, and therefore had nothing of value to bring back to their home countries. At Dipabhavan's seven-day retreat for foreigners, international meditators are told they can enjoy a different type of relaxation in this secluded environment. Simon, a retired American pilot, had attended Dipabhavan's retreat several times because he felt refreshed and recharged in this natural setting. The retreat center is located on a hill that offers sea and mountain views. Retreat participants are also taken to a nearby garden and forest where meditation within nature is possible. The scenic settings, curiosity of tourists, and the sometimes boring beach vacation are what teachers find make their retreats popular.

For international tourists, a natural location is one of the main criteria for choosing an international retreat center. They seek solace within these temples, something they cannot find at home, as the imaginary of meditation creates an image of sitting silently under trees in a lush forest. Romantic imaginaries of the 'East' as untouched by modernity fuel part of this image. Through these Romantic motivations, the feeling of peace is the goal of the practice, rather than Buddhist teachings of *nibbāna*. What I highlight here is the strong connection between nature and meditation for

82 *Narratives of international meditators' experiences*

international meditators. Certainly Thai Buddhists choose to meditate in such beautiful settings and both Buddhadasa Bhikkhu and Ajan Pho of the International Dhamma Hermitage and Dipabhavan Meditation Center laud the benefits of nature for one's practice and understanding of the Buddha's teachings. However, for international meditators these natural settings mark the 'authentic' and 'exotic,' decontextualized from Thai Buddhism. Another prominent motivation for seeking out a meditation center is the goal of therapeutic healing and well-being.

Therapy and health

Unlike the curious tourists focused on Romantic imaginaries of meditating in nature, meditators interested in well-being are more singular in purpose with an orientation towards the 'universal' benefits of the practice, aligning with Rational Orientalism. Within the context of colonialism certain Asian religious teachers associated their traditions with discourses of modernity, such as rationality and science, hoping to build their authority and legitimacy. Meditation as a global religious practice that can be separated from its religious context is exemplified today in the discourse between psychology and meditation, the most recent instantiation of Rational Orientalism. This prominent and popular dialogue has led to partaking in meditation retreats as a means for therapy and healing. A young woman from Holland named Helena, who was traveling around Asia, had just completed a yoga retreat in Bali and wanted to try a meditation retreat at Wat Doi Suthep as well. Koh Samui is known for its spa and detox treatments. Neil, an American in his mid-forties was completing his detox program on the island with the seven-day retreat at Dipabhavan. In this way, meditation is often conflated with yoga and spa treatments as both are utilized for health and well-being. This imaginary of meditation therefore is secular in nature, focusing on overcoming specific problems. Some meditators arrive at an international meditation center not only because of its beauty or its convenient location within a natural setting in a tourist area, but in order to deal with a difficult period in their lives. These international meditators expect to be transformed by the meditation retreat. The experience is seen as an opportunity to change oneself and one's life, an impetus for personal development and transition.[5] The idea that meditation can help alleviate their problems leads international meditators to seek out a place with a recommended teacher, usually found through a friend, by word of mouth, or Internet discussion forum.[6]

One middle-aged American meditator named Steve at Wat Chom Tong exemplifies this. He became interested in meditation while he was coming out of a long and difficult relationship and had lost his job. Because of this situation, he felt that there was nowhere else to go but a meditation retreat. In his state, he did not have any expectations of the retreat, only a hope that the experience could be healing. Steve was trying to let go of some painful experiences and found that the meditation technique helped him to be less reactive and more detached from his thoughts. He attended a twenty-one-day course and then a ten-day review retreat a few months later. He continues to meditate a short period every morning and goes back to the breathing technique every time he is stressed. Some meditators use the practice as a way to deal with emotional trauma. After meeting Sally, a middle-aged woman from Ireland at the Wat Kow Tahm meditation retreat, we communicated via email about her experiences. She first arrived at Wat Kow Tahm because she was deeply unhappy, suffering periods of depression. She also had a drinking problem and was in an abusive relationship. Her first retreat and experience meditating was transformative, as she reports she was able to see suffering in her own body clearly. After this, she attended many more retreats and became a teacher's assistant. After returning home to Ireland, Sally remains an enthusiastic meditator.

International visitors may also use the discipline of meditation as a substitute or complement to twelve-step programs to combat addiction. Paul Garrigan writes about his specific reason for wanting to practice meditation in Thailand, "My life had become unbearable because of an alcohol addiction, and it was my goal to beat it at this Thai temple" (Garrigan 2009, no page). He had read about *vipassanā* meditation, but since Wat Rampoeng was his first retreat experience in Thailand, he did not know what to expect. He discusses his goals for the retreat, writing, "At that time, I would have been ecstatic if they could just help me to get and remain sober – Enlightenment was far too ambitious a goal for me" (Garrigan 2010, 138). Garrigan, who is now a recovering alcoholic, writes of his experience after the retreat,

> [F]or the next few days my mind felt wonderful and free; the world was so much simpler. Unfortunately it didn't last as I once again began drinking . . . still I really give the meditation retreat in Chiang Mai a lot of credit. It created a taste in me for mental freedom that once tried could never be forgotten.
>
> (Garrigan 2009, no page)

Those interested in therapy, healing, and recovery are searching for mental freedom and distance from their problems and addictions. They have more of a purpose and seriousness in their practice than those interested in authenticity and difference. However, in both cases these international meditators draw from the same imaginary of meditation as a decontextualized global religious practice.

Apart from recovering from addiction and learning how to deal with difficult personal relationships, meditation is also used to boost health. A significant discourse surrounding meditation is its ability to reduce stress and improve one's overall well-being, with scientific studies often cited. Al, from America, who is over 70 years old, is a frequent visitor to Wat Suan Mokkh's International Dhamma Hermitage, and practices the long-breathing technique taught there, strictly for health benefits. Being out of shape and overweight, Al first attended an International Dhamma Hermitage retreat through the recommendation of a friend as a way to detoxify. He did not find the retreat psychologically challenging; he simply followed the schedule and reaped the positive health benefits. His weight has reduced significantly, he incorporates the vegetarian diet he learned from the retreat in his daily life, and continues the long-breathing practice for at least a half hour each day. In six years, he has gone on the retreat eight times and continues

84 *Narratives of international meditators' experiences*

to use it as a time to detoxify, saying he is not interested in *nibbāna* or anything spiritual. He writes in a *Nation* article that, "Three strengths of Buddhism stand out that no other religion or way of life offer collectively. They are deep mental meditation, extremely healthy long breathing exercises, and environmental awareness" (Eberhardt 2010, no page). His doctors have found that he has improved liver function and lower cholesterol level. His main purpose in his first trips to the International Dhamma Hermitage was strictly for weight loss. The last five retreats Al attended he instead sought also to explore his 'inner self,' along with the health aspects of long breathing. Al told me that he does not attend for the Buddhist teachings, as these are too complex for him. For health reasons, the meditation retreat lifestyle stands out as the most important part, although he has become interested in broader benefits of the retreat over time.

As seen from these international meditators, when the purpose of attending a retreat is for health, Buddhist goals such as *nibbāna* are not mentioned. The meditation practice is exclusively devoted toward aims of therapeutic or bodily well-being. For this avenue of access, the individual teachers, specific retreat programs and one's goals stand out more than natural settings or temple architecture. These individuals seek a center or teacher known for effective and secular methods. One of these centers is Wat Chom Tong with its foreign lay teachers. Others visit the Southern temples such as Wat Kow Tahm and the International Dhamma Hermitage for their attempts at healing. In this way in one center, international meditators are accessing the retreat in multiple ways. Because of the discourses of meditation regarding these benefits of the practice, international meditators seek to meditate in a secular way. Therefore, international meditators select the parts of the meditation retreat that cohere with their goals and motivations. For those interested in health, the long-breathing and vegetarian food is appropriated, and for those wishing to live in nature and explore the culture beyond the beaches, the natural settings and experience of living in the temple are most significant. These are the avenues through which many international meditators come to Thailand's international meditation centers, showing the extent to which meditation has become divorced from its Thai Buddhist context. Rational Orientalist discourses of Buddhism as a non-dogmatic, non-theistic religion that coheres with science and empiricism has given way to the ways international meditators access meditation today. Meditation is now considered a secular aid to health and well-being, a form of therapy, and a cure for addiction. However, for some, the Buddhist teachings are also incorporated into one's religiosity, where a long-term engagement with meditation is formed.

Long-term meditators

Long-term meditators have the most sustained engagement with Thai Buddhism. Over a prolonged period they engage with the particular contexts of Thai Buddhism rather than the universalizing ideas of modern Buddhism. They came to Buddhism as a decontextualized global religious practice but in relationship with Thai teachers have come to learn much about meditation and Thai Buddhism. The roles they take

Narratives of international meditators' experiences 85

on show the deep commitment possible for international meditators who engage with the practice over time. In Thailand's international meditation centers, spaces have been created for long-term international meditators to volunteer and teach meditation. It is not only Thai monks who are authorized as meditation teachers but Thai meditation teachers also allow foreigners to teach other foreigners hoping that the teaching will be well-suited to the audience of a similar cultural background and language. From recording the history of teaching foreigners at many international centers it is clear that when an experienced English-speaking teacher is available, Thai meditation leaders often ask them to teach or be in charge of the foreigners in some way. Whether these international meditators choose ordination or remain lay Buddhists, it is possible to become meditation teachers within international meditation centers. Others seek temporary sustained visits and become cultural brokers who return to the same temple and community each year. It is the meditation that attracted them to Buddhism and their experience with the practice that led them to incorporate it into their lives in a significant way.

These long-term meditators sometimes begin their practices as tourists interested in understanding the culture and people of their destination. Phra Ofer Thiracitto, an Israeli monk,[7] has practiced meditation since 1983. He first attended a retreat at Wat Rampoeng in Chiangmai as a traveler.[8] Early on, he was not interested in meditation or the spiritual life but in traveling and learning about other cultures. He found at Wat Rampoeng he could further this interest through observing Thai Buddhists and living in the temple with them. At some point Phra Ofer's interest in travel turned into a desire to learn meditation. Upon returning to his native Israel, he became sincerely interested in meditation and continued to practice. At one stage he started to practice meditation more seriously, and began to learn from Ajan Tong at Wat Chom Tong. After some time Ajan Tong gave Phra Ofer permission to teach in Israel, still as a layman. He wanted to become a monk at that time but knew he needed permission from his parents and that it would be hard for them to understand his decision.

For international meditators from non-Buddhist countries ordination can be a difficult choice to explain to one's family and friends. In this social context renouncing the lay life and becoming part of a foreign religion is often not met with joy as it would be in most Thai families. Phra Ofer ordained, at first temporarily, but after his father passed away his mother gave him permission to ordain fully. After his ordination he taught in Germany for several years and began teaching again in Israel in 2005. Since then he spends half the year in Germany and the other half in Israel fulfilling his duties as a meditation teacher. Therefore he is part of the movement and exchange of Thai Buddhist meditation to other parts of the world. For him meditation is not only a global religious practice but a large part of his life. Through their ordinations and roles as teachers, these long-term meditators' imaginaries of meditation are much broader. Now Phra Ofer is part of the lineage of Ajan Tong and has helped many international meditators access Ajan Tong's meditation method and teachings.

Ordination was similarly a difficult choice for Austrian *mae chii* meditation teacher, Mae Chii Brigitte Schrottenbacher, most recently of Wat Prayong

86 *Narratives of international meditators' experiences*

Gittavararam.[9] Mae Chii Brigitte was married while in her twenties, but because of a strong fear of death that emerged following the birth of her children, she started to explore ways to cope with this. She discovered meditation and completed her first two-month intensive retreat in 1989. But this wasn't enough for her and soon she was back, wanting to become a nun. She eventually decided to leave her children with her husband after they lived with her for a short time in Thailand. She did not want to disrobe and even though it was very difficult she felt it was the best decision for her life and her family. When I spoke with Mae Chii Brigitte, she related to me that since this time she has given her life to meditation and the monastic life.[10] Taking up the lifestyle of an ordained person and leaving family are evocative themes of the life of the Buddha. In the social context of her native Austria this was an unusual choice, which would have been viewed with suspicion and concern by her family. Negative reactions from family to the unfamiliar choice of becoming a renunciate are something that foreign monastics usually face. This emulates the Buddha's life story, as in both cases there is a high social cost to renunciation and conversion. In this case, Mae Chii Brigitte felt monasticism was a valuable choice as her commitment to meditation grew into a profound dedication to Thai Buddhism. She too is a meditation teacher who has immersed herself in the world of Thai Buddhism. Through donations she is able to organize alms and offer funds to female renunciants (*mae chiis*) and poor families in Central Thailand along with several other social welfare projects including aid to victims of the 2011 flooding. She won an Outstanding Women in Buddhism Award in 2009 for her efforts.[11] For her this is not a temporary engagement of a decontextualized practice utilized for tourists seeking an experience in a natural setting or physical well-being but a lifelong commitment embedded within Thai Buddhist communities.

Some long-term meditators choose to move to Thailand and then become interested in its variety of Thai Buddhist practices. Phra Frank,[12] an American monk, came to the dhamma through teaching English in Thailand and meeting his first teacher, Ajan Helen Jandamit of the House of Dhamma. Today he teaches the foreign meditators at Wat Sanghathan in Bangkok. One lay meditation teacher, Peter,[13] at Wat Chom Tong, traveled to Bangkok in search of a teacher and at Bangkok's Wat Mahathat was instructed to seek out Ajan Tong in Chiangmai. After he finished the basic course at Wat Chom Tong and then sat five more retreats, he was asked to start teaching. It was through traveling to Thailand and first being an international meditator or working in Thailand that led these dedicated practitioners to stay and teach others. Their initial engagement as tourists blossomed into a long-term commitment. In both of these cases, these international meditators found a lineage and community that they wanted to be a part of as well as an alternative lifestyle where they could teach and continue to practice meditation.

Foreign meditators often experiment with different teachings as sampling is the norm for long-term international meditators. Luang Pi River,[14] a British monk at Wat Dhammakaya, teaching at the Middle Way retreat, had a circuitous route to finding a temple where he wanted to ordain. He had tried a number of meditation methods prior to attending Wat Dhammakaya's Middle Way retreat. Luang Pi River attended two retreats at the International Dhamma Hermitage, taught at a spa in Koh Phangan, and participated in an Ajan Tong retreat in Chiangmai during his travels. During this sampling, he heard of Wat Dhammakaya and went there to practice. He attended the Middle Way retreat and this experience caused him to seek ordination at Wat Dhammakaya because he wanted to be a part of developing this retreat program. He has been teaching at Middle Way since October 2009. It is often the connection with a certain place, community, practice, or teaching method that leads to sustained engagement and participation. Luang Pi River's dedication and motivation to explore meditation in Thailand helped him find a place to ordain, teach, and maintain his practice.

But one does not have to ordain to teach meditation at Thailand's international meditation centers. Often international meditators who are frequent attendees are asked to volunteer to help manage group retreat centers that accommodate a large number of retreatants at once. Thus there are opportunities for further involvement and exchange, and a few international meditators take advantage of these roles. Reinhard Hoelscher,[15] German layman, is an example of a meditator who contributed to a retreat center through volunteering and teaching. He had been attending retreats each month at the International Dhamma Hermitage for a few years, and living at the main Suan Mokkh monastery between the ten-day retreats. In this way he became very familiar with the retreats and the people responsible for the organization. From 2004 to 2008 he lived permanently at the retreat center and was asked to take responsibility for the organization of the monthly foreigner retreats. Similarly German laywoman, Mady, had a transformative first experience[16] at the International Dhamma Hermitage retreat and continued to participate in many retreats to follow. She related this story in a dhamma talk to the participants at the Dipabhavan Meditation Center retreat I attended,[17] in which she was a volunteer. Her first retreat experience caused her to reevaluate her life, which she changed to focus more on meditation and living a simpler life in Thailand, moving to a nearby island for half of the year each year. These long-term meditators demonstrate that the imaginaries of meditation do not always have to be of a tourist searching for an idealized picture of meditating in nature or a secular decontextualized practice. They represent one end of the spectrum of engagement with Thai Buddhism that does not fade into other discourses. Instead they are embedded within Thai Buddhism, particular communities, and in relationships with their students and teachers. This chapter next discusses the details of the meditation retreat experience, highlighting the main areas of significance for international meditators.

International meditators' daily practices

Focusing more closely on the intricacies of international meditators' experiences, I highlight two retreat centers, Wat Rampoeng and the International Dhamma Hermitage of Wat Suan Mokkh, which have quite different programs designed for their international meditators. This section takes a close look at the reactions

88 *Narratives of international meditators' experiences*

of international meditators to the schedules, practices, activities and ceremonies, meditation teachings, and daily living environments of these respective retreat programs. I have chosen these two centers for closer analysis for a number of reasons. These places are among the most populous and oldest international medication centers in Thailand. They represent the two basic possibilities of a retreat format, the individual program of Wat Rampoeng based on the method of Ajan Tong and the group retreat of Ajan Buddhadasa Bhikkhu. And finally, writings capturing international meditators' experiences on travel blogs and websites are most prolific concerning these two sites. The following information is mostly drawn from travelers' blogs of their experiences. In this way these daily practices are described in a more informal manner, giving the reader a more candid reaction to each aspect of the retreat programs.

Wat Rampoeng

Wat Rampoeng is one of the most popular meditation retreat sites for foreigners, especially in the North of Thailand. It is easily accessible from the city of Chiang Mai and it has a large amount of space to accommodate many meditators. This is an intense retreat program that follows the method of Ajan Tong. Because of the strictness of this method, a popular idea exists that Wat Rampoeng is for serious practitioners and the retreats in the South, such as the International Dhamma Hermitage, are filled with retreat tourists or backpackers who are not as motivated. One discussion on the Thai Visa Forum sums up the opinions of these two popular options for retreat in Thailand, "I live not too far from Wat Rampoeng but the flower thing and other rituals really put me off. Wat Suan Mokkh could be a solution, but don't fancy sitting with half motivated backpackers" (Thai Visa Forum 2009). Here the forum participant is referring to the opening ritual of the retreat where all meditators formally receive the Eight Precepts and offer flowers, candles, and incense to their meditation teacher. In Wat Rampoeng foreigners are taught the basics of Thai Buddhist behavior but often feel confused and nervous about conducting themselves correctly. Through investigating the motivations, expectations, difficulties with the practice, and reflections, what follows is a comprehensive view of international meditators' experiences.

Motivations and expectations

Many international meditators who attend the Wat Rampoeng retreat often don't know what the practice entails or even its goals, but are interested in experimentation. Most international meditators stated that by the end of their experiences at Wat Rampoeng, they found some value in it. From learning a little about Thai culture to being able to sit still for more than fifteen minutes, there is usually something about the experience that makes it rewarding and that travelers do not regret.

One traveler who kept a blog about her experiences writes that she had some knowledge about meditation that she wanted to take further:

[A]bout a year and half ago I came across a website for the Northern Insight Meditation Center in Chiang Mai, Thailand. Having dabbled in martial arts and meditation courses in the past, I was intrigued by the opportunity to take my practice even further and get the benefits I had seen in more dedicated meditators. While other wats [temples] like Suan Dok advertised three day courses, the Wat Rampoeng offered a 26 day beginner course . . . a year and a half later, we were walking through the front gates with packed bags, big smiles, a lot of optimism, and no idea of what we were getting ourselves into.

(Stewtchell 2008)

This highlights how international meditators are willing to try meditation because of its cache and positive cultural association, despite not knowing anything about the conditions, retreat center, or method of practice. Another traveler also went to Wat Rampoeng specifically for this intense twenty-six-day course and found it difficult to handle. She describes the end period of the experience, called 'determination,' when one meditates for three straight days:

Food is brought to your room, but curtains are to be kept drawn, and escape is solely permitted for your daily visitation to the teacher. You aren't allowed to wash, you aren't allowed to change your clothes, and you aren't allowed to brush your teeth. This is hardcore. They just about stop at putting you under lock and key. I always knew it was coming. It had been my whole reason for going. The drama appealed. But on the first night reality overwhelmed me. What on earth was I doing? How could I possibly have the stamina, precious middle-class me, with my prerequisite nine hours sleep a night? Did I really want to make myself terminally ill and incurably insane?

(Davies no date)

The idea of meditation is exoticized but the practice and retreat experience itself does not convey the 'otherness' imagined. Instead the experience is marked by struggle and challenge. Some are intrigued by the promise of this intense experience, but do not expect the amount of effort needed. Part of the reason for this might stem from the way meditation is situated within the tourist agenda. Another travel blogger writes,

[O]n the morning after the mahout training we donned the all white clothes that we'd previously bought at the Chiang Mai night market, got in a *songthaew* (adapted pick up truck with benches in the back and used like a bus) and went to Wat Rampoeng for the toughest 10 days of our trip so far.

(Garrettt 2008)

This shows the link between experiences and how they are connected for tourists. Elephant training, learning massage, and Thai cooking are bundled together with learning meditation. This creates the idea that meditation is another fun activity to learn that reifies a Thai cultural artifact. But soon travelers come to apprehend

90   *Narratives of international meditators' experiences*

that meditation is qualitatively different from tourist activities. Early on within the retreat experience at Wat Rampoeng this difference is obvious.

Fear and nervousness

Many travelers do not know what to expect when passing through the temple gates at the start of a retreat. This is an unfamiliar environment with regulations of behavior that are unfamiliar to newcomers. This traveler writes about her stressful preparation for the retreat and first day:

> [W]e had signed up for 10 days of vipassana [sic] meditation at the wat [temple] which is just outside Chiang Mai and were feeling quite nervous. The website we'd seen promised a wake up bell at 4am, no food after noon, 10 hours of meditation a day and no talking at all, amongst a host of other rules and regulations. We had visited the wat earlier in the week to sign up and the surprisingly hostile monk who took our details and put us through a rather difficult interview asking us why we wanted to undertake the course had only served to heighten our anxiety about how hard the 10 days would be.
>
> (Garrett 2008)

Wat Rampoeng is a dramatic example of the fear and nervousness that can accompany a meditation retreat because of the requisite bowing and comportment during the opening ceremony and for the interviews with the teacher. When new international meditators arrive, having just learned the multi-step process of bowing and not remembering the motions exactly, they often feel intimidated when called to enter the abbot's office. Sometimes meditators freeze and hesitate to enter while the abbot waits for them, continuing to call out to his new students that he is ready for them. When arriving in the office, many beginners bow incorrectly, or too many or too few times. Commenting about the initial instructions one traveler writes, "It's fast, intense, and serves to raise the nerves of everyone in the room. Heck, one girl was crying within the first few hours of arriving and I assured her that we all felt pretty much the same way" (Stewtchell 2008). The first meeting with the abbot also causes anxiety:

> [T]he stress only grows as we are herded into the waiting room of Prah Adjarn Suphon's [sic] office, the Abbot of Wat Rampoeng and our teacher for the meditation course. After a very quick run down of what we're expected to do upon entrance and exit of his office, we feel very ill-equipped to face the big man and we whisper to each other trying to remember our lines and actions.
>
> (Stewtchell 2008)

Another traveler finds that his nervousness was unnecessary. Intimidation and worry soon become relief that the abbot is not concerned about these minor gestures. The instruction was given in order for the meditators to pay proper respect to the abbot, who the meditators imagine will be watching them carefully, and if a mistake is made, will be unhappy.

> [W]e waited outside the abbot's room nervously until we were all ushered in and prostrated and greeted both the abbot and his translator. He then led us in the opening ceremony which involved following chants and offering up the lotus flowers, candles and incense sticks to Buddha . . . Far from being the intimidating, distant figure we had expected, he was actually very warm and friendly.
>
> (Garrett 2008)

This nervousness stems from their new and unfamiliar environment. The basic modes of behavior are quickly learned, but the practice of meditation remains another challenge.

Difficulties with the practice

Because of the lack of knowledge and in some cases exotic ideas about meditation, beginners often find the practice itself difficult. Even for those with some experience meditating for an hour or more each day, this does not replicate a retreat where one meditates anywhere from seven or eight to twenty-four hours per day. Both mentally and physically strenuous, the practice can put undue strain on one's knees and back muscles. Because of the imaginary of meditation as peaceful, relaxing, and blissful, the hard work involved comes as an even greater shock. One traveler writes after a retreat how stressful the experience was,

> [Y]ou see, every time you meet with the teacher he gives you a new step or instruction, as well as an extra five minutes on your meditation sessions and increase in total hours. In no time, you're logging 30 minute sessions for a total of ten hours a day.
>
> (Stewtchell 2008)

The amount of meditation expected in a retreat is known to those who do some reading and research about the program at Wat Rampoeng, but for many the reality of how challenging this will be does not become clear until a few days into the retreat.

The end of the retreat, the determination period, is especially challenging. One traveler wrote about her experience:

> [T]wenty-four hours into the exercise, heart pounding down to my toes, I lay down on my bed and gave up. I wept with relief. I awoke an hour later, responding to some deep-buried pang of guilt. Excellent, I remembered, I was free. I could be in the glittering metropolis of Chiang Mai a whole two days earlier than planned.
>
> (Davies no date)

92 *Narratives of international meditators' experiences*

It is not only the meditation practice itself and the amount required each day but also the fact that the international meditators are compelled to remain within the temple compound that is also demanding. After exploring many different places, the travelers on a meditation retreat are now asked to remain in a limited space for a period of no less than ten days. One traveler felt the rules were too demanding,

> [I] was pretty sure I was in Buddhist hell. If the road to nirvana was paved with starvation, sleep deprivation, and painful body manipulations, how much worse could it be? It was as if the Christian missionaries came to Thailand and told the people about hell and the Buddhists started taking notes.
>
> (Stewtchell 2008)

This inability to adjust points to the reasons why some international meditators engage in rule-breaking and dissent from the strict schedule.[18]

Descriptions of other activities

Living within a temple complex is often completely new to foreign meditators. Their reactions and responses to these daily temple activities illustrate this level of engagement and adjustment. Along with meditation throughout the day, there are other activities such as the interview with the abbot, meals, and ceremonies within the temple compound that international meditators write about and find confusing. The opening and closing ceremonies are usually something new and strange for international meditators. One informant commented "The opening/closing ceremony done by Ajarn Suphan was lots of chanting asking the gods for protection or something I guess and I'm fine with that, need all the help I can get."[19] It is clear from this comment that not all of the procedures are fully understood by the international meditators.

One traveler describes the interview process:

> [E]very time we go to their room we had to kneel at the entrance, edge into the room on our knees and prostrate to the buddha [sic] statue in the room three times, then to Ajahn Suphan (the abbot) three times, then to Bhikkhune Akayanee (the translator) three times. Then we must say hello to them both in Thai which is "Sawat de ka" for a woman, and "Sawat de krab" for a man. To prostrate you kneel, put your hands together in front of your chest, touch them to your forehead then lean forwards and place them on the ground. Then you touch your head to your hands, rise back up to your knees, put your hands together again and touch them to your chest, then forehead, then chest again. All this must be done slowly and with mindfulness.
>
> (Garrett 2008)

The recounting of this procedure shows that the international meditators learn this well and that the interview process is part of their experience of the Other as evidenced by this meditator's choice to write about this in detail. The dining

Narratives of international meditators' experiences 93

hall experience is also a ritualized procedure new to most international travelers. Many are surprised that non-vegetarian food is an option, not realizing that most Theravāda Buddhists do not maintain a vegetarian diet. This demonstrates how little is known about Buddhism despite the curiosity toward its meditation practice. The chanting that precedes the meal is also a new experience. Chanting with the monks in Pāli and Thai is necessary for all participants before eating the meal. Sometimes this process can take up to a half hour as everyone waits for all participants to be seated with their plates in front of them. For English-speaking meditators there is a separate sheet with a translation of the Pāli into English—however the English words are not said aloud. During the Thai part foreign meditators are instructed to read the words in English silently.

Some international meditators enjoy this process of being able to take the time to reflect on their meals before eating, while some are not so positive about the experience. "I say 'endured' the prayers and singing, as the difficulty – after the uncomfortable sitting and hunger – was the inaccessible ancient language of Buddhism used" (Edwards 2009). This can be an interesting experience at first but loses its exoticism quickly. One traveler writes:

> [A] shaven-headed nun with a microphone turned up much too loud would sing phrases we would try to repeat. Fun the first few times. Then the monks would chant a couple of primitive-sounding ditties, with stirring rhythms and eastern modes. The monks – about 50 or 60 of them, aged from ten to 70 – would then start to eat, having been served by the nuns. We would then sing further songs to them about how we mustn't enjoy our food too much, and how suffering gave us 'bright skins', or so the translation read. It did seem an odd way to begin a meal, singing anti-gluttony propaganda songs to scoffing monks.
>
> (Edwards 2009)

This again shows the lack of understanding concerning Thai Buddhist rituals and how the lure of the exotic can quickly fade. A lack of respect for the ritual and monasticism is seen here. This also can contribute to leaving the retreat early or intentionally dissenting from the rules of the program.

Most foreigners are able to experience the weekly Buddhist holiday, *wan phra*, at Wat Rampoeng. This is the only ceremony that is explained in any detail to the international meditators. The dhamma talk by the abbot is conducted mostly in Thai with some English describing the ritual for the international meditators. If English-speaking monks are present they will explain the reason for the ceremony and how to participate. This is a positive experience for many participants and the only group activity they take part in with the Thai meditators. Although they do not fully understand the significance of the ritual, the circumambulation around the stupa with flowers, candlelight, and burning incense is a memorable experience. One traveler reveals, "Partly due to the fact the ceremony was carried out at night by candlelight, it was a very ethereal and beautiful hour or so and definitely one that neither of us will ever forget" (Garrett 2008). This ritual is often perceived to be an 'authentic' Buddhist and Thai cultural experience.

94 *Narratives of international meditators' experiences*

But this feeling does not occur with every ritual aspect that international meditators comment about.

Another activity conducted during the rains retreat is an almsround ceremony, where laypeople place food into the monks' almsbowls inside the temple. Unlike *wan phra* in which foreigners are included, in this ceremony the international meditators do not know this ceremony is taking place and when they see it, are not sure what is happening. Therefore the confusion doesn't elicit the allure of the exotic, only negative aspects of the unfamiliar.

> [O]ne ceremony of the monks I didn't at first grasp was held at eight o'clock each morning. Some of the white-dressed students, shaven-headed nuns and assorted locals would line one side of the main thoroughfare through the temple, standing behind trestle tables laden with packaged food. At first it looked like they were having a cake stall; . . . Into these bowls [the monks' almsbowls] the stall holders would place various juice boxes, chocolates and sometimes money. I'm not sure what the monks then did with the food – hopefully not eat it all. I imagined that it went back to the shop for sale.
>
> (Edwards 2009)

Because of the focus on meditation for the foreigners these confusions about temple life arise frequently. "We learned a lot about the religion of Buddhism and

Figure 4.2 Almsround, Wat Rampoeng

about the Thai culture, though we had to learn it all through observation as nothing is explained when you can't talk and everything is in Thai" (Stewtchell 2008). These activities are interesting and produce much speculation and chatter by the foreign meditators. These are exotic moments for international meditators that can also be met with discomfort and criticism.

Reflections on the retreat experience

Meditators often reflect upon their retreat experiences, soon after they finish, in a positive way. International meditators may resolve to integrate their meditative practice in their home countries or while continuing their travels. But the idea of going to another retreat is not as interesting as incorporating the meditation in smaller ways. One traveler writes,

> [A]t the closing ceremony Ajarn Suphan said that he hoped we would continue with our meditation in our daily lives and we have both agreed that we will try. It is an excellent way to clear your mind, even if we only manage half an hour after work when we get home.
>
> (Garrett 2008)

In addition to wanting to continue meditating and giving the practice value, many meditators recommend it to anyone who would like to have less stress and learn about their minds.

Travelers often go abroad at a point when they experience a kind of impasse in their lives. Meditation is seen as a way to aid in the process of breaking through whatever issues they may face, and some meditators say it helps to make difficult decisions for the next stage of their lives:

> [W]hile I was in the retreat I felt myself becoming more focused, and really believed I had more control over my thoughts. I also felt I very quickly gained an improved perspective on my life, and especially about what I hoped to do once my current trip had ended . . . I hope the mindfulness will continue to be a part of my life, but perhaps in more subtle ways than the leg-breaking meditation.
>
> (Edwards 2009)

Travelers sum up their experience by talking about their states of mind. They say their minds appear more clear and focused and that they understand the suffering of an impatient mind. However, they also know that this is difficult to maintain. One traveler writes, "We came away with strong backs and more focused minds . . . I now know more than ever that meditation can clear the mind, help me to live in the moment, and to focus" (Stewtchell 2008). Many informants have a positive experience when they leave the temple, feeling balanced and happy about the time spent there. They are grateful to abbot of Wat Rampoeng, Phra Ajan Suphan (Phrakru Bhavanavirach) for his teaching and some who have done the ten-day retreat are

96 *Narratives of international meditators' experiences*

inspired to go back for the full twenty-six-day course. The confusion and disorientation of living in a Buddhist temple and difficult aspects of the practice are forgotten, and for the most part fond memories and benefits from the experience remain.

Wat Suan Mokkh's International Dhamma Hermitage

Wat Suan Mokkh's International Dhamma Hermitage presents a marked contrast from the meditation retreat at Wat Rampoeng. In addition to being a group retreat where all meditation hours are practiced together, this retreat is quite secular, with no Buddha statues, rituals, or ceremonies. However, there are many teachings about Buddhism and the thought of Buddhadasa Bhikkhu. The disciplined nature of the retreat as well as the drop-out rate are commonalities between Wat Rampoeng and the International Dhamma Hermitage. In both cases the imaginary of meditation lies in stark contrast to the actualities of the retreat experience. Longtime volunteer and manager of the retreat center, Reinhard, states this about the motivations of participants at the International Dhamma Hermitage:

> [F]rom the interviews on registration day one can get the impression, that most beginners to meditation (which are about 70–80%) of the participants come out of curiosity. Many have no idea at all why they did come – it's just on their agenda while traveling in Southeast Asia – and this is why about 25% drop out. We always tell the participants that the best attitude to attend the retreat is to have no expectation at all, but they have and will not tell us – maybe some fantasies about supernatural powers originating from hearsay from India. But this is my speculation, no facts. Unfortunately meditation is very much misunderstood in the West.[20]

Nature and surroundings

As described earlier, a significant trope for international meditators is the connection between meditation and nature. A striking feature commented on by many international meditators attending this retreat is the importance of nature. Compared with Wat Rampoeng, international meditators who choose the International Dhamma Hermitage hardly ever comment on the orientation or the management of the retreat. Instead, as demonstrated from the comment book and the insight sharing that takes place in the evening on day ten, what is most significant for these foreign meditators is the environment of the hermitage. One international meditator described water as the significant part of his retreat experience. At the International Dhamma Hermitage the retreatants have communal wells of water for showering and separate ones for laundry, as well as the use of hot springs during breaks and foot baths to wash off one's feet. The meditation hall is filled with sand and is located in an open *sala*, adding to the natural feeling and resonates with the imaginary of meditation as a practice to be done in a forest or other natural setting. However, this spartan lifestyle is both praised and criticized as extreme by foreign participants. One travel blogger writes:

Narratives of international meditators' experiences 97

[T]his sandbox of a meditation hall proved to be quite the challenge, as most days it rained and your feet would be wet and then would be completely covered with sand by the time you reached your place. Sand would get on your cushions and in your clothes and could be quite irritating and a distraction while you meditated.
(Azurra 2007)

Similar to Wat Rampoeng, the exotic becomes difficult and challenging. Some beginning meditators find the adjustment to this lifestyle testing. Each meditator's room consists of a cement bed and a wooden pillow, a demanding aspect of this retreat. But along with these challenges comes the realization that this is part of the natural lifestyle and retreat experience sought after. Another travel blogger comments about the living conditions, "I expected simple accommodation, not something that was frankly, oppressive. I found it [the concrete bed] pretty much impossible to sleep on it, it didn't much help going to bed at 9:30pm" (Freeman 2009). Getting used to the surroundings and the lifestyle can be rewarding for those who stay. Because of this many travelers spend time writing about the layout of the retreat center and how they dealt with living in this way for the duration of the retreat.

Well, it must have taken some time that I actually realized that THIS 'room' will be my place for eleven nights. It is comparable with a cell or even a prison. The room is approx [sic] 8 sq meter, has openings to all sides (even to the next room), it has a STONE Bed, a WOODEN pillow, just a mat and a blanket. There is also a cloth line [sic] and some hangers. More disturbing for me was the thought that all sorts of creatures moved in before me in my "room" and it did not look like they will leave. After working in a five star hotel environment and knowing Housekeeping Brand Standards – I had to make some compromises here. . . Well, it is part of the big picture and that's what I wanted – back to basic and living in and with nature.
(Lang 2007)

Remembering the Romantic imaginary of meditation in nature helps this tourist accept the lack of amenities in her living space. Those who seek nature and dismiss modern lifestyles are confronted with not just the beauty but also the challenges of this lifestyle, such as insects and other animals.

Aside from the discomfort of a wooden pillow and stone bed, there are positive aspects of the retreat environment. Many meditators comment on the serene experience of evening group walking meditation around the pond and standing meditation while looking up at the stars. Waking before dawn and being able to see the sunrise is also an awe-inspiring part of the experience. Another travel blogger comments,

so much of my time was spent observing all the minute details of this area and so much effort was dedicated to learning how to truly live in and as a part of the surroundings. The sand, the concrete bed, the mosquitoes, the wet ground, the slippery floors and the dark. All influenced my experience in its own way.
(Azurra 2007)

Figure 4.3 Bathing wells, International Dhamma Hermitage

Despite discomfort and lack of amenities, this traveler comes to have a more realistic imaginary of meditation.

Schedule

What stands out for many travelers who come to the International Dhamma Hermitage is the schedule. As expected, people who have participated in a retreat before find the timetable manageable, but first-time retreatants often find it quite grueling. But, since there are other daily activities besides meditation such as yoga, chanting, and time set aside for dhamma teachings, it is a less demanding schedule than that of Wat Rampoeng. Compared with Wat Rampoeng, there is significantly less meditation time and more sleep. Like the living space of the retreat and proximity to nature, the schedule is so different from most daily lives, it is worth commenting on in detail. Many travel bloggers write out the entire day's schedule to give their audiences an idea of their experiences.

During the last days of the retreat the schedule changes so that there is only one daily meal and there are no teachings—only meditation practice. This gives students a taste of a more advanced retreat. Also on the last day the silence is broken so that the retreatants can share their experiences with one another in an event called Insight Sharing. I have noticed that this can become more of a confessional atmosphere that has more to do with personal histories than meditation experiences. Others comment on the lifestyle and schedule of the retreat and how difficult the experience was for them—how they wanted to quit but felt good about staying in the end. For the most part these are very positive comments when most of the hard work is finished.

Meditation and teachings

Once international meditators at the International Dhamma Hermitage become accustomed to the schedule, the next important aspect of the experience is the meditation practice and the teachings about Buddhism. British monk Than Dhammavidu is the main teacher at this retreat site. He mostly explains concepts within Buddhism that Buddhadasa Bhikkhu emphasized in his writing. Even if Than Dhammavidu's teachings aren't precisely remembered by his meditation students of over ten years, his personality and presence are easily recalled. His delivery and dry humor are memorable and he makes the complex ideas of Buddhadasa Bhikkhu relatable with his daily lectures. Along with his teachings are talks by the various volunteers that manage the retreat. Some lay foreigners, Thai laywomen, and Thai *mae chiis* also talk about their meditation experiences and offer some teachings to the group. One travel blogger discusses the difference between Than Dhammavidu's teaching and a Thai nun's, along with why he is attracted to Buddhism:

> [I] enjoyed the lectures quite a bit. The first thing they told us was to not blindly believe anything they say, to try and experience it for ourselves and build our own belief system. I was immediately attracted to a religion that supports their belief system with empiricism rather than faith. Half of the lectures were done by the Thai Buddhist nuns who of course had all of the religious dogma of a Thai Theravāda Buddhist such as ghosts, karma, reincarnation and an afterlife. The other half and my favorite half was done by a British, Atheist, Buddhist monk, an interesting combination to say the least. He had a way of teaching with such comical cynicism that it made the whole chamber laugh. His teachings of Buddhism were very down to earth, philosophical and really got to the nuts and bolts of what the Buddha actually taught, without the religious dogma that generally comes with this particular spiritual practice.
>
> (Quest 2010)

This international meditator reveals, through this rational Orientalist imaginary of meditation, the kind of religiosity he is seeking. The writer gives value to atheism and the Buddha's teachings while labeling the Thai nuns' teaching negatively as dogma with its antimodernist elements of rebirth and invisible beings. This highlights the prevalence of the ideas of modern Buddhism and the contextual nature in which Buddhist teachings are received as well as the importance of the secular imaginary of meditation as a decontextualized global religious practice.

Reflections on the retreat experience

Reinhard sums up the international meditators' reflections from the International Dhamma Hermitage:

> [P]eople liked the silence, the simple living conditions, the close contact to nature. To me the takeaway for most is the experience that a place like the International Dhamma Hermitage exists, that it is possible to live a different life than they have grown used to and that meditation provides a tool to deal with the challenges of life. Most then will not make any use of this knowledge once they have left the monastery gate until they run into problems or a crisis in their lives. Then they will remember that it is possible to calm and to train the mind in order to solve their difficulties and may give it another try – this is what many "old friends" are telling us.[21]

Even though many of the travelers seem less than serious in their approach to the retreat—the practice can still be meaningful. One traveler, after his experience at the International Dhamma Hermitage, recommends meditation for all people:

> [I] urge everyone who reads this to seek a class or two in the practice of meditation. It doesn't matter if you are faithful to a certain religion, meditation is non-denominational, if anything it will help you grow closer to your beliefs. Meditation and mindfulness is such an important skill to have. With just a basic understanding of the practice, I am able to be proactive when a negative emotion enters my mind, and allow it to pass before it takes hold and I become a victim of it.
>
> (Quest 2010)

Figure 4.4 Meditation hall, International Dhamma Hermitage

One young traveler who was curious about Buddhism found that, for a long time after his retreat experience at the International Dhamma Hermitage, his life was simpler and he felt more clear-headed. He continues to do part of the yoga routine taught at this retreat and meditate a few times a month.[22] There are a variety of responses and reflections on the meditation experience at the International Dhamma Hermitage including the imaginary of meditation in nature. The reactions of international meditators demonstrate the ambivalence of this initial enchantment with nature. The natural lifestyle and strict schedule are the main challenges of this retreat, revealing the contextual nature of each retreat program.

Conclusion

It is not only the meditation itself, but also the schedule, surroundings of the retreat center, and other activities of living in the center, that make up the content of the meditation retreat experience. From those accidental religious tourists who happen upon a scenic temple and are invited to learn meditation to those who plan a retreat to deal with a certain problem in their lives—there are many different kinds of international meditators. For those interested in therapy and healing, the discourse between meditation, psychology, and well-being is the most attractive, highlighting the consequences of Rational Orientalism. But for others interested in cultural exploration and being in nature, the Romantic imaginary is prominent. Thai Buddhists of course seek out natural settings for their practice and enter retreats because of specific instances of suffering. However, for them usually the retreat is embedded within the world of Buddhism including ideas of merit-making, fulfilling vows, offering to monks, and other ritual practices, as well as an understanding of the temple and its functions for Thai society.

Some international meditators have found a place where they benefited and have eventually become teachers and volunteers at these sites. The same imaginaries that led to limited engagement can also lead to long-term commitment. International meditators' reactions to the details of the retreat program reveal confusion and lack of prior knowledge at first but this can deepen to an understanding of the practice and a wish to integrate it into one's life. These narratives illustrate the paths international meditators take to the retreat and the imaginaries that motivate them to participate. The next chapter looks closely at the commodification of this experience, revealing that promotional materials draw from similar imaginaries when advertising a spiritual vacation.

Notes

1 The number of interviews I was able to conduct varied at each site depending on the number of international meditators present while I was conducting research. Often it was difficult to talk during the retreat so in this case, I contacted the meditators after completion of the retreat. Depending on the site this could vary from three to ten interviews. From my findings both genders were represented almost equally at each site and the age range varied from 20- to 70-year-old participants. The most common group is the twenty to thirty age range, the next being middle-aged participants.

102 *Narratives of international meditators' experiences*

2 Nyanatiloka Mahathera (1878–1957) was one of the first Western monks to be ordained in Sri Lanka. He was a scholar-monk who is most known for his booklet *Fundamentals of Buddhism: Four Lectures.* (www.accesstoinsight.org/lib/authors/nyanatiloka/wheel394.html), and
  The Buddhist Dictionary (www.budsas.org/ebud/bud-dict/dic_idx.htm).
3 The Tourism Authority of Thailand calls Wat Doi Suthep "the most important and visible landmark" of Chiangmai (www.tourismthailand.org/See-and-Do/Sights-and-Attractions-Detail/Wat-Phra-That-Doi-Suthep--145). City Life Chiangmai also calls Doi Suthep "Chiangmai's most popular mountain." (www.chiangmainews.com/ecmn/viewfa.php?id=1958). A widely reported local saying is that if a visitor has not yet visited Doi Suthep, then they have not really arrived in Chiangmai.
4 Interview with Ajan Pho, Dipabhavan Meditation Center, June 25th, 2010.
5 This is true of meditation retreats but also of tourism in general. Bruner (1991) and Noy (2004) discuss tourism undertaken for personal change.
6 There are over twenty discussion threads directly related to meditation retreats in Thailand for foreigners on the Thai Visa Forum Website (www.thaivisa.com/forum/) and five on the Dhamma Wheel Website (dhammawheel.org).
7 See Phra Ofer's biography here: www.vipassana-dhammacari.com/weitere_eng.html.
8 Interview with Phra Ofer, Wat Chom Tong, Lineage of Ajan Tong, March 22nd, 2010.
9 For more of her biography see, www.meditationthailand.com/.
10 Interview with Mae Chii Brigitte Schrottenbacher, Wat Prayong Gittivararam, March 10th, 2010.
11 The Outstanding Women in Buddhism award began in 2002 in collaboration with the United Nations' International Women's Day. From 2002 to2010 this award was given to many Buddhist women throughout the world who have engaged in social projects. The award seems to have discontinued in 2011 as the Outstanding Women in Buddhism Website is no longer functioning.
12 Interview with Phra Frank Gavesako, Wat Sanghathan, June 18th, 2010.
13 Interview with Peter, Wat Chom Tong, April 28th, 2010.
14 Interview with Phra Luangpi River, The Middle Way Retreat, June 10th, 2010.
15 Email correspondence with Reinhard Hoelscher, International Dhamma Hermitage, via email, February 22nd, 2010.
16 This is a shared trait of many long-term international meditators. For some this transformative experience entails an insight into one of the three characteristics of suffering, impermanence, or non-self. For others, as international meditation center teachers have related to me, this can be a spontaneous entrance into the first *jhāna*. This kind of initial attainment is motivating to continue to practice meditation in a serious and dedicated way.
17 I attended the June 20th–June 27th, 2010 retreat at Dipabhavan Meditation Center.
18 This tendency toward dissent is considered more fully in Chapter 7.
19 This quote is from an email correspondence with Kelvin on May 19th, 2011, an international meditator I have contacted via my research website, Wandering Dhamma (wanderingdhamma.org).
20 Email correspondence with Reinhard on May 20th, 2011.
21 Email correspondence with Reinhard on May 19th, 2011.
22 Email correspondence with Mike on May 20th, 2011.

5 Meditation for tourists in Thailand

Commodifying a universal and national symbol

While the term globalization implies a borderless, fragmented, and fluid world, there exists at the same time an impulse to identify, distinguish, and reify. Henrietta Moore writes that "cultural diversity is both eroded and recreated by processes of globalization, and information technologies are playing a significant role in preserving and disseminating cultural heritage and traditions" (Moore 2013, 273). We can see these two tendencies at play within international meditation centers in Thailand. The practice of meditation is contextualized within Thai culture and the country itself while it is also decontextualized as a universal practice in which anyone can participate. Advertisements present meditation as both a universal practice and a cultural icon that links Thailand's current society to its ancient past. This chapter discusses these constructions of Thai Buddhism and meditation through a discourse analysis of tourism publications relating to meditation.

Advertisements utilizing social imaginaries of Thailand and meditation signal to the international community the Romantic nature of this practice, where one can escape into an exotic, timeless activity, removed from modern ills and malaise. At the same time as Thailand's difference is highlighted, meditation is also connected with universal systems of science and rationality. Similar to the Orientalist imaginaries of international meditators described in the previous chapter, both poles of Orientalism—Romantic and Rational, are accessed in promotional materials. Meditation comes to be portrayed as Romantic and rational, modern and an antidote to modernity, familiar and exotic simultaneously. Through advertisements about meditation targeting the international community, Thailand is imagined as a 'spiritual oasis,' evoking discourses of Romantic Orientalism. Thomas Tweed describes how a Romantic interest in Asia began in the early nineteenth century. His typology of early American Buddhists includes a 'Romantic' type consisting of individuals interested in the exotic culture and aesthetics of Buddhist Asia, including its customs, architecture, and music, among others (Tweed 1992, 70). Romantic Orientalists thought that knowledge of Asia could combat the materialism and rationalism of the Occident. Therefore the primary interest of Romantic Orientalists was how Asia could be used to balance the West's worldly tendencies and help them know their true selves better (Said 1978, 115). As we will see today these ideas are used to promote travel to Thailand to international visitors. Simultaneously, meditation is also constructed as a familiar modern practice

104 *Meditation for tourists in Thailand*

through discourses of Rational Orientalism. Orientalist scholars sought to understand and construct Buddhism through the textual tradition, focusing on the earliest documents. They held in high regard traditions that followed science and appeared modern despite their origins (Almond 1988, 24). Today this carries into common tropes of Buddhism as cohering with science, rationality, and pragmatism. Utilizing these tropes in promotional materials, meditation becomes both a universal and national symbol. This chapter critically investigates this tension and its relationship to commodification by looking at primary sources of meditation guidebooks and promotional materials. Second, in this chapter I demonstrate how these selective elements serve to reinforce consumer values and constitute a commodification of meditation for international tourists. Through the appropriation of postcolonial imaginings of the 'exotic spiritual East' and the scientifically proven beneficial practice of meditation for personal health and well-being, the experience of meditation is commodified to promote travel to Thailand. In this section my goal is not to evaluate commodification as negative or positive or make any judgments regarding what constitutes 'authentic' Buddhism. Instead I look at the dynamics of discourses and practices involved with promoting meditation and how they are situated in regards to the international audience in Thailand.

Religious tourism has become especially vibrant and dynamic in Thailand in part through promotion by Thai Buddhists. In *Meditation in Modern Buddhism*, Joanna Cook writes,

> [B]uddhism, as well as being closely associated with Thai national identity in the minds of Thai people, is an important part of Thailand's self-presentation to outsiders. Today meditation and Buddhism are incorporated into the tourism project of the Thai government as a presentation of the modern state and nationalism. Grounding the nation on the traditions and practices of Buddhism as signifiers of authenticity, meditation is presented as an attractive, accessible and authentically Thai experience for foreign and Thai tourists.
>
> (Cook 2010, 36–37)

Here Cook highlights how Buddhism in Thailand is one way for Thai people to present themselves to the international community. Meditation becomes a national symbol of Thailand because Buddhism is closely associated with the nation as is demonstrated through statements like 'To be Thai is to be Buddhist,' and as one of the pillars of the Thai state—Nation, Religion, and King. At the same time meditation is also promoted as an inclusive practice that is universal in its reach. I demonstrate that this commodification does not detract from the practice for foreign communities, but offers innovative possibilities for expressing Buddhist practices.

Consuming meditation in Thailand

International meditation centers are entangled with the market, with Thai Buddhism, international networks of Buddhists, and their own local lineages and contexts.

Discourses about meditation within publications from Thailand show how the product of meditation has been attuned to match these desires of international tourists. Richard Gombrich has noted that the lay meditation center takes as its fundamental model the capitalist logic of supply and demand. He writes,

> [T]he meditation centre is thus in Weber's sense a 'rational' institution, based not on heredity, place of residence, or other ascription, but on the demand for and supply of a service, namely the teaching of meditation and opportunity for its practice under qualified supervision.
>
> (Gombrich 1983, 21)

Through the emergence of the institution of the meditation center, meditation has widened its reach beyond monastics to the masses. Given this, Gombrich asks, "whether the provision of any commodity previously reserved for an elite to a mass market can fail to affect the nature of the commodity—even if the commodity is meditation" (Gombrich 1983, 30). Certainly the nature of the commodity has changed as simplified, easily replicable meditation methods were introduced to accommodate the rapidly increasing number of participants.

This change in the nature of meditation as a commodity is multiplied for a foreign audience, as seen in promotional materials from Thailand. Jane Iwamura (2011) discusses the ways the 'Oriental Monk' figure within popular culture, through his nonsexual solitary spirituality, is made acceptable and appealing for mainstream consumption. In similar ways the practice of meditation and its manifestations in Thailand are represented to the international community as a desirable commodity for the widest possible range of participants. Beginning in the 1960s, especially American religiosity consisted of an individual seeker on a journey in search of new forms of ancient wisdom (Roof 1999). Through these images of the lone spiritual seeker and meditation as a 'universal' and 'authentic' practice, it becomes commodified and inserted into an eclectic religiosity of individual tourists. Advertisements for Thailand's international meditation centers carve out a space for international meditators by tapping into their cultural and religious frameworks, shaping meditation as both a national and universal symbol of Thailand. The promotional materials have clearly drawn from images of both Thailand as an exotic paradise where one can embark on a relaxing meditation retreat in natural settings and Buddhism as a rational, scientific set of practices for transforming the mind.

However, for international meditators, commodification of anything connected to the Buddhist temple or meditation center is in direct contrast to their vision of an 'authentic' culture and religious tradition, which should be 'pure' and 'untainted' by commerce. The presence of market items such as amulets and even street food and drinks is seen by some international meditators to mark an inauthentic or unnatural space to practice meditation. Like Peter Moran finds concerning Western travelers to Bodhanath's Tibetan Buddhist monasteries, international meditators in Thailand fear that meditation will become "yet another 'commodity' produced by the monstrous forces of modernity" (Moran 2004, 58). Moran's study reveals

106 *Meditation for tourists in Thailand*

that the presence of money was disturbing in contrast to the supposed spiritual ideals and the traditions of Tibetan Buddhists, and an imagined 'pure' Buddhism (Moran 2004, 78). The relationship of the economy to meditation are seen to be antithetical to some international meditators. My discussions with the meditators revealed that many do not realize that monasteries are a social organization and part of a community that needs monetary funds in order to function. Because of this some temple abbots allow laypeople to sell food, drinks, lottery tickets, and sometimes massage within temple grounds. Therefore the temple has its own economy and sources of income through the reciprocity of exchange and consumption. Through this lack of knowledge concerning the economic functioning of temples, some international meditators share criticisms of temple practices between one another while attending a meditation retreat, or they simply decide not to engage at all, disenchanted by this seeming lack of authenticity.

Meditation is marketed, advertised, and disseminated within the tourism market but it is also part of the Buddha's teachings that are offered by donation, or *dāna*. *Dāna* is a practice of generosity in Buddhism where laity give to the monastic community in various ways, from offering food to monks on morning almsround to sponsoring the construction of a temple. *Dāna* is part of the core social practice of Buddhism, referred to as the economy of merit. This practice of *dāna* helps lay people acquire spiritual rewards or merit when monastics ritually receive their donations. As discussed in Chapter 3, monastics provide this opportunity for laity by serving as a field of merit through their ascetic lifestyle. Monastics do not themselves give merit but this transference is thought to occur as a natural result of the good act through the impersonal process of *kamma*. Monks offer teaching and perform rituals freely, not in exchange for the laity's donation (Cook 2010, 138). Therefore the economy of merit is the market within which Buddhism primarily operates. Meditation retreats in Thailand exist outside of the traditional monetary exchange market because the experience of meditation, for most international meditation centers, is offered freely.[1] At the end of a retreat meditators make their donation to the center itself, not an individual teacher, therefore avoiding a personal exchange.[2] Although not a direct exchange of money, monastics and laity depend on each other to enact their roles properly. Meditation is offered, as it was told to me by many international meditation center teachers, to all out of compassion to help end human suffering. Meditation teaching by donation is a traditional aspect of Buddhist teaching. In Thailand and elsewhere in Theravādin Southeast Asia there is a history of monks acting in this role as a source of donation for the temple.

Dāna is an aspect of Buddhism that international meditators typically do not understand. A number of international meditation center teachers commented to me that international meditators are not known for their generosity. It is the Thai meditators who are distinguished for their large donations because they are accustomed to this practice.[3] In fact, at Wat Kow Tahm and the International Dhamma Hermitage, where there are mostly international meditators, the organizers request a fee to be paid by all retreatants to cover the costs of food, as they found their students did not donate enough money to cover these expenses. Steve and Rosemary Weissman, teachers at Wat Kow Tahm, give a speech near the last day of the retreat about donation, encouraging their students to follow this practice and give generously for their teachings and maintenance of the center. Although international meditators themselves do not often understand the practice of giving and merit-making in a Buddhist context, international visitors become a status symbol for the Thai Buddhist community. Along with the motivation of compassion, having an international center with foreign meditators increases the reputation and thereby the funds from Thai Buddhist laity. This was evident when, as I was writing my name in Thai in a meditation center guestbook, I was instructed instead to use Roman letters so that the Thai Buddhists would know there are visitors from around the world. Thus the mere presence of foreign visitors can generate offerings from Thai Buddhists.

Although participation in a meditation retreat program lies outside of the traditional market, the promotion of meditation is connected with consumerism and the business of tourism. Market forces act on the advertising of the experience of meditation, highlighting some aspects of Buddhism and the retreat while obscuring others, such as rituals, interactions with Thai Buddhists, and daily life in the temple. These aspects are not part of the image used to promote the meditation retreat experience. Unlike Buddhist tourist site destinations such as Bodhgaya, the place of the Buddha's Enlightenment, or Tibetan Buddhist enclaves such as Dharamsala and Kathmandu,[4] where local businesses surrounding the site often capitalize on foreign income, Thailand's international meditation centers are diffuse and not always located near tourist areas.[5] Tourism organizations in Thailand promote meditation vacations in order to boost the economy in general through spending on airfare, food, and lodging preceding and following retreats. Motivations for marketing Buddhism and meditation include countering negative images of Thailand through the proliferation of sex tourism. Additionally, promoting and exposing others to meditation is a meritorious activity. These goals are likely at work together with economic motivations of increasing tourism.

Buddhist commodifications in Thailand

Commodification within the context of Thai Buddhism is not unusual. Writings on the commercialization of amulets by Stanley Tambiah (1984) provides a backdrop for the possibilities of commodifying meditation in Thailand. Tambiah discusses the belief in and trade of amulets within Thai Buddhist society (Tambiah 1984, 335–336). He argues that for Thai Buddhists, amulets hold the power and charisma of the depicted monk or holy figure. The amulet represents a materialization of the ascetic monks' discipline. The transmission and objectification of the monks' religious powers then is directed toward the material world. Tambiah writes,

> [I]t is inevitable in the Thai case that this process of vulgar materialization, this law of gravity, should have further consequences. One is that the amulet moves from a context of donation and love (*metta*) to a context of trade and profit. It is converted into a highly salable good and enters the bazaar and marketplace.
> (Tambiah 1984, 336)[6]

108 *Meditation for tourists in Thailand*

Since Tambiah's important study, the amulet industry in Thailand has increased further with amulet stalls now located in most modern shopping malls and hypermarkets like Tesco Lotus and Big C as well as roadside stalls. The proliferation of amulets through magazines and specialized markets attests to the dynamic material culture and promotion of Buddhist objects. Chalong Soontravich describes how market forces, when mixed with the exchange of amulets, created not only supply and demand but also a method through which some amulets became more popular, valuable, and expensive (Soontravanich 2013, 200).

Instead of looking at material objects being negatively affected by commodification, I follow Vineeta Sinha (2011), Justin McDaniel (2011), and Pattana Kitiarsa (2012), all of whom argue that commodification allows for creative engagement and adaptation of the tradition. Sinha contends that the industry of religious items does not contaminate or diminish the sacredness of the object but rather enhances its value as the object is now widely available for everyday religiosity (Sinha 2011, 201). Religion and commerce are often entangled in complex, intimate ways proving that the assumed polarity between religion and the marketplace is unfounded. Rather than leading to the degradation and fragmentation of religious traditions, Sinha asserts that "consumption could be an imaginative and creative process, involving the participation of active agents—the consumers—who appropriate goods and commodities for their own specific, meaningful purposes" (Sinha 2011, 198). Practitioners do not simply acquire the religious objects on offer. Instead these commodities are mediated, influenced, and shaped by the preferences and feedback of practitioners and consumers. Therefore the relationship between commerce and religion needs to be framed outside of a critique of consumerism and fear of secular mundane effects on sacred realms (Sinha 2011, 203).

McDaniel demonstrates the ways that amulets and other Buddhist material objects have become creative forces within Thai Buddhism. He argues that scholars should "talk about Buddhist material and artistic culture without simply lamenting modern Thai commercializing of religion, the creation of an 'occult economy,' or the materialistic corruption of spirituality" (McDaniel 2011, 166). McDaniel hopes for a change in scholarship from framing commodification of Thai Buddhism as a crisis or consequence of the negative effects of globalization (McDaniel 2011, 190). McDaniel finds instead that these material objects and art have inspired Buddhist practice more than doctrine has. These objects help to create new communities of tourists, pilgrims, Buddhists, and amulet traders. Kitiarsa discusses how commodification is a significant process through which popular Buddhism is shaped within Thailand (Kitiarsa 2012, 1). He argues for scholars to acknowledge the importance of popular and commercialized religion for both Thai Buddhists as well as scholars (Kitiarsa 2012, 6–7). Like McDaniel, Kitiarsa finds that markets, more so than traditional religious institutions, spread and express Buddhist teachings in Thailand.

The meditation retreat experience forms part of the complex system of Buddhist merit-making as well as the tourism industry in Thailand. The experience of meditation is marketed and consumed but not sold in the sense of traditional market exchange. Because there is no outright monetary exchange for the teachings or retreat program itself, publications advertising meditation use the available popular imaginaries of Thailand and Buddhism to increase tourism within the country and disseminate information for those seeking to attend a retreat.

Meditation promotional materials

There is a significant amount of promotional material about meditation sites in Thailand, conveying the intentionality of commodifying meditation in particular ways. These materials point to the ways that Buddhist and tourist institutions "draw upon wider cultural imaginaries" (Salazar 2010, 48) as they target the English-speaker's vision of a meditation retreat. The remainder of this chapter addresses the content of the material publications related to international meditation centers in Thailand. Along with international meditation centers, Thai and Buddhist institutions called the Tourism Authority of Thailand (TAT) and the World Federation of Buddhists (WFB) figure prominently in the creation, proliferation, and dissemination of information about meditation in Thailand. Promotional materials produced internally at meditation centers also reveal similar modern Buddhist discourses. These materials are produced for Thai Buddhists as well and comparison reveals the ways Buddhist teachings are translated for the international audience. In conclusion, I analyze the images of these materials that convey the imaginaries of meditation for tourists.

Next, I will address how these publications, in the form of guidebooks, brochures, and booklets, use the selected presentation of meditation as a national symbol of Thailand and a universal symbol of Buddhism in order to commodify this practice. The TAT's commodification is more targeted and oriented toward increasing tourist numbers, while WFB's focus is on disseminating information. However, the selective elements follow a similar pattern of promoting the experience of meditation.

Promoting meditation through guidebooks

Peter Moran writes that the "function of any tour book is to explain the unfamiliar, to feed the desire among a great many travelers to make the Other familiar, to domesticate alterity" (Moran 2004, 35). The meditation guidebook serves a similar function of offering information and making intelligible the uncommon setting of Buddhist meditation temples in Thailand. Below is an extensive publication history of these guides in English and an analysis of their contents, beginning with the WFB. Since its inaugural meeting in Colombo, Sri Lanka in 1950, the WFB has sought to propagate the Dhamma and promote solidarity and unity of Buddhists all over the world. Founded by Dr. Malalasekera, a well-known Sri Lankan Pāli scholar, the WFB has over 140 Regional Centers in thirty-seven countries around the world, with its current headquarters in Bangkok, Thailand.[7]

110 *Meditation for tourists in Thailand*

The WFB began the genre of meditation guidebook in Thailand in the late 1970s, making it the first institution to publish meditation guides for foreigners in English. Based on the research of then monk, Sunno Bhikkhu, now well-known as Jack Kornfield,[8] WFB published *A Brief Guide to Meditation Temples in Thailand*. This guide was an important early document and the first of its kind to help foreigners learn and practice meditation in Thailand.[9] Kornfield undertook this publication because he found that the large numbers of Buddhist temples and teachers had left spiritual seekers confused as to the best places to learn and practice meditation. As a longtime student of Thai Buddhist meditation and a former monk, his familiarity with Thailand made him an important interlocutor who could understand both international meditators' needs and the possibilities available to them. To this end, Kornfield's guide offers a selection of temples, which have instructors with previous experience teaching foreigners and who can transmit the teachings in English or through an interpreter, and with a suitable diet and accommodations for foreigners' needs. In this way Kornfield helped foreigners identify the opportunities open to them by providing a guidebook to select meditation temples that were receptive to and familiar with the habits and practices of international visitors.

Through the selective choices of meditation centers that were deemed appropriate for foreign visitors, the guidebook format lends itself to commercial practices. Because of the increased demand for this information about meditation, a communication system developed to disseminate this material. In this way, guidebooks shaped the ways meditation as a commodity created a perceived demand among spiritual travelers. Instead of foreigners interested in meditation choosing a temple they encountered at random, or none at all, this group now had a list of handpicked temples from which they could choose. This demonstrates how commercialism can both create new religious communities as well as adapt religious institutions based on participant feedback for a wider dissemination of teachings. These marketing and dissemination practices are conducted in order to introduce international visitors to Thai meditation retreats and facilitate the interaction between international meditators and centers.

A committee of the National Identity Board authored a second edition of this meditation guidebook under the title *A Brief Guide to Buddhist Meditation Centres in Thailand*. The 'Preface' of this book explains that the revised edition of the guidebook was necessary in response to the increased interest among foreigners seeking meditation instruction in Thailand. The 'Preface' goes on to present meditation as an ideal practice for combating modernity:

> [A]s the world rushes towards the 21st century and the stress and strain of daily life become greater, more and more people are looking for ways to bring peace and tranquility into their lives. For some years now the trend has been to turn towards Eastern philosophies, and while many people have already found the answer in Buddhism, others are beginning to recognize that the path of the Buddha can lead them to what they are seeking. This quest for a peaceful existence has resulted in an influx in the number of foreigners visiting Thailand in spiritual pursuit.
>
> (National Identity Board 1988, no page)

Meditation for tourists in Thailand   111

This quote speaks to the disenchantment of modern society as well as the search for wisdom in the East.[10] The guidebook authors here assert that the stresses of modern living cause spiritual seekers to look to the past, to an ancient practice of peace, identified here as meditation. This example evokes the Romantic Orientalist discourse of meditation in Thailand that constructs the practice and place as an exotic 'Other,' and further illustrates that Romantic Orientalism remains influential for the popular understanding of Buddhism. These benefits attributed to meditation, somewhat ironically, add to the value of the commodity and contribute to the conception of meditation as an experience to be consumed.[11] This meditation guidebook edition draws from these familiar tropes within the cultural imaginary of Buddhism.

After the publication of this edition, opportunities for foreigners changed as new monasteries and meditation centers became popular and other locations were no longer able to host foreigners.[12] For this reason a third edition by Bill Weir[13] appeared in print in 1991 and online in 1994.[14] Yet another guide was needed ten years later as the number of foreigners and demand for knowledge about meditation centers continued to proliferate. The fourth edition of the WFB guide, titled *A Guide to Buddhist Monasteries and Meditation Centres in Thailand* by Pataraporn Sirikanchana, was published in 2004. The 'Foreword,' written by WFB president Phan Wanamethee,[15] states that there are many guidebooks to Thailand that give information on famous temples but this book "is meant to meet the needs of those seeking knowledge about reliable places in Thailand where meditation is taught according to Buddhist traditions" (Phan Wannamethee 2004, no page). Thus conceptualizing meditation as part of an economic model wherein lies a demand to be met continues in this more recent edition. Phan Wannamethee also asserts that the continual updating of this guidebook series reflects the growing interest in meditation centers among international visitors. Meditation is presented as the antidote for chaotic modern living, and Thailand is the place to find such a practice. This demonstrates meditation's role as a national symbol and extension of Thailand's exotic allure as well as a universal symbol of peace, relaxation, and anti-modernity.

Since the first WFB guide, the structure and format of the international meditation center listings, which make up most of the content of these guidebooks, have been strictly consistent.[16] The standard format includes the teaching method, teachers, language, size, food, accommodation, possibility of ordination, and pertinent contact information of the international meditation center. This practical information also includes the type of meditation and daily schedule, helping the international meditator imagine a routine day at the center. Travelers can choose based on meditation system, language availability, quality of food, location or amount of group practice, and availability of the teacher. This information is beneficial for those already interested in attending a retreat; however, it does not offer a picture of Buddhist rituals, daily almsround, morning and evening chanting, temple activities, or whether one will be able to participate in such routines. Meditation is the focus of these guides, not engagement with Thai Buddhism, even though at most meditation centers this engagement is inevitable.

112 Meditation for tourists in Thailand

In addition to the WFB guides, long-time Thailand resident Joe Cummings (1991)[17] published *The Meditation Temples of Thailand: A Guide*. In his 'Introduction' Cummings describes why he decided to write this book:

> [W]ith the rising general interest in Theravāda Buddhism and in insight or mindfulness meditation in particular, the time seems right to make the study of Buddhism in Thailand even more accessible to westerners, if possible. This book was written to serve that purpose. In the past, many foreigners have arrived in Thailand with the name of one wat [temple] or none at all; it is hoped that this guide will alleviate some of the problems experienced by first-time visitors, as well as open up a wider range of possibilities for the serious student.
>
> (Cummings 1991, vii–viii)

Cummings found in the 1990s that international meditators were searching for information on suitable centers that was not widely available.[18] As a Westerner fluent in Thai, Cummings, like Kornfield, is a significant interlocutor in transferring knowledge of meditation centers to international visitors.

This guidebook mostly focuses on the national appeal of meditation. Cummings asserts that, of the Theravāda Buddhist countries, Thailand is the most open to foreigners, has a strong social and cultural support, the instruction is given freely, and the teachings are offered with no motive to convert practitioners (Cummings 1991, vi–vii). He writes that, although Theravāda monasteries exist in predominantly English-speaking countries, Thailand offers the experience of the Buddhist tradition in its "millennium-old cultural setting" (Cummings 1991, vi). Also, one benefits from the generous hospitality of Thais within an environment that is "non-cultish with no motive to 'convert' students" (Cummings 1991, vii). This particular guidebook, therefore, creates and hopes to fill a desire not just for meditation but rather the chance to practice meditation as it is uniquely taught and experienced in Thailand. Further chapters on Buddhism in Thailand discuss the social roles of laypeople and monastics, well-known teachers, and teaching systems. Therefore Cummings explains more about temple life and Thai Buddhism than the authors of the WFB guides. He focuses on assuaging international meditators that they will be accepted and giving them the information they will need to feel comfortable in this new environment.

The most recent guide, "Meditation in Southeast Asia,"[19] was compiled by Dieter Baltruschat (2007), translated by Katharina Titkemeyer, and was published online. The information on retreats collected by the Members of the Munich Buddhist Society intentionally follows the format of the WFB guide publications. The editors have also added even more practical information such as advance preparations, medical care in the area of the center, and the best time of year to attend. In the 'Introduction' to the section on Thailand, this author, like Cummings, discusses meditation as an important part of Thailand's tourist offerings:

Meditation for tourists in Thailand 113

> [I]t [Thailand] has some outstanding meditation teachers. Some monasteries have excellent conditions for practice. Thailand also offers a broad spectrum of retreats. Whether you are a beginner wishing to combine a beach holiday with a meditation course, a meditator who wishes to ordain in a forest monastery, or simply want to practise intensely, you will find a suitable place.
>
> (Baltruschat 2007, 6)

A particular kind of religiosity is implied here where all levels of engagement with Buddhist meditation are considered equivalent. One can be a tourist who mixes meditation with holiday-making, a serious practitioner who primarily attends meditation retreats, or a meditator who is interested in becoming a monastic. These various levels of commitment create a desire for meditation by demonstrating the different avenues through which one can enter into meditation practice in Thailand. This information is now easier to access online but builds on the history of the WFB guides, using the same structure. Following previous guides, this information helps the international meditator feel mentally prepared for what they may experience physically during the retreat and gives potential meditators the ability to choose a program that fits his or her personal criteria. This guide, although compiled by individuals who attended retreats in Thailand, does not include narratives of the intensity of the practice, issues with translation and understanding the teacher, or interactions with Thai Buddhists. Dissemination of practical information and promoting the benefits of meditation in Thailand are more important for these guidebooks than describing the actual experience of meditation in particular centers.

These guides have been important sources for Buddhist travelers and the history of foreign meditation in Thailand. Many travelers visit several of these spots over a long period of time, making personal meditation tours of Thailand. This would not be possible without the information in these guides. These meditation guidebooks provide opportunities for increased engagement with meditation within a global religious tourism industry that promises an escape from modernity and a uniquely Thai tourist activity. Meditation guidebooks remain seminal for their importance in creating an information system for international meditators. Although currently they are not widely available in print, this information system exists today on websites and in mainstream guidebooks about Thailand. Bill Weir's edition is readily available online and print copies of Srikanchana's are sold in Buddhist bookshops, mainly in Bangkok. Guidebooks to Thailand, such as those in the popular Lonely Planet and Rough Guide series, provide some information, drawing from these meditation guidebooks and recommending that those interested should seek them out. Like meditation guidebooks, Thailand guidebooks list temples accepting foreigners but unlike meditation guidebooks do not offer much detail. Because this information is constantly changing, today the Internet is a more reliable way to select a meditation retreat. However, much of the format and content of listings of meditation centers in Thailand is taken from the initial work of these guidebooks.[20] This intersection of tourism and meditation extends further with the publications by the Tourism Authority of Thailand.

114 Meditation for tourists in Thailand

Tourism Authority of Thailand's meditation booklets

In order to promote and develop the tourism industry, The Tourism Organization of Thailand (TOT) was established in 1960 by the federal government. The name was changed in 1979 to the Tourism Authority of Thailand (TAT).[21] Today, the TAT is headquartered in Bangkok, with offices throughout the country and overseas. In order to counter the sexual image of Thailand's tourism industry, the TAT concentrates its publicity on other activities (Meyer 1988, 92), producing promotional materials about tourist destinations, holidays and festivals, and themes such as recreation and spirituality (Tourism Authority of Thailand website, no date).

The TAT has published three glossy booklets,[22] highlighting a number of international meditation centers throughout Thailand as well as offering basic information about Buddhism and meditation. In 2010, the TAT published and distributed 10,000 booklets. The target markets for these booklets are the USA, Europe, and Australia; the secondary market is Asia, which includes China, Hong Kong, Japan, Korea, Singapore, India, Chinese Malaysia, and Israel. The TAT began creating and publishing these materials because they believe religious tourism, especially meditation, is widely popular. The TAT also asserts that religious tourism has shown rapid growth and an increasing amount of foreign travelers are becoming interested in this kind of tourism every year.[23]

The most overt forms of promotional advertising of meditation are captured in these booklets. The TAT wants to be certain that Thailand is internationally known as a religious tourist destination with a plethora of meditation locations equipped with modern facilities that are ready to accommodate international visitors. The Bangkok Post quotes the director of the TAT's Attractions Promotion Division, Kulpramote Wannalert,

> [A]s a Buddhist country, Thailand is one of the world's significant Buddhist centres where interested foreigners could study Buddhism and meditation . . . We see it as imperative to implement tourism packages for foreigners who are interested in Buddhism and meditation.
>
> (Bangkok Post 2009, no page)

Through this promotion, Buddhism is part of a marketing strategy to increase tourism to Thailand. By depicting Thailand as an international center of Buddhist learning and teaching, Thai meditation becomes a national symbol and a way to enhance Thailand's image abroad.

The ideas presented in the TAT's three meditation booklets and its E-magazine demonstrate distinct ways discourses of meditation are presented to foreigners. The TAT promotes meditation by focusing on both its appeal as a Romantic Orientalist practice as well as themes that resonate with a Rational Orientalism. Rationalist Orientalist discourses include the atheistic and anti-dogmatic nature of Buddhism as well as its coherence with science. These discourses have been used to contrast Buddhism with Christianity as well as align Buddhism with secularism

Meditation for tourists in Thailand   115

through demonstrating its rational and empirical nature. The TAT both appropriates positive aspects of modernity to promote meditation and also maintains that the negative aspects of modernity can be reversed by meditation.

In the TAT's 2010 publication, under the subheading of "What is Buddhism?," Buddhism is discussed in contrast to theistic religions.

> [B]uddhism, one of the major religions of the world, is a spiritual religion based on the teachings of the Buddha. In Buddhism there is no deity; Buddhism is focused on personal development and liberation from suffering through selflessness and self-mastery.
> (Tourism Authority of Thailand Booklet 2010, 5)

This section claims that Buddhism does not teach belief or faith, attributing the Buddha as saying, "Believe no one, not even me, but discover the truth for yourselves" (Tourism Authority of Thailand Booklet 2010, 5).[24] Many of the characteristics lauded by a Rational Orientalist interpretation of Buddhism are replicated here, such as Buddhism as a non-theistic religion, an interest in the 'original' teachings of the Buddha, and the non-dogmatic nature of the tradition. The TAT takes advantage of these popular and positive conceptions of Buddhism in its advertising to the international community.

Buddhism's coherence with science is also a noted theme within the modern presentation of Buddhism and also connects with a Rational Orientalist understanding.

Meditation is advertised as coalescing with scientific fact and common knowledge about health and well-being.

> [T]here is an understanding around the world that meditation plays a role in sustaining a healthy lifestyle, with the practitioner seeking some degree of detachment from the material world, and drawing on inner peace for a sense of well-being. Meditation is a safe way of balancing one's physical, emotional, and mental states. Today, physicians recommend meditation as a way of relaxing from the stress of everyday life.
> (Tourism Authority of Thailand Booklet 2008, 5)

The physical benefits of meditation listed here, the TAT asserts, are internationally known. It is notable that science is used to support these claims.[25]

At the same time, the TAT also uses discourses of Romantic Orientalism and anti-modernism in order to commodify meditation for international consumption. These discourses show how the past is constructed nostalgically so that, although meditation is portrayed as a modern practice, it also evokes the 'authentic' and 'exotic' ideals of Eastern wisdom. These TAT meditation booklets depict both Thailand and meditation as a place and practice where one can find peace and respite from modern living. In its 2008 booklet, the TAT asserts that visitors can search and explore Thailand to discover its hidden practices

116 *Meditation for tourists in Thailand*

and techniques. The writers assert that "each year Thailand has attracted visitors from all over the world who wish to discover the secret of the peaceful and meditative lifestyle" (Tourism Authority of Thailand Booklet 2008, 5). Here meditation is seen as a mystical secret, evoking a Romantic Orientalism where meditation is described as an ancient practice that the modern tourist, like the colonialist before her, can unearth.

In these publications tourists are made to feel as though their present life circumstances are lacking something in their busyness and chaos. The relaxation of the meditation retreat provides the antidote for this modern affliction. Meditation provides an alternative to modern living and the symptoms of it manifested in mental illnesses and stress. The TAT's publications draw on these ideas of modernity to argue that meditation can provide the balance needed for hectic lives. This is evidenced in the TAT's E-magazine called "Thailand, Center of Buddhist Learning and Traditions," where the authors write,

> The West is becoming increasingly enamored with the ways of the East. Early interest in martial arts like karate and tae-kwon-do has matured to embrace more peaceful practices such as tai chi, yoga, Ayurveda, Thai massage, and of course, meditation.[26]

The meditative practices of the East are presented as the solution to stressful living in the West and are seen to combat negativity created by worldly conflict and busy schedules in modernity.

Meditation publications portray Thailand's international meditation centers as part of an unchanging, ancient practice that combats the effects of modern disenchantment and malaise, a cultural trope culled from the West's portrayal of itself. Instead of participating in physical commodity consumption to ease modern malaise, international tourists are offered an opportunity to consume the experience of meditation. Both the meditation guides and promotional booklets of the TAT have Romantic and Rational Orientalist influences and both portray Buddhist meditation as a universal and Thai symbol. However the TAT publications give equal attention to Romantic and Rational Orientalism stemming from a Thai tourism perspective while the guidebooks pay more attention to meditation as a national practice of Thailand. The TAT's audience of general tourists perhaps resonates more with a Rational, universal perspective. Those specific tourists looking for meditation retreats would seek out meditation guidebooks, which promote meditation more as a Romantic and national practice. Both the TAT and WFB use Rational Orientalist discourses in order to argue that in addition to meditation being a part of Thai culture, it is also a modern and universal practice. Therefore both sources promote meditation using similar resources and drawing from the same popular imaginations of Thailand and meditation. While focusing on these imaginaries, the texts of these publications do not include the rigorous mental and physical toll of an extended meditation retreat, daily temple activities, communication problems, and possible interactions with

Thai Buddhists. These promotional materials both constitute a commodification of meditation for the international community as well as spread the Buddhist teachings to a wide variety of audiences.

International meditation center retreat pamphlets

Another source of literature advertising meditation is found within Thailand's international meditation centers. While the TAT promotes meditation as part of the larger tourist experience in Thailand, international meditation centers themselves provide information for tourists interested in specific retreat centers. Most meditation retreat centers have informational pamphlets for foreigners about what to expect when staying at a particular center or temple and detail the schedule and practice at that particular site. Therefore these are more realistic than the TAT's depictions of Thailand and its meditation traditions but still show similar consumerist rhetoric that specifically targets the international audience.

International meditation center brochures are often designed to gloss over the disjunctures of cultural understandings of the self. These significant disjunctures are ignored because the promotional materials are directed to foreign communities with different cultural frameworks. In order to demonstrate this, it is instructive to compare Thai and English brochures for the same meditation center. The brochures in Thai and English of Diphabhavan Meditation Center in Koh Samui, Southern Thailand illustrate this. The brochure for Thai meditators refers to major Buddhist topics including suffering, the four path stages to *nibbāna*, the Four Noble Truths, *paticcasamupatta* (dependent co-origination), and *ānāpānasati* (mindfulness of breathing). There is no description of why the retreat would be beneficial or who should enter the retreat, as presumably Thai Buddhists would be familiar with this. The international brochure in English does not contain these teachings, as many would not recognize these terms.

The English brochure, in contrast, highlights the advantages of the retreat at Dipabhavan. These include secular benefits regarding well-being such as 'getting to know oneself,' learning about one's feelings, having a less scattered mind, letting go of worry, and applying these benefits to cope with daily life.[27] These tropes relate to the discourses we have already seen in other meditation promotion formats as the benefits point to a Romantic, nostalgic longing for a time and place free from stress and chaotic daily routines as well as discourses of therapy and healing. Travel is often constructed as a journey of self-discovery, so that only by leaving one's familiar lifestyle can one come to find one's 'true' self. Proclaimed benefits of meditation like 'getting to know oneself,' tap into these ideas. The English brochure from Dipabhavan retreat center states that the meditation retreat is a special time to explore the inner side of oneself and to learn what one really wants in life, and it concludes that "This retreat might just be a start towards discovering such important things about oneself." However, there is a large difference between 'knowing' oneself, and 'finding' oneself. A traditional goal of meditation is to experience the reality of non-self—that there is no permanent

118 *Meditation for tourists in Thailand*

entity or 'soul.' Therefore there is no self to discover or find, but there are qualities, tendencies, and habits one can come to know in order to understand how to overcome defilements and aid in cultivating the direct experience of reality.

The Middle Way Meditation Retreat organized by Wat Dhammakaya takes these discourses of modern disenchantment further still. As this temple's strategies of commodification are taken to an international audience, the message is attuned to the cultural repertoires of English-speaking visitors. The key tagline for the brochure is "Relax your body, rest your mind and find inner peace." The brochure also describes the purpose and benefits of the Dhammakaya method. It states that the technique

> is about self-discovery, relaxation and purification of the mind . . . The meditation cleanses your mind making you more gentle, kind, and unharmful, it helps to quit a bad habit and acquire good ones, helps with personal development and career progress.

It is particular to the Middle Way retreat to emphasize career progress, the formation of good habits, and personal development. In this instance the practice of meditation moves beyond its depiction as a national symbol and universal ideal of peace and relaxation and taps into the self-help market, and highlights well-being and self-improvement. This focus aligns with the current trend of popular psychology and self-improvement publications and speakers, especially in the USA (Ehrenreich 2010). These pamphlets therefore represent another instantiation of the interpretation that meditation can be consumed in order to help escape modernity and the malaise associated with it.

Themes of disenchantment, the appeal of finding oneself in a serene environment, personal development, and meditation for non-Buddhists all draw on subjects evocative for an international audience. In all of these writings about the rising interest in meditation by foreigners, no mention is made of converting to Buddhism. It is assumed that the international meditators are interested in meditation for the secular benefits of peace and relaxation. These selective themes reveal the ways meditation is advertised as a commodity meant to attract international tourists. It is not only the text in these brochures but also images that suggest an ideal, picturesque experience for an international audience.

Images of meditation

Diverse media create impressions and assumptions of the tourist destination that connect with tourists' fantasies, expectations, and nostalgic sensibilities (Salazar 2010, 22). A significant part of the commodification of meditation presented to tourists exists in carefully selected images. Meditation retreat promotional materials utilize certain sets of imagery that the international market will respond to. Commodities are not always linked to their precise function but appeal to the logic of desire (Baudrillard 1998, 77). Images of meditation retreats are not realistic depictions but connect with this social logic of international travelers and

Meditation for tourists in Thailand   119

positive projections of Buddhism, meditation, and Thai tourism. Culture can be used to satisfy demand just as any other consumer object. Jean Baudrillard theorizes that "need is never so much the need for a particular object as the 'need' for difference" (Baudrillard 1998, 78). The images in promotional materials for meditation retreats serve as symbols of participation in religious otherness.

Tourists are in search of viewing and experiencing the images of difference within their destinations. They perceive scenery, practices, objects, behaviors, buildings, etc., as symbols that typify the otherness of the region being toured. In this way, traveling becomes a series of spectacles in which modern man grasps different cultures. What results is a desire to see, experience, and consume the cultural symbols, as John Urry argues in his important work, *The Tourist Gaze* (Urry 2002, 13). For Thailand one of these symbols is a quiet, natural setting inside a Buddhist temple with a person sitting peacefully in meditation. Images depicting such scenes in meditation retreat advertisements reinforce these symbols and the desire to see and experience them in person. Therefore, Thais and foreigners are made self-conscious of Thai culture and meditation's role as a commodified practice that can be adapted for international consumption.

The creation of desire through images is another way that these promotional materials implant a consumerist logic around the practice and retreat center. These types of images are utilized in both TAT publications and international meditation retreat pamphlets. The first way this is done is again through Romantic pictures of a single international meditator as the focal point of the image. From an international meditator Photoshopped onto a lotus flower to a tan woman meditating in a black bikini with a temple rising in the background, some of these images show the extremes of advertising meditation. Both of these images portray a tourist meditating in an exotic, almost fantastic scene. The image of a young woman meditating on an enlarged lotus flower depicts the 'magic' that can occur within this practice. The woman in a black bikini, however, illustrates the association of beauty and well-being with meditation that is only tangentially related to Buddhism, as the pagoda takes a backseat to the image of the woman. These images demonstrate the tropes of meditation present within the content of meditation retreat advertisements in a dramatic way. Other images of foreign meditators depict them alone, dressed properly, either in white clothing or loose-fitting multicolored outfits, meditating in nature. Significantly, there were no images of Thai monastics teaching the foreign meditators, Thai Buddhists practicing with foreigners, or foreigners in groups in the pamphlets that I reviewed.

Thai meditators featured in these tourist materials are both part of the meditation retreat scenery as well as cultural markers, as Graham Dann argues in a study of tourism images, reminding travelers that they are in a different place (Dann 1996, 70). They are not central to the images but rather incidental as evidenced by brochures for Thailand. Images of a single Thai meditator within the backdrop of temple scenery evoke this difference of space. However Thai meditators are not seen from a close vantage point as international meditators are. The distant images of Thai meditators serve as a metaphor for the ways international meditators engage with their Thai counterparts because of the language barrier and

120 *Meditation for tourists in Thailand*

separation of the two groups at most centers. In these images Thai meditators add to the exotic and unfamiliarity of the meditation retreat. They become part of the construction of meditation as a symbol of Thailand.

The second main depiction of Thai meditators displays them in groups, always wearing the traditional white clothes. Foreign meditators usually enter a retreat alone and think about spirituality as an individual pursuit. The relaxation of the retreat comes from being alone, away from others and in the beautiful natural surroundings. However, pictures of groups of Thai meditators seated in a meditation hall or practicing walking meditation in a long line together demonstrate how Thai people act as cultural markers of the host culture (Dann 1996, 70). This is how foreign meditators usually encounter Thai meditators—not as individuals but as groups. These images of Thai meditators represent the dynamism and vivacity of Thai Buddhism and the continuing importance of meditation practice to the populace. This evokes a tradition that is alive and well and something that foreigners could participate in.

Meditation retreat advertisements also play on the Romantic gaze, a term used by John Urry (1995), not only through images of people but also ones that portray ornate temple structures and pristine nature within the meditation center. From the glistening heads of dozens of golden Buddha statues to damp, lush forests, these images capture for the international meditator the idea of a Romantic and tranquil experience. Many images show sweeping landscapes of nature while others focus closely on bells, the hands of a Buddha statue, or a single flower. All of these express the natural beauty of the temple environment as well as the allure of Buddhist imagery in Thailand. These promotional strategies and tropes reveal meditation as a national commodity that can be linked with popular images of the country. Through this promotion, meditation becomes an extension of Thailand's public face to the international community—part of its tourist identity. To be associated with this extremely popular global phenomenon is an advantageous connection to make.

Conclusion

These three sets of sources used in this chapter—meditation guidebooks, TAT booklets, and international retreat center pamphlets—demonstrate the connections between cultural imaginaries of Thailand and meditation, as well as how tourism creates new pathways and recognitions for the interweaving of religion and commercialism. The pamphlets and brochures create a desire to experience and consume the practice of meditation within a Thai Buddhist temple. Guidebooks and TAT publications shape the experience of international meditators and their interactions with Thai Buddhists and international meditation teachers. These publications have certainly made it easier to obtain information on meditation retreats. The presence of the publications and their numerous editions indicates that there has been and continues to be an interest in this information. Meditation guidebooks have also directly affected the Internet information available about the centers, revealing that these guidebooks are an important foundation for international engagement with Thai Buddhism. Images also create a fantasy of the Thai meditation retreat, portraying the experience as magical, exotic, and peaceful. These images reinforce the imaginaries of Thailand and meditation.

International meditators, through these publications, are attracted to this practice that is simultaneously modern and authentic, familiar and exotic. The producers of these promotional materials, writers and staff of large institutions as well as volunteers from international meditation centers, are part of the production of meditation as a cultural commodity. This both empowers Thai Buddhists through their control over these discourses, as well as reinforcing the otherness of Thailand's Buddhist practices.[28] These publications respond to the popular imagination of Buddhism and Thailand and offer international meditators a chance to experience the reality of a Thai meditation retreat. This commodification of meditation is another instantiation of the entangled nature of religion and commerce and how religious practices are now adapted at an international level to reach a diverse and widespread audience.

This chapter's first aim was to illuminate how Thai meditation publications, similar to the narratives of international meditators, utilize both poles of Orientalism—Romantic and Rational. Romantic Orientalist discourses in these guidebooks and promotional materials imagine Thailand as an exotic and intriguing Other, revealing how the appeal of meditation is commodified to promote travel to Thailand. Meditation is also constructed as a familiar and modern practice as a consequence of Rational Orientalist discourses. Through these tropes meditation becomes both a national and universal symbol. The second aim of this chapter was to demonstrate that the appropriation of these discourses has served to reinforce consumer values and constitute a commodification of meditation for international tourists. Drawing on familiar imaginaries, this commodification highlights the creative possibilities for bringing a Buddhist practice to a much larger audience. Within the economy of merit system of Thai Buddhism, promoting meditation aids with the dissemination of the teachings and thus produces merit. Described as both modern, with its rational and scientific approach, as well as rooted within the traditional Thai monastic setting, meditation provides an ideal commodity, which can be constructed and transformed in order to advertise a religious vacation and promote meditation retreat possibilities for international visitors while in Thailand.

Notes

1 The Middle Way Retreat charges for its retreats where they rent facilities in Phukhet, Chiangmai and Loei. These fees cover transportation to retreat center, food, lodging, and course materials. Their website states that the fees are used to maintain the retreat facilities and promote The Middle Way meditation retreat (www.mdwmeditation.org).
2 This generalized exchange is not always ideal as Gutschow describes the unequal support of Buddhist monks and nuns in the Himalayas (Gutschow 2004, 84). Because of the different functions each group performs, they are valued differently. Also, in Thailand some monks are known to have a greater field of merit and donations to them personally garners much support.

122 *Meditation for tourists in Thailand*

3 Moran (2004) has found similarly among Western patrons of Tibetan Buddhism in his study of Bodhanath, Kathmandu. From speaking with Tibetan teachers he has found that Western people rarely give large sums of money to support the monasteries. However, Taiwanese patrons are known among Tibetan lamas for their large donations toward monastic building projects.

4 For an analysis of Buddhist commodification practices in Kathmandu see Moran (2004), and in Bodhgaya see Geary (2008).

5 International meditation centers are mostly concentrated within Central, Southern, and Northern Thailand. Although tourist temples such as Wat Doi Suthep have an international meditation center, these meditators are not a primary source of income for the temple. The international meditators comprise a small percentage of the tourism market, which primarily consists of tourists on day trips. In the South of Thailand the number of tourists on beach vacations fueled the creation of two large group retreats, the International Dhamma Hermitage in Chaiya and the International Meditation Center at Wat Kow Tahm on Koh Phangan. However, it is not the international meditation centers themselves that create an economy surrounding tourism; they are a consequence of tourism and account for a small portion of the tourists who travel in the South.

6 The language used in Thai is 'renting,' not 'buying' an amulet. The desire to displace the language of commerce from amulets underscores Tambiah's point that amulets were part of a practice of donation. In fact some temples explicitly suggest a donation, rather than a fee for their amulets.

7 Regional centers carry on "various activities based on propagation and practice of the Dhamma for securing peace and happiness of humankind" (World Fellowship of Buddhists website).

8 Jack Kornfield found his way to Thailand through the Peace Corps. In 1972, after five years meditating with teachers throughout India and Southeast Asia, he returned to America. He became a graduate student in clinical psychology and today teaches a merging of psychology and Buddhist meditation. Kornfield is known as one of the key figures in bringing *vipassanā* to America and the West. He is one of the founders of the Insight Meditation Society in Barre, Massachusetts and founded and currently teaches at Spirit Rock Insight Meditation Center in Woodacre, California.

9 Practicing *vipassanā* meditation in Thailand for foreigners was only possible at this moment because the practice had already undergone laicization among Thai middle class urbanites. See Jordt (2007) and Cook (2010) for the history of this process in Myanmar and Thailand respectively.

10 This quote recognizes a particular kind of Western engagement with Buddhism, the Romantic perspective. Tweed characterizes this type of interest in Buddhism as an attraction to Asian culture (Tweed 1992, 69). Some international meditators are attracted to all things 'Asian,' and meditation, through its mainstream popularity, meets this criteria.

11 This development is not unique to Thailand. There is a precedent for this association of modern disenchantment and *vipassanā* meditation in Myanmar (See Houtman 1990; Braun 2008). The institutions seen here therefore take advantage of a preexisting trend.

12 Often, if the abbot or Thai monk meditation teacher does not speak English, the meditation center will rely on an English interpreter. Interpreters, either lay or ordained, are usually young and do not permanently reside in a given center. Because of this flux of interpreters, many meditation centers are only able to host international visitors on an irregular basis.

13 Bill Weir began his writing career for Moon Handbooks after embarking on a series of long-distance bicycle tours. He has written several titles for Moon including Arizona, Utah, and the Grand Canyon. Weir contributed text to *National Geographic Traveler, Arizona* along with updating the third edition of *A Guide to Buddhist Monasteries and Meditation Centers in Thailand* in 1991.

14 For the online edition see: www.hdamm.de/buddha/mdtctr01.htm.
15 Phan Wannamethee was formerly a president and rector of the World Fellowship of Buddhists. He oversaw publication of the fourth edition of *A Guide to Buddhist Monasteries and Meditation Centers in Thailand*, published by the WFB. He is currently the secretary general of the Thai Red Cross Society and lives in Bangkok.
16 For a sample list of categories and information provided for each listing see: www.hdamm.de/buddha/mdtctr01.htm.
17 Joe Cummings was one of the first writers for *Lonely Planet Thailand*, which is regarded as one of the best guidebooks about the country. Having traveled the country for over twenty years, Cummings has written several other Lonely Planet guidebooks, Moon Handbooks, and a number of photography books. He is also a correspondent for CPA Media, Hong Kong, and Travel Intelligence.
18 Unlike the WFB guides and Joe Cummings' popular series of Thailand travel guidebooks for Lonely Planet, there is only one edition of this book.
19 See www.insightmeditationcenter.org/site/wp-content/uploads/2009/06/Asian_Retreat_Centers.pdf.
20 See for instance dhammathai.org, sawasdee.com, www.buddhanet.info, dharmaweb.org.
21 For more information on the TAT, see: www.tourismthailand.org/about-tat/. Both the Tourism Authority of Thailand and The National Identity Board are responsible for the dissemination of cultural information about Thailand but these organizations have no formal connection or relationship.
22 "Meditation in Thailand, Learn and Practice Buddhist Meditation in the Traditional Thai Surroundings" (2010); "Meditation in Thailand, The Path to Inner Peace and Well-Being" (2008); "Experience Buddhist Meditation (2003); TAT E-magazine "Thailand, Center of Buddhist Learning and Traditions" (no date).
23 This information is taken from email correspondence with the assistant to Mrs. Kulpramote Wannalert, Director Attractions Promotion Division, Tourism Authority of Thailand, June 15th, 2010.
24 This quote refers to the Kalama Sutta (AN 3.65).
25 There is a long-standing dialogue between Buddhism and science (See Cho 2012; Lopez 2008; Wallace 2003). This is another aspect of the conversation connecting Buddhism with modernity. Buddhist leaders have argued for their tradition's coherence with science, thus claiming Buddhism is more modern than theistic religions. Meditation has become a significant aspect of this dialogue as the practice has become an object of scientific inquiry.
26 Quote taken from the Tourism Authority of Thailand E-magazine "Thailand, Centre of Buddhist Learning and Traditions." See: www.tatnews.org/emagazine/2146.asp.
27 Dipabhavan Meditation Center Brochure for International Meditators, collected June 21st, 2010.
28 Not only Thai Buddhists, but foreign monastics and laity contribute to the production of promotional meditation materials. Even though this is the case, Thais make the ultimate decisions on what is published. As Ooi (2010, 83) has noted in Singapore, tourist institutions may attempt to self-Orientalize themselves in order to attract tourists through drawing on the Western imagination of 'Asia.' Thai tourist and Buddhist institutions attempt to self-Orientalize their portrayals of meditation through reinforcing the perceptions of Buddhism in the West.

6 Pedagogical techniques for translating *vipassanā* meditation

Advertisements represent a broad, large-scale effort to promote meditation. However, international meditation center teachers provide nuanced understandings and translations of the Thai Buddhist retreat program, utilizing decontextualized modern Buddhist discourses and imaginaries of meditation. Along with translations of the Thai Buddhist meditation retreat, international meditation center teachers must learn the cultural assumptions of their international students. The initial orientation period, daily interviews, and closing ceremonies are the primary student teacher interactions, but these exchanges occur throughout the retreat. This excerpt from my fieldnotes demonstrates some of the difficulties involved in this dialectical process:

> [D]anni and I were a bit upset that our teacher didn't show up on our last day of the retreat. We thought that he would give us a final teaching or words of wisdom for how to meditate when we are back in Ireland or on our travels. Sara said this to me in our conversation before she and her partner departed from Wat Umong. When I spoke to Phra Viriya about this couple he said he did not want to teach them anymore because he found their actions disrespectful. They arrived late to the morning group discussion and would often be near one another's rooms, which are restricted from the opposite sex. Rather than speaking directly to them about this issue, Phra Viriya stopped teaching them.

This situation demonstrates some of the difficulties these two groups face in dialogue with each other. The two Irish students thought it was acceptable to not adhere strictly to the rules of the retreat program, demonstrating their lack of submission and understanding of the retreat norms. This offended Phra Viriya; but instead of explaining the retreat program more carefully, he left them to practice by themselves. This highlights the informal way international meditators sometimes approach a retreat and how their teachers can choose to respond in a variety of ways ranging from educating to ignoring. This chapter discusses this range, from successful translations to ineffective ones.

Mary Louise Pratt (2007) uses the term 'contact zone' to analyze encounters between disparate groups. She writes:

Translating vipassanā *meditation* 125

> [A] 'contact' perspective emphasizes how subjects are constituted in and by their relations to each other. It treats the relations among colonizers and colonized, or travelers and 'travelees,' not in terms of separateness or apartheid, but in terms of copresence, interaction, interlocking understandings and practices, often within radically asymmetrical relations of power.
>
> (Pratt 2007, 7)

This is the space where "peoples geographically and historically separated come into contact with each other and establish ongoing relations" (Pratt 2007, 6). In this chapter I analyze the international meditation center as such a contact zone and shed light on the resulting dialogues and interactions. Although international meditation center teachers, to varying extents, understand that one way to practice meditation is as a decontextualized global religious practice, their comprehension of meditation, even if they are lay foreign teachers, is much broader and embedded within a complex ethical, cosmological, and social worldview. When different imaginings of Buddhism interact with each other, some aspects of the meditation retreat take on new importance, some aspects retain their original significance, while others are brushed aside or deleted altogether.

Focusing on practices of translation, this chapter distills the voices of international meditation center teachers and their pedagogical strategies. Teachers translate the retreat format from a standard Thai Buddhist program into a global one that resonates with a decontextualized religious practice. Translations utilizing psychological, universal, and secular imaginaries of meditation are effective in this context. I show how international meditation center teachers cater to these imaginaries of Buddhism, stemming from historical contexts of Orientalism and modern Buddhism. International meditators spur this translation through their reactions and feedback to the retreat program. However, some international meditation center teachers do not speak in modern Buddhist discourses and do not recognize the imaginaries of meditation that their students hold. A retreat program with this kind of teacher cannot be translated easily, if at all. Therefore some international meditation center teachers understand how to translate the retreat and others do not or are unwilling to. Additionally, despite some international meditation center teachers' efforts at translation, the retreat program remains confusing and demanding for international meditators. The end of the chapter analyzes what happens when international meditation center teachers' translations are ineffective and international meditators dissent from the retreat program.

Some of these translations are intentional as teachers articulate specifically why they adapt the retreat in particular ways; however, other translations are not conducted with such intention but are reactions over time of interactions with international meditators and their imaginaries of Buddhism. Following trends of modern Buddhism we see translations of international meditation center teachers toward secularization and universalism of Buddhist practice, using psychological, therapeutic language to explain the teaching and selecting elements of the meditation retreat that resonate with international meditators and discarding those that do not.

126 *Translating* vipassanā *meditation*

Translation within Thailand's international meditation centers

Translation constitutes a bridge to the target audience where the translator crosses boundaries between culture and languages in order to enable understanding. I use the term translation to describe a process not only of translating one language into another but from one set of cultural contexts and worldviews into another. Therefore translation within Thailand's international meditation centers is not only from Thai to English, but also from the Thai Buddhist cultural idiom into a secular and psychological framework. Some teachers, whose audiences are both Thai and international meditators, must be able to think between cultures and continually refine his or her translation in dialogue with international meditators. Talal Asad writes that the "acquisition of new forms of language from the modern West—whether by forcible imposition, insidious insertion, or voluntary borrowing—is part of what makes for new possibilities of action in non-Western societies" (Asad 1993, 13). These translations create new opportunities for exchange with international meditators about Buddhism and meditation. Through translations that make the retreat program comprehensible and familiar, international meditation center teachers create a space for learning and dialogue. They use categories of individualism, psychology, secularism, and universalism in their translations for modern international audiences. This is not simply 'dumbing-down' the meditation retreat but selectively reinterpreting aspects, removing some of the standard retreat format and adding new parts. It is true that this translation at first minimizes the degree to which Buddhism can seem strange or challenging, however, the meditation retreat itself is certainly a daunting enterprise, especially for tourists with little knowledge of Thailand or Buddhism. Translation aids the international meditator in being able to participate in the retreat and offers an understanding of how the retreat program facilitates meditation practice.

These translation practices have a history within Buddhism as it entered Southeast and East Asia and indeed throughout Buddhism's history of movement to new cultural contexts. John Holt (2009) argues that because the indigenous religious substratum of Laos was spirit cults, Buddhist concepts were translated through these conceptual categories. The indigenous religious substratum provided the framework in which Buddhism could enter and one that was used to convey Buddhism at the popular level (Holt 2009, 45). Joseph Cheah (2011) also concludes that Theravāda Buddhism was not successful in Burma until it was rearticulated to incorporate spirit cults, or *nats* (Cheah 2011, 62). When King Anawrahta, in the eleventh century, failed in his effort to cleanse Buddhism of pre-Buddhist elements, he instead sought to contain the power of the *nats* by subsuming them under a Theravāda Buddhist framework. Therefore religious change does not always concern purification of indigenous beliefs and practices, but flexibility and creative translations that work with the worldviews and frameworks of new potential followers.

Translation was also used during the historical interaction as Buddhism moved from India into China (Mollier 2009; Sharf 2002; Zurcher 2007; Chen 1973).

Translating vipassanā *meditation* 127

Christine Mollier (2009) argues that Mahayana Buddhism's encounter with Taoism in China shaped them both in significant ways. Erik Zurcher writes that this translation necessitated selection of elements that were congruent with preexisting Chinese worldviews and that could be easily adapted and incorporated (Zurcher 2007, 2). In similar ways Buddhism's encounter with discourses of modernization such as science, universalism, and secularism has shaped its formation more recently in non-Buddhist countries. When translating Buddhist teachings and practices in international meditation centers we do not see simple borrowing of external ideas but a selective application of these discourses in the presentation of the tradition to foreign communities. This is done in order to appeal to new cultures and communities of practitioners. Mollier writes that Buddhism and Taoism integrated practices of one another in order "To attract or keep faithful followers by providing them with the most fashionable religious trends, even if this meant borrowing conspicuously from the opposing camp's heritage" (Mollier 2008, 19). International meditation center teachers do not combine discourses of other religious traditions as much as secular and scientific discourses meant to appeal to modern international audiences.

In this way, translation is not about exactness or precision of meaning but rather which aspects resonate with the culture over time and how they are incorporated and imagined anew. In one of the most recent translations of Buddhism from various centers in Asia to America, scholars have noted a lack of Asian norms of authority in regard to monastic hierarchies as well as student-teacher relationships (Sharf 2002; Baumann 1997, 2001, 2012; Prebish 1999; Queen 1999). Instead self-authority predominates. This authority of individual experience is part of modern religious trends (McMahan 2008, 212). Despite the widespread availability of texts and teachers, many interested Americans find resonance with the way Buddhism is presented as a personal choice consisting of elements they can selectively incorporate into their religious repertoires. Clearly, Protestant values have become assimilated into the American translation of Buddhism and they are utilized by both Western and Asian teachers in America. American audiences did not receive or hope to receive an 'authentic' or 'unadulterated' Indian Buddhism but accepted and rejected elements in order to domesticate the tradition to their specific cultural and historical concerns. In this way translation of texts was just as important as cultural translations that developed through constant exchange and contact within Buddhism's history. The use of Daoist terminology helped Chinese make Buddhism meaningful, the incorporations of spirit cults within Buddhism in Southeast Asia aided in making connections to local ways of thinking, and possibilities of self-authority made Buddhism resonate with American audiences. In the same way Buddhism is molded to fit into modern sensibilities in Thailand to international audiences through integrating discourses of secularism and science.

Although translation becomes a way of claiming universalism, it also entails apprehending difference at a cultural level. This translation is most notable upon reflecting that there are hardly any Thai Buddhist terms that international meditation center teachers use. In rare cases students may be required to greet their

128 *Translating* vipassanā *meditation*

teacher using the Thai greeting '*sawatdii*.' Buddhist terms are often kept to a minimum so as not to alienate newcomers.[1] For foreign non-Buddhists only a small number of key teachings are presented. These Buddhist teachings are all related to developing their meditation practice. For example the Five Hindrances[2] are a key teaching for overcoming problems during meditation. This is one of the only teachings presented during the retreat at few international meditation centers. In addition, as part of the orientation at the outset of many retreats, some teachers delineate the Four Foundations of Mindfulness. Teachers only discuss these concepts as they relate to meditation practice; they do not educate international meditators on the broader context from which they developed. Therefore students learn some basic Buddhist terms but do not know the referent or context of the concepts. International meditation center teachers state that insight knowledge is considered to be the only knowledge necessary. Insight knowledge produces deep understanding at the experiential level. Intellectual knowledge, comparatively, is much more superficial. Therefore it is the experience of insight that is sought after through the meditation practice and all of the rules and regulations of the retreat program promote this. Terms and intellectual understanding of Buddhist teachings are not necessary as experiential learning is the most important and sought-after kind of learning.[3]

Understanding which beliefs and practices need to be translated and how to do so is the most significant task for international meditation center teachers. In this way, international meditation center teachers function like anthropologists, in many cases with vast ethnographic knowledge of their students. Paula Rubel and Abraham Rosman (2003) write,

> [T]he central aim of the anthropological enterprise has always been to understand and comprehend a culture or cultures other than one's own. This inevitably involves either the translation of words, ideas and meanings from one culture to another, or the translation to a set of analytical concepts.
>
> (Rubel and Rosman 2003, 1)

International meditation center teachers are taking part in ethnography as translators of one culture into another, of analytical concepts and practices of Thai Buddhism into ones that English-speakers will understand. Some international meditation center teachers think about this explicitly and themselves as translators and others do not. But they are all performing this role to various extents and with different strategies.

Translation strategies

Because of their unfamiliarity with the culture and traditions of Thai Buddhism, international meditators are treated as a distinct group by the meditation teachers and among themselves. International meditation center teachers implement various translations that are specific to each temple or retreat center environment as it is not only the teachings that are translated for international meditators but

Translating vipassanā *meditation* 129

oftentimes the physical space and practices of the meditation center are altered to accommodate this audience. Some of the earliest Buddhist teachers to attract large numbers of foreign audiences offer models of strategies of translation that continue today within Thailand's international meditation centers.

Burmese monk Ledi Sayadaw[4] is an early example of a teacher who attracted lay Burmese and foreign followers. Erik Braun argues that in Ledi Sayadaw's book, *The Manual on Insight Meditation*, which was translated into English in Burma in 1915 and intended for a European audience, he did not change his presentation of meditation in any significant way. He only emphasizes the role of the laity and the importance of their study (Braun 2013, 128). Ledi Sayadaw corresponded with Westerners such as Pāli scholar Caroline Rhys-Davids, and found that they were interested in analytical analysis (Braun 2013, 129). Rhys-Davids and Ledi Sayadaw shared ideas about Buddhist doctrine and philosophy. However, they did not think of Buddhism in the same way. Rhys-Davids exhibited an Orientalist decontextualized vision of Buddhism, while Ledi Sayadaw's view was embedded within a more traditional cosmology (Braun 2013, 130). This demonstrates a history of Buddhist teachers maintaining a consistent message for foreigners and international meditators. International meditation center teachers also are not adopting the worldview of their students but are knowledgeable about what attracts them and will be familiar.

Sri Lankan Buddhist leader, Anagarika Dharmapala, provides another early model.[5] Steven Kemper compares how Dharmapala taught Sri Lankan and international audiences:

> [T]o Sinhala audiences, he offered moral instruction and practical advice about handling money, table manners, and personal hygiene. For Western audiences, preaching in a way that resembled a Christian sermon made it an easily recognized social practice . . . nothing was lost, he thought, by sloughing off the repetitive and time-consuming quality of the traditional form. Westerners were not likely in any event to be interested in making merit. They could convert by taking the Three Refuges; they could participate if they liked; or they could come and go. The one thing non-Sinhalas were certain to find engaging was meditation.
>
> (Kemper 2005, 29)

Dharmapala argues that his reductive translation does not affect the quality of the teachings received by non-Buddhists. International meditation center teachers in Thailand today often have large programs for Thai audiences including dhamma talks, chanting sessions, and preaching, while international meditators focus exclusively on their individual meditation practice. This is not to say that all international meditation center teachers know about and explicitly draw from these earlier figures but that these issues of cultural translation have resulted in similar strategies of action. Other models for Thailand's international meditation center teachers will be discussed as I outline their primary strategies below.

130 *Translating* vipassanā *meditation*

Translating for individual choice

Choice and flexibility is a feature of religion in modernity.[6] International meditation center teachers translate the meditation retreat into a range of personal preferences and optional activities for international meditators. International meditation center teachers who teach both Thai and international groups know that they must switch from a group which mostly conforms to established roles and authority to the more subjective orientation of the international visitors who follow inner sources of authority and individual orientation (Skilton 2013, 165; Heelas & Woodhead 2005, 6). Much writing about contemporary religion describes the emergence of choice, of the possibility of subscribing to a number of religious beliefs and practices without identification or conversion. Spiritual marketplace is a common term scholars use to explain the process of how people choose which practices and beliefs are best for them at various moments of their lives (Houtmann & Aupers 2010, 101). This spiritual marketplace is connected to the sacralization of the self, which advocates people to follow personalized paths that do not rely on any established external models or hierarchies of authority (Houtmann & Aupers 2010, 102). In this way, although modern individuals are to some extent limited by the cultural resources available, they are not bound to one religious option. Throughout their lives, modern individuals' religious identities may include a single dominant tradition and group but may also include creative adaptation, expressing religiosity differently when in different contexts. As well, they may be open to add decontextualized global religious practices to their religious and cultural repertoires. International meditation center teachers often realize that their students' religiosity, identities, and commitments are diverse, fluid, and complex.

The most important aspect of this individual and contextual religiosity is the primacy of one's personal experience. Within any religious experience, feeling and intuition come to be the primary ways to gain knowledge. David McMahan (2008) writes, "Buddhism, according to many modernist interpretations invites self-discovery, interior exploration, and inner freedom" (McMahan 2008, 191). In this way one common perception of Buddhism is that it allows individuals to pursue their own truths and identities. Similarly to *vipassanā* meditation, the intellect plays a secondary role within the privileging of experience. However, in meditation, it is not one's 'inner self,' that guides, but the Buddhist doctrines revealed as one progresses within meditation practice. Stef Aupers and Dick Houtman (2010) write that "New Age, with its characteristic rejection of restrictive religious traditions, institutions and doctrines, and its emphasis on the primacy of subjective life and personal experience, has become a full part of the Western cultural mainstream" (Aupers & Houtmann 2010, 18) and "ideals of individual liberty, personal authenticity and tolerance have come to permeate the core institutions of modern, Western countries" (Aupers & Houtmann 2010, 22). International meditation center teachers, to varying extents, create the flexibility for their students to practice in a way that privileges individual preferences.

An important strategy to translate the meditation retreat for international meditators is to allow the students to tailor the experience to their comfort level. Ajan

Translating vipassanā *meditation*   131

Buddhasak, of Wat Prathat Doi Suthep,[7] has led retreats for some foreign meditators who are resistant to activities such as prostrating to the Buddha and teacher and attending morning and evening periods of chanting because they are only interested in meditation, rather than any other religious practices at the temple. They want the experience of meditation, but not that of living in a Thai Buddhist temple. In these cases Ajan Buddhasak advises them not to be concerned about participating. He emphasizes that participation is a choice available for each person, and meditators can simply continue meditating if they do not wish to partake in other activities. One activity that causes tension for international meditators from other faiths or who hope to focus exclusively on meditation is chanting. At the Dipabhavan Meditation Center on Koh Samui, it is emphasized that chanting is optional. The website states, "Some people may feel that 'Buddhist' chants conflict with their own religious beliefs. If so, you need not chant along, if it makes you uncomfortable."[8] Thus international meditation center teachers display the ability to translate retreat practices so that they fit within a model of personal preferences and experimentation.

At Section 5 of Wat Mahathat, Bangkok, international meditators also decide their own levels of participation. Phra Ajan Suputh Kosalo estimates that for over thirty or forty years foreigners have come to Section 5, to spend the day meditating and receiving instruction through a translator. But since the arrival of Ajan Suputh Kosalo in the late 1990s, foreigners have had two choices—they can practice for the day as in the past, or if they agree to follow the regulations, they can stay overnight at Section 5. These regulations include wearing white clothing, taking the Eight Precepts, paying respect to the Buddha statues and monks, and participating in chanting. This choice accommodates those with other religious affiliations as well as reinforcing personal preferences and individual choice as the norm within religious experimentation. However, we see here that there are limits to this flexibility. If students are unwilling to abide by the Eight Precepts and other non-negotiable rules, then they cannot live at the temple. Therefore the rules of the temple are not compromised but international meditators are still allowed to add a decontextualized meditation practice to their religious repertoires and follow their own authorities.

Some international meditation center teachers are compelled to offer these individualized choices based on feedback and reactions from the international meditators themselves. Phra Bart used to have a ceremony giving the Eight Precepts to each participant at Wat Luang Por Sot, but some of the foreigners told him they were not Buddhist and did not want to follow these rules. Now foreign visitors are offered the choice to take the Five or Eight Precepts. Throughout Thailand's international meditation centers, teachers recognize that international meditators are different from Thai Buddhists and that the retreat should be more flexible to accommodate these differences. However, wearing appropriate clothing and keeping the basic rules of the retreat are necessary, especially within a mixed retreat where Thai meditators are also present.

Pluralism, choice, religious experimentation, and individualism all characterize the assumptions of many international meditators and their experiences at the

132 *Translating* vipassanā *meditation*

international meditation centers. The retreat format is transformed into an experience where one can choose the degree to which one participates and experiment with Buddhist meditation. Because international meditators determine their levels of participation, they feel comfortable experimenting with this practice, and the teachers have learned to be more accommodating. In this way, the meditation retreat fits within the modern, pluralistic notion of sampling religious practices without compromising important rules and values of Buddhist conduct, which remain necessary for international meditators to conform to.

Psychological translation

Besides individual choice and self-authority, psychology also plays an important role in many international meditators' frameworks for meditation and international meditation center teachers' translations. As we have seen in Chapter 4, psychology and therapy is a significant pathway through which international meditators engage with the meditation retreat. The dialogue between Buddhism and psychology consists of both critics and those who praise the possibilities of integration. Caroline Rhys-Davids wrote one of the first books on this topic called *Buddhist Psychology* (1914). She argues that because Buddhism is focused on human experience rather than belief, its meditation practices of self-examination would be valuable for the West (Rhys-Davids 1914, 9). She praises the Buddhist tradition as offering a significant analysis of cognition and the processes of the mind, which are much closer to modern day psychology than Western religious traditions (Rhys-Davids 1914, 4).

This dialogue between Buddhism and psychology continues to be especially prominent in American society. As far back as the late nineteenth century Americans believed that Buddhism was compatible with psychology (Tweed 1992, 104). The religious crisis of the Victorian era linked with the rise in scientific forms of knowledge, and the increased ethnic and religious pluralism led to an awareness of different perspectives outside of the Protestant faith (Tweed 1992, 94). Thomas Tweed writes:

> [P]robably the most crucial source of Buddhism's appeal in nineteenth-century America was the perception that the tradition was more 'scientific' than other available religious options . . . it seemed more adaptable to, for example, the findings of the new geology, the new biology, and the new psychology.
>
> (Tweed 1992, 103)

The therapeutic has been labeled America's primary social orientation (Metcalf 2002, 353). Because of this, American *vipassanā* teachers translate meditation psychologically in order to make the practice more accessible and familiar. This is witnessed by the high percentage of American *vipassanā* teachers who are also trained psychotherapists, especially at Spirit Rock Meditation Center.[9]

Most conspicuous among these teachers is Jack Kornfield. He demonstrates his preference for translating meditation using the idiom of psychology in one of many books on this topic called *Wise Heart*.[10] In this work, Kornfield finds Buddhist texts are incomprehensible for his students. He writes that many of the most important and revered scriptures by Buddhists, although treasured by him, are impenetrable to the average reader. For example he asserts that the Heart Sutra consists of indecipherable puzzles and can sound like fantastical mythology, while some Tibetan writings are as difficult to understand as the biochemistry of a life-saving drug (Kornfield 2008, 50). Complex diagrams that exist in temples in Asia about consciousness he compares to physics or systems theory. The Buddha was a list-maker, Kornfield asserts, but for people who find math difficult this is con-fusing. Instead Kornfield prefers to discuss Buddhist psychology. What he means by this is his interpretation of Buddhism, translated through a psychological lens. He asserts that Buddhism is a practical psychology for living, which transcends all national and sectarian traditions of Buddhism. He believes this practical psy-chological method is central to bringing Buddhist teachings to a new culture, and forging an accessible and nonsectarian approach.

However, others engaged in this dialogue critique the possibilities of integrat-ing Buddhism and psychology. In Roger Walsh's (1981) creatively titled article "Speedy Western Minds Slow Slowly" in *Revision*, he finds that Western medi-tators are actually limited by psychology. Rather than being complementary, as many Western teachers argue, Walsh writes that:

> [B]oth Achaan Cha and the Burmese monks commented that Western practi-tioners seem to become trapped in doing psychotherapy on themselves rather than meditating . . . Psychotherapy focuses primarily on changing mental contents at the symbolic level . . . However, the Eastern teachers thought that while this might sometimes be useful, for a significant number of Western practitioners this focus proved to be a limiting factor preventing an awareness of more subtle mental mechanisms.
>
> (Walsh 1981, 76)

Jack Engler (2003) too has studied Western practitioners of meditation and finds that the practice unfolds differently from their Asian counterparts mostly because of varying ideas of the psychological self. One of the goals of Buddhist practice is to discover that the idea of a continuous self is a construct, that in reality there are only momentary events that arise and pass away. Engler's studies and observa-tions of Western *vipassanā* meditators found that many of the practitioners after a three-month intensive retreat "found themselves unable to sustain mindfulness practice in its traditional form because they encountered so much unresolved grief, fear, wounding, and unfinished developmental business with parents, sib-lings, friends, spouses, children, and others" (Engler 2003, 44). This resolution of psychological trauma and personal issues became the focus of practice, rather than the arising and passing away of objects (Engler 2003, 44). Jeremy Carrette and Richard King (2005) also critique the project of translating Buddhism through the familiar lens of psychology. They contend that instead of a comple-mentary integration, the influence of psychology has reinforced individualism.

134 *Translating* vipassanā *meditation*

When psychology and individualization combine together they make personal well-being and one's self-esteem primary (Carrette & King 2005, 57). Therefore, they argue that psychology does not add anything to Buddhism and that Buddhism does not add anything to this dominant discourse of psychology.

Some international meditation center teachers are, through their students, aware of these modern religious discourses that are significant fields through which their audience comes to know and understand Buddhism. They use psychology to help their students understand the goals of *vipassanā* meditation and as a way for them to mark meditation retreat practices as accessible and familiar. One of the foreign lay teachers from Wat Chom Tong related to me why he chooses to use psychology in his teaching. In my fieldnotes I wrote:

> Psychological terms can be like a mini-dhamma that can lead to the bigger Dhamma. Using terms like anxiety, depression, anger, hatred, paranoia is helpful for Westerners to label their feelings so they can identify it, know they can deal with it, and think that it's normal. Western psychology is a useful translator and stepping stone to understand deeper Buddhist concepts.[11]

Therefore Western teachers use psychology in their teaching to other foreigners. Foreign monk meditation teachers are often put in a mediator position between two cultures and find that psychology is helpful for understanding. Phra Bart of Wat Luang Por Sot specifically stated to me that it is appropriate for Westerners to teach other Westerners as they understand each other's point of view.[12] He is in favor of divorcing meditation totally from Buddhism, and not introducing any faith. He argues that Westerners respond to psychology, as they are not interested in religious ideas.

Like the broader modern Buddhist dialogue about the integration of Buddhism and psychology, some teachers do not find them complementary. Other lay teachers at Wat Chom Tong explicitly do not use psychological terms because they would rather the method and process of *vipassanā* meditation do the work on its own. One lay teacher told me that if students can finish the basic course of twenty-one days at Wat Chom Tong, they will not need psychology and their practice will be purer. Thai Buddhists are usually taught that insight is an experience that illuminates the three universal characteristics of *anicca*, *dukkha*, and *anattā* (impermanence, suffering, non-self), and is not a secular or pragmatic understanding of one's personal psychological processes. This lay teacher found that international students can perceive 'insight' as any kind of psychological transformation that allows one a sense of clarity in regard to one's own life. Therefore, insights are thought of as personally meaningful rather than as a demonstration of Buddhist truth.[13] At other international meditation centers also, teachers find psychology should be divorced from Buddhist teaching. Venerable Sander, teacher at the Middle Way retreat from Wat Dhammakaya, had studied psychology in school. When he came to Thailand looking to ordain, he wanted to learn orthodox Buddhism, not more Western science.[14] International meditation center teachers are mixed about utilizing the discourse of psychology. Some assert it is not helpful

Translating vipassanā *meditation*   135

to integrate as this would change the retreat experience while others feel it is an appropriate complement.

Some international meditation center teachers do not recognize psychological discourses or comprehend when their students use psychological language. It is difficult for international meditation center teachers, especially when they are not native English-speakers, to anticipate and understand the assumptions of all international meditators. Similarly, it is difficult for international meditators, in some cases, to frame their questions and concerns for international meditation center teachers, revealing their different imaginaries and understandings of Buddhism. This was demonstrated during a question and answer session I attended about meditation meant for interested English-speakers by Vietnamese monk, Phra Viriya at Wat Umong.[15] Phra Viriya began by discussing meditation from the scriptures as he has a deep knowledge of the Satipaṭṭhāna Sutta. It was clear that these foreigners were more interested in meditation as a psychological practice helpful for daily life. The foreigners there asked questions about how to control emotions, letting go of bad memories, and depression. Because of the different assumptions, the two groups found it difficult to communicate. For Phra Viriya, the Buddhist scriptures hold the most authority so that is what he drew from in his teaching. His audience, however, had no knowledge of the scriptures or the Pāli terms he was using. They spoke to him as if he were a Western teacher, using psychological terms for their questions and concerns. Therefore in this case the teacher was unable to use or understand psychological terms and the students were not familiar with Pāli ones.

International meditation center teachers then are cautious in the ways they use the discourses of psychology. Their approaches vary on the strategy of psychology. Some feel it is a stepping stone to more important teaching and others think it is a distraction. Some studied psychology and came to meditation because of the relationship and integration of the two within modern religion. Psychology is an important venue of understanding for international meditators and the international meditation center teachers I talked with grapple with the issue of psychology and how to incorporate it or leave it out of the retreat.

Secular translation

Secularism is another discourse of modernity that international meditation center teachers address in their translations. Charles Taylor (2007) discusses secularization not as a decrease in religion but a change in Western societies from one where God was inseparable from public life and politics to one where disenchantment is apparent. (Taylor 2007, 65–67). In this way, modern secular societies are characterized by an increase in personal religious commitment in isolation as opposed to collective ritual. Taylor writes that within the context of Christianity "the point of declaring that salvation comes through faith was radically to devalue ritual and external practice in favor of inner acknowledgment of Christ as savior" (Taylor 2009, 37). Along with external communal ritual, repression of magical elements or spirits becomes sidelined as science predominates

136　*Translating* vipassanā *meditation*

(Taylor 2009, 38). Now rituals are performed for the psychological and therapeutic effects on one's mental state, not in order to transform the world in some way (Taylor 2009, 52). This is the way many international meditators approach ritual and this attitude influences the ways international meditation center teachers translate the meditation retreat.

International meditators notice the lively public role of religion for Thai Buddhists in some centers within a temple. As we saw in Chapter 4, narratives of the meditation retreat by international meditators reveal that some rituals, such as the collective evening *wan phra* stupa circumambulation at Wat Rampoeng, are intriguing to international meditators. The beautiful candlelit ceremony, invitation, and explanation of the ritual by English-speaking monks helps international meditators gain access to the ritual and feel connected to the community for a short time. However, other rituals that are not explained and do not illicit international meditators' participation are considered confusing and often dismissed. International meditation center teachers often intentionally do not explain these rituals, as one of their strategies is to create a secular atmosphere focusing on meditation as a decontextualized global religious practice. If meditation is embedded in rituals and communal activities it no longer can be seen as decontextualized from Thai Buddhism or as a portable, secular, universal practice. International meditation centers which host both Thais and international meditators do not include rituals for the international group, and those group retreats with only international meditators avoid or leave ritual out of the retreat program altogether.

International meditation center teachers, in addition to avoiding devotional activities, also intentionally present meditation in a culturally familiar way to international meditators, introducing secular discourses within the Buddhist meditation retreat format for international meditators. Phra Bart of Wat Luang Por Sot[16] taught aspects of Buddhism to those who are interested and recommended attending evening chanting for a cultural or 'touristy' experience, but when he taught meditation, he focused on its compatibility with a scientific and psychological worldview. This deritualized presentation serves to assuage international meditators that meditation is a secular enterprise, allowing them to place meditation practice within a secular framework useful for relaxation, therapeutic healing, and as an antidote to hectic modern lifestyles. Secular translations that decrease ritual and devotional activities help international meditation center teachers relate to their audience and make the retreat program familiar.

At Wat Chom Tong, teachers find that international meditators are usually curious about Thai Buddhism after completing a basic twenty-one day course. But they continue to question the teacher and the rituals—always wanting to know why these practices exist and what the benefits are. After this course, international meditators have a period of rest and transition before leaving the temple. Some of them use this time to explore Thai Buddhism, attending evening and morning chanting, circumambulating the stupa, and participating in *wan phra* almsgiving. After all of the meditation practice within a secularized international meditation center, international meditators begin to explore their opportunities to learn about the religion. At Wat Chom Tong there is also one dhamma talk about pain during

Translating vipassanā meditation   137

meditation. The lay teachers here feel that this is something all meditators will be interested in—how to deal with and understand pain. As secular as they make this talk, they have encountered resistance from students who dismiss their teachings as an ancient Eastern philosophy that will not work in the West. Because of this, teachers ask their students to have an open mind demonstrating that no matter how secular they attempt to make the retreat, it will not fit everyone's imaginaries. Public collective rituals are disconcerting for international meditators, especially in those centers attached to a temple and mixed with Thai Buddhists. This is not seen as an important part of the retreat for international meditators as many of their teachers do not explain or compel their students to participate.

Universal translation

Claims to universalism characterize modern religions and translation strategies used by international meditation center teachers. Embedded within discourses of the modern and scientific, universal claims purport to speak for all of humanity in all contexts and times and yet are set within highly nuanced and contingent historical, social, and cultural conjunctures (Chatterjee 1993). World religions such as Buddhism are called such because they propose an image of the world, universally true in all places and times. These claims, however, are themselves set within particular social and historical contexts, and must be seen within these contingent circumstances of competition and debate. In the Buddha's time, universalism was an argument against the particularism of Brahmanical religion (Collins 1994, 62) and today the universalism of Buddhism is directed toward modern discourses.

During the colonial era, universal reason became a global form of knowledge and power as particular nations and cultures were depicted as static and unable to develop (Tsing 2002, 9). The colonizer held this power of universal reason but the colonized remained in the realm of the particular. The universal, in contrast to the particular or local "opens the way to constantly improving truths and even, in its utilitarian forms, to a better life for all humanity" (Tsing 2002, 9). This 'universalism' is often posited in religious discourses, and the modern *vipassanā* meditation revival draws on this significantly. International meditation center teachers utilize the power of the universal to make meditation meaningful and important to their international audiences from all different backgrounds and religions.

S.N. Goenka is a well-known example of a teacher who asserts that *vipassanā* meditation transcends the local through its universal applicability.[17] His strategy of teaching meditation uses words that appear universal in nature rather than particularly Buddhist. When asked how he teaches meditation in India and the West, he responded that

> there is no difference in the actual teaching, but there is in the way of presentation. For example, I don't use the word 'Buddhism' which is commonly used for the teaching of the Buddha. Nor do I use the word 'Buddhist' for those who follow the teaching of Buddha.
>
> (Goenka 1998, 175)

138   *Translating* vipassanā *meditation*

He finds that if he used these words, people from different religious backgrounds would consider him to be religious and his retreats would not be well-attended. Because Goenka doesn't want to portray *vipassanā* meditation as a Buddhist practice, he uses the words "dhamma" and "dhammist," which he believes appear more universal. He teaches *vipassanā* meditation as something that rises above all religions because he believes it is universal and secular. In many of his publications he calls *vipassanā* a 'universal law of nature.' He expands on this here:

> [T]he law of gravity exists with or without Newton. The law of relativity exists with or without Einstein. Similarly the law of nature remains whether or not there is a Buddha. It is cause and effect. Two parts of hydrogen and one part of oxygen make water. If either is missing on a planet, there will be no water. This is a law of nature.
>
> (Confalonieri 2006, 21)

Here he likens a meditator to a scientist who 'discovered' *vipassanā* as Newton 'discovered' gravity. Therefore to practice *vipassanā* one does not need to know anything about the Buddha, his teachings or the context from which Buddhism arises out of and continues to be reimagined within.

Goenka discusses his teacher, U Ba Khin's strategies for explaining Buddhist meditation for non-Buddhist, English-speaking Western people, saying that "the explanation was made more palatable to those who were coming to learn, but the actual practical teaching remained the same" (Confalonieri 2006, 88). U Ba Khin developed a new frame and vocabulary for foreigners and non-Buddhists. He states that it is not the Buddhist religion that is universal but the teachings of the Buddha. U Ba Khin and Goenka were forerunners of this universal translation, and international meditation center teachers in Thailand utilize similar strategies. Many of these international meditation center teachers state that they adapt the presentation of *vipassanā* but this does not alter the practice in any way. This distinction between presentation and actual *vipassanā* practice highlight the ways Buddhists argue for universalism. It is the practice itself, the effort and experience of sitting and walking meditation that constitutes the universal content as *vipassanā* is meant to work on human bodies and minds in similar ways. However, the ways people understand the practice, their goals and motivations are in the realm of the particular. Teachers argue that once meditators begin the work of *vipassanā*, they will transition to the universal.

There are a few international meditation center teachers in Thailand who have thought deeply and written about teaching meditation to non-Buddhist practitioners utilizing universal discourses. The late and well-respected scholar-monk, Buddhadasa Bhikkhu, was one of these teachers who was able to adapt his message to a non-Thai audience. When discussing the Buddha's teachings with foreigners in 1986, he compared the dhamma to a strange and special medicine because it can be taken by anyone, regardless of religion, nationality, ethnic background, education, class, or language. Santikaro, the translator for Buddhadasa Bhikkhu, writes:

Translating vipassanā *meditation*   139

[I]n speaking to Western meditators, Achan Buddhadasa uses a straight-forward, no-frills approach. He does not go into the cultural interests of traditional Thai Buddhists; instead, he prefers a scientific, rational, analytical attitude. And rather than limit the instruction to Buddhists, he emphasizes the universal, natural humanness of Anapanasati [mindfulness with breathing].
(Santikaro 2001a, xvi)

Buddhadasa Bhikkhu delivered these talks to foreigners at Wat Suan Mokkh in the late 1980s and early 1990s. Through the emphasis on *vipassanā* meditation as a method divorced from faith, Buddhism is explicitly contrasted with theistic religions and constitutes a secular, scientific practice. Arguing that Buddhist teachings are universal is a significant discourse within the translation of Buddhism for foreigners. In order to make non-Buddhist participation possible and comfortable for participants, international meditation center teachers emphasize the universal nature of meditation and how it does not conflict with other religions.

When entering the meditation hall of Dipabhavan Meditation Center on Koh Samui, one can see large banners in Thai and English stating the three resolutions of Buddhadasa Bhikkhu: "That all people strive to realize the heart of their own religions, that all people make mutual good understanding of essential principles among the religions, and that all people liberate themselves from the power of materialism." What is most striking about the teachings of this retreat is how each talk, especially those from the tapes of Buddhadasa Bhikkhu, discusses the universal nature of Buddhism. These talks all compare Buddhism with Christianity or contain references to how Buddhism coalesces with the other religions of mankind.[18] The universal application of Buddhist practice is stressed in the dhamma talks for foreigners as each demonstrates that meditation and this retreat are intended for people of all religions.

During the course of fieldwork, I asked many teachers if they teach Thai and international meditators in different ways. Many responded that yes, there is a big difference between these two groups, but were quick to clarify that the dhamma is universal. These teachers argue that cultural differences create a need for different presentations of the teachings. At Wat Tam Doi Tohn, Phra Ajan Nawi Piyadassi[19] stated that he cannot start by teaching foreigners about the Buddha because this group does not yet have belief or faith. So instead he starts with the teachings, or dhamma. He finds that Thai people have faith in the Buddha first and come to the dhamma later. In this way he observes that both groups reach the same results but from different starting points. Mae Chii Brigitte[20] similarly finds that foreigners have much conceptual knowledge from reading books about Buddhism but lack faith; this is the opposite of Thai Buddhists.[21] Thus international meditators' statuses as non-Buddhist and non-Thai lead teachers to establish different didactic approaches. They emphasize a universal translation of Buddhist teachings and practices within the meditation retreat.

Secular, universal, psychological, and translation for individual choice are all discourses international meditation center teachers use in their adaptation of the meditation retreat program. Drawing from modern Buddhist discourses, the teachers'

140 *Translating* vipassanā *meditation*

presentation of meditation resonates with their students' cultural assumptions and imaginaries of meditation. After years of this translation work, these teachers utilize these imaginaries to make meditation a familiar addition to their students' cultural and religious repertoires. However, despite this understanding through dialogue, sometimes translation does not work. The next section explores what happens when the purpose of *vipassanā* and the meditation retreat is not understood completely by the international meditators.

Subversion and dissent

James Clifford argues that, within the process of translation, it is important to distinguish what is missing and distorted (Clifford 1997, 42). As such this section takes into account examples of what is ineffective or lost in translation for international meditators. Webb Keane (2007) theorizes about the translation of Christianity in Indonesia in his ethnographic monograph, *Christian Moderns*. He primarily utilizes the term semiotic ideology, which he defines as cultural concepts that mediate between selves and signs and contain moral and political assumptions that are embedded within social contexts, habitus, practices, and ways of thinking (Keane 2007, 16–18). He shows how Calvinist missionaries and Sumbanese Indonesians express differing semiotic ideologies. The two groups have different assumptions about the moral and political aspects of their communicative acts, and about the relationships between self and signs, words and objects. In addition to encounters with missionaries, multiple imaginaries also clash at travel destinations. Tourism can help to shape the frameworks for these encounters where cultural differences are most prominent. Through these interactions, modern religious practices create new meanings and dialogues. Because of this, encounters between different religious worldviews should not be studied as a way of pointing out difference, but, as Henrietta Moore argues, as fluid connections and productions with a plurality of possibilities and contributions (Moore 2011, 6).

International meditation center teachers utilize strategies that integrate discourses of psychology, secularism, and universalism in order to translate teaching the meditation practice and how it relates to the goals of *vipassanā*. However, even though these teachers remove rituals and make devotional activities optional, they do not translate every aspect of the retreat process. This is cause for much of the difference surrounding semiotic ideologies between international meditation center teachers and their students. Therefore, although international meditators and international meditation center teachers often both consider meditation as an inclusive practice, both groups are not completely aligned. As much as international meditation center teachers try to understand their international students, some aspects of the retreat will inevitably be lost in translation. It is difficult to translate the meditation retreat and its goals when the strategies used all mark *vipassanā* meditation as universal and decontextualized from Thai Buddhism, while practicing within a particular temple and within a particular meditation method and lineage. No matter how much international meditation center teachers discuss the secular, universal practice, the teachers are still embedded fully within

Translating vipassanā *meditation*   141

a Thai Buddhist context. This section demonstrates what occurs when translation is either ineffective or incomplete. In the cases I discuss here international meditation center teachers and international meditators diverge in their understanding of the purposes and benefits of the retreat program. They have varying views on the proscribed behaviors of the retreat, the ways a temple should function, and the nature of authority. Many first-time international meditators do not understand the goals of the meditation retreat. These international meditators are prone to evaluate what is being offered to them, and appropriate what they deem works for their own particular imaginaries and semiotic ideologies.

One of the ways international meditators subvert the intention of the meditation retreat program is by leaving early. This usually occurs after the first few days of a retreat. In either a group retreat or an individual one, when faced with the reality of the schedule for the next ten days, some international meditators leave before the scheduled end date. One college student from American, Sandra, wrote this to me in a follow-up interview:

> [I] was at Wat Rampoeng for a total of 4 days. Originally signed up for 10. Had no idea really what I was getting myself into, just knew that I wanted to explore more about Buddhism but particularly meditation. I thought the retreat would entail, a group of foreigners or Westerners much like myself, who would live in a temple for 10 days and be instructed by monks on meditation techniques, Buddhism precepts, et al. My 'expectations' certainly were not met, making it particularly challenging and puzzling in the beginning. I realized the schedule for the day did not entail any 'group' learning, nor lectures really, and this is what I felt was missing.

This international meditator decided to leave because she felt she did not experience any learning about Buddhism. She realized that her expectations were unrealistic but would have preferred time for formal instruction and learning, not only individual meditation sessions. The retreat format was not translated for this particular audience, whose imaginary of the meditation retreat was not the mass meditation movement model but instead an intellectual understanding of meditation practice.

The reason that ten days is an important number is because it is thought that this is the amount of time it will take to reach the equanimity phase of the cycle of insight. One has not completed a full cycle of insight, but has reached an acceptable level to leave a retreat and reenter the world. The importance of remaining in the retreat is not always explained. This international meditator hoped for an intellectual understanding of Buddhism, but the meditation retreat is designed so that one would come to experience Buddhist principles through the practice. By leaving early, meditation teachers worry that meditators will be stuck in a phase of the cycle that is not suitable for leaving the retreat program. If one leaves within the first few days, meditation teachers state that one cannot attain a level of concentration or get used to the schedule. In this way the meditation is rendered ineffective, as one cannot yet follow the retreat program fully.

142 *Translating* vipassanā *meditation*

Differing imaginaries of the meditation retreat are present here, placing value on different kinds of knowledge.

Another reason for leaving the retreat early is feeling trapped in the monastery grounds. Patrick, a young traveler from Ireland, admitted that he felt imprisoned by the monastery gates of Wat Rampoeng, which he was not allowed to go outside of during the retreat. This containment however, is intended to mark the boundaries between the inside and outside world. The spaces of the meditation retreat create a heightened concern for the interior, forcing meditators to give up control. International meditators' ideas of personal freedom are thus in conflict with the meditation retreat structure, which has constraints in place for optimal meditation progress. Travelers are often used to a significant amount of freedom in their lives, in fact that is a typical reason for travel. Being limited to one location for an extended period of time therefore can be strange and difficult.

There are small ways in which international meditators can dissent from the rules of the meditation retreat. In some centers, meditators are watched closely and told that if they are caught using their phones they will be expelled from the retreat. At the Wat Kow Tahm International Meditation Center there are strict rules in place regarding silence and communication. All participants' phones and electronic devices are stored away during the retreat. Silence is also well-maintained through the work done before the retreat to instill into the meditators that this is serious practice. They sign an agreement and must read about the rules in place that they are compelled to obey before they choose to participate in the retreat. Through their experience with international meditators on the tourist island of Koh Phangan, the Weissman's of Wat Kow Tahm have learned how to instill these rules into their participants.

However, at centers where the meditation teacher is not always present and meditators have more time amongst themselves, there are often opportunities for subversion and dissent of which meditators take advantage. When new international meditators are not informed or repeatedly reminded of the goals of the retreat and its purposes, they frequently find other activities. One young Canadian woman confided to a small group of international meditators at Wat Doi Suthep that she found the meditation technique too difficult. Instead of practicing, she stayed in her room watching DVDs on her computer for most of her time there. This was possible because the teacher only monitored the behavior of international meditators during the short, daily interviews. In some cases too much translation for individual preference, or lack of explanation or monitoring leads to dissent from the retreat program. Other international meditation center teachers are aware of this tendency and make sure their new students understand the discipline required to complete a retreat. They don't want students who are just 'waiting for the bus,' as one teacher at Wat Umong put it. In other words, international meditators who are not seeking a meditation retreat primarily but a couple of free nights' stay before their next destination. But the reality of a meditation schedule with seven to eight hours of meditation per day is too much for some international meditators.

Dissent and subversion can also be observed among international meditators who discuss their experiences during the retreat with their travel partners. Some

Translating vipassanā *meditation*   143

international meditators do not exclusively speak with their meditation teachers during interviews as proscribed. This group identifies a spot to meet their friends and discuss their experiences. This was evident in centers that allowed walking meditation away from the meditation halls. Participants would find each other to chat instead of finding a quiet spot to notice the movement of their bodies. At international meditation centers with English-speaking Thai monks besides their teacher, international meditators told me they believe it is beneficial to talk with them about Buddhism, the monastic life, or their meditation experiences. This kind of discussion, about their own meditation to a person other than one's teacher, is banned at retreats because such conversation could leave one confused and interpreting one's experience incorrectly. This ban on conversation is a difficult point to get across for international meditation center teachers to their audience, who are used to dialogue and discussion. In some cases, ineffective explanations and little focus on the details and reasons for all aspects of the retreat program cause international meditators to question the retreat rules.

In Thailand's international meditation centers some international meditators come and go quickly, never speaking to anyone, but some collect everyone's email addresses, promising to keep in touch as if in summer camp. It is natural to be curious about the other meditators—to want to know their reasons for taking on a meditation retreat. Foreign tourists are often lonely and looking for others to travel with. At these centers no one talks during meditation or in the meditation halls. However, meditators can find places to talk during afternoon tea breaks, at night before bed, or before leaving. These are times when international meditators discuss their backgrounds and their travels around Thailand and Southeast Asia. Foreign tourists are used to meeting other travelers and conversing about their plans, and often do not understand the significance placed on keeping noble silence. After the retreat, some international meditators make plans to continue traveling together. International meditators, in some mixed centers, constitute a small portion of the population. Discussing their choice to take part in this experience is less isolating and makes their decisions seem less strange.

Jessica from Canada discussed why she decided to speak during the retreat at Wat Doi Suthep. Here are her sentiments from my fieldnotes:

> [J]essica told me that she could tell that talking affected her practice but the meditation was too boring and difficult to maintain throughout the evening. She was anxious to discuss this with the other meditators and felt better knowing many of the others felt the same way.

Depending on the meditation center, the response to talking can be silent disapproval, or a warning of expulsion from the retreat. Meditation centers make clear from the orientation and written instructions that one of the rules is to remain silent. However, some international meditators do not think this rule is significant and choose to ignore it. Others, like Jessica, understand that silence aids one's concentration practice but still feel compelled to share their experiences with others. One international meditator, André, a student from Ecuador who

144 *Translating* vipassanā *meditation*

completed the basic course at Wat Rampoeng, described to me his dissent from the ban on speech:

> [A]lthough it was forbidden, at the 5th day I made friends with an English and a German guy, having little conversations with them. Not having any contact with people was the hardest rule for me because I am very interested in people and I like to connect with them but I knew it was important to follow the rules and avoid any conversation and eye contact.

Even though this international meditator understood the rules and completed the retreat, this ban on talking was not considered crucial, and because of his sociability and loneliness chose to subvert this rule occasionally.

Even though some international meditators would like the ability to talk freely, they still seek a center that is quiet with a vast forest and natural settings. This can be difficult at some meditation centers located in busy temples. Many international meditators expect silence and tranquility and are disappointed when distractions arise such as the noisiness of ceremonies, Buddhist holiday celebrations, or construction around the center. When the meditation center is not situated within an idyllic environment, spending ten days meditating is less appealing. The semiotic linkages between meditation and peace are too strong for some international meditators to adjust their imaginary of what a meditation retreat might entail. Although international meditation center teachers are aware of the need to translate into secular, universal, psychological terms for international meditators' personal preferences, they are unable to account for all of the differences.

Another issue related to dissenting from the retreat program is the self-authoritative orientations of many international meditators. International meditators, without much knowledge of disciple-teacher relationships, trust themselves over their teacher. In Thai Buddhism, although the mass lay meditation movement created opportunities for more meditation teachers, lineage and discipleship are still important. Most international meditators have not experienced such a relationship and therefore some do not give authority, respect or trust to their meditation teachers or the meditation retreat program. An example of this is the schedule of the retreat, which consists of little sleep. International meditators have told me adamantly that they know their bodies and that they can meditate better with more sleep. The lack of sleep is a particular problem for many travelers who attend the Ajan Tong retreats in Chiangmai, who are not expecting this aspect of their lives to be disrupted. One of the rules is to remain wakeful and in a meditative state throughout the day with decreasing hours of sleep as one progresses. International meditators dissent by waking up after the morning bell, and napping after breakfast and lunch. As discussed briefly in Chapter 4, lack of sleep is one problem that is often cited as a reason for leaving or causing difficulty with the practice. After talking with Paul, a middle-aged professional at Wat Chom Tong, I wrote this in my fieldnotes:

Translating vipassanā *meditation*   145

[P]aul didn't know that a major challenge of this retreat for him would be the lack of sleep. This aspect of the rules was not explained to him in full when he arrived. He was very surprised when the meditation teacher continually asked him to sleep less and less.

Although Paul obeyed the rules it is clear that some international meditators assume that certain aspects of the meditation retreat are not important, especially those that interfere with the freedoms they are more accustomed to. Points of subversion expose the semiotic ideologies of international meditators that have particular imaginaries of meditation and place importance on aspects of the retreat experience divergent from the design of the retreat program. The rules and regulations international meditation centers impose challenge international meditators' capacity for difference. International meditation center teachers and their students discuss *vipassanā* meditation practice as a decontextualized global religious practice. Its meaning and goals draw from psychology, individual choice, secular, and universal discourses. However, some of the particulars of the retreat process are not translated and the self-authority and freedom of travelers lie at odds with the rules of the retreat program.

Conclusion

Annette Sanger (1988) studies how barong dances in Bali have been translated for tourists. She finds that tourist reactions to the shows have caused adaptations to its presentation in order to appeal to the audience's tastes. Through feedback from tourists, barong dances became shorter, more entertaining sequences were added, females were asked to play the female roles, and sections unpleasant to tourists, such as eating live chickens, were removed from the performance. But Sanger finds that these changes are not seen as affecting the tradition or authenticity of the dance. Balinese justify this in a number of ways, including that the barong costume is used without desecration and the show is performed respectfully. Therefore this tradition has been modified by the addition of tourism but the translation has occurred in ways that Balinese feel do not affect the integrity of the tradition.

The examples of Bali as well as international meditation centers demonstrate that cultural forms become reconstructed in the context of tourism and international engagement. Shinji Yamashita (2003) also writing on Bali states:

[T]he surprising thing about Bali is not that its essence has survived being corrupted by modern Western civilization and has come down to us intact at the present day, but rather that is has survived by flexible adaptation in response to stimuli from the outside world . . . As a result, what we need are not narratives of homogenization or loss, but of emergence and invention.

(Yamashita 2003, 10)

146   *Translating* vipassanā *meditation*

This can be compared with the translation practices for international meditators throughout Thailand. It is clear that translation practices are inevitable within sites of encounter or contact zones, where different cultural groups' interactions foster creativity and invention. Within Thailand's international meditation centers, intercultural dialogue and discourses of modern Buddhism act as a frame for continued translations. Many international meditation center teachers understand how to translate aspects of the retreat and Buddhist teachings into universal and secular discourses that privilege individual choice. However this is sometimes not sufficient to impart complex purposes and goals of the meditation retreat. We have seen the outcomes of this through small acts of dissension and those who leave the retreat early.

International meditation center teachers feel that the changes they make for international meditators do not impinge on the regulations of temple living or the ways meditation is practiced. These teachers argue that there is no loss from these changes as they serve to spread meditation throughout the world. International meditators return to their home countries—some discussing their experiences with friends, some joining local meditation centers, and others forming long-term connections to their teachers in Thailand. Members of the latter group often return to Thailand and even sponsor their teacher's meditation teaching tour within their home country. I will discuss this further in Chapter 8.

International meditation center teachers help to illuminate one trajectory of translation processes within the globalization of Buddhism. David McMahan (2008) points out that historically Buddhist traditions "selectively and creatively re-present elements of Buddhism using the local vernacular, sometimes diluting it with local custom, accommodating it to local dialects, adapting it to local practices" (McMahan 2008, 262). McMahan argues that this translation does not constitute a loss of the traditional goals of Buddhism. In his review of Donald Lopez's *Buddhism and Science* (2010) he discusses how Lopez laments the adaptation, disenchantment, and reduction of Buddhism and its meditation practice to relaxation and stress reduction (McMahan 2010, 857). Instead, McMahan (2008) argues that modernity does not have to be detrimental to Buddhism but can enrich it just as Buddhism can challenge modernity. International meditation center teachers' translations to modern discourses of Buddhism are not reducing the dhamma or goals of meditation but presenting them in new ways as Buddhist leaders have done since Buddhism moved out of its Indian context 2,500 years ago. Bringing meditation into dialogue with present-day concerns brings Buddhist values into contemporary contexts (McMahan 2008, 213).

International meditation center teachers don't simply repeat modern discourses and make them align with Buddhism but bring meditation into dialogue with psychology, secularism, individualism, and universalism. They affirm the value of these discourses but do not let them completely ensconce the retreat, choosing carefully where to incorporate modern discourses. This is demonstrated when international meditation center teachers refuse to be flexible or when the overly psychological or secular language of international meditators is incomprehensible. International meditation center teachers do not consider their translation

Translating vipassanā meditation   147

practices to affect the goals of the meditation retreat. Buddhist teachers deem the goal, the experience of insight, to be extra-linguistic and beyond translation. Therefore the translations used to explain how to attain insight are not seen to affect the experience of insight itself. However, these translations are not without their consequences, as the section on subversion and dissension in this chapter illustrated. In the next chapter I discuss more of the results of translation as they relate to the bodily performance of meditation.

Notes

1 Campbell (2011) has written of similar findings in her ethnographic account of meditation centers in Toronto, Canada, attended primarily by practitioners from non-Buddhist backgrounds.
2 The Five Hindrances are a list of mental states that hinder a meditator's ability to concentrate the mind. These are sensual desire, ill-will, tiredness and sleepiness, restlessness and remorse, and doubt.
3 Within Theravāda Buddhism, one's experience is not authoritative without verification by one's teacher. Jordt describes ways teachers in the Mahasi Sayadaw lineage determine the level of insight attained by their students through their dialogue in daily interviews (Jordt 2007, 68).
4 Ledi Sayadaw (1846–1923) was an important scholar-monk during the British colonial period in Burma. He wrote many important works for other scholar-monks but more importantly for the Burmese lay people. His accessible writing and interest in lay understanding of Buddhism have made him a key figure in Burmese Buddhism. See Braun (2013).
5 Anagarika Dharmapala (1864–1933) was one of the key figures in modern Sinhalese Buddhism. He founded the Maha Bodhi Society in 1891 in order to develop the site of the Buddha's Enlightenment as a pilgrimage destination for all Buddhists, and he represented Buddhism in the World Parliament of Religions in 1893. See Kemper (2005).
6 This tendency toward the subjectivist and individualistic in modern religion has been noted by many scholars (Heelas 1996; Bruce 1996; Sutcliffe & Bowman 2000).
7 Interview with Ajan Buddhasak, Wat Prathat Doi Suthep, May 1st, 2010.
8 Quote taken from the Dipabhavan retreat website (no date): http://dipabhavan.weebly.com/retreat-guidelines.html.
9 Spirit Rock Meditation Center (spiritrock.org) was founded by Jack Kornfield in 1987. The teachings of this center maintain that the *dhamma* should be integrated into one's life, including how to work with trauma and conflicts. Some of their retreats offer a mixture of mindfulness meditation with psychotherapy, drawing from Western psychology (Kornfield 2007).
10 Jack Kornfield's other books about this integration include *A Path With Heart* (1993), *After the Ecstasy, the Laundry* (2001), *A Lamp in the Darkness: Illuminating the Path through Difficult Times* (2011), and *Bringing Home the Dharma* (2012).
11 Interview with lay meditation teacher, Wat Chom Tong, April 28th, 2010.
12 Interview with Phra Bart, Wat Luang Por Sot, June 28th, 2010.
13 Interview with lay meditation teacher, Wat Chom Tong, May 28th, 2010.
14 Interview with Venerable Sander, Middle Way Retreat, Loei Center, June 10th, 2010.
15 Observations from Wat Umong meditation group meeting with Phra Viriya, June 16th, 2012.
16 Interview with Phra Bart, Wat Luang Por Sot, June 28th, 2010.
17 S.N. Goenka (1924–2013) began his format of ten-day courses, in the tradition of his teacher U Ba Khin, when he was authorized to teach *vipassanā* in 1969. He left Burma to bring this teaching to his homeland of India. From here the Goenka method has

148 *Translating* vipassanā *meditation*

become a worldwide phenomenon with centers in North America, Europe, Australia, the Middle East, Africa, Latin America, and Asia. See Chapter 2 for more information on the lineage of U Ba Khin.

18 Based on fieldwork at Dipabhavan Meditation Center, June 20th–June 27th, 2010.

19 Interview with Ajan Nawi Piyadassi, Wat Tam Doi Tohn, September 26th, 2010.

20 Interview with Mae Chii Brigitte, Wat Prayong Gittivararam, March 10th, 2010.

21 This bifurcation between the faith of native Buddhists and the questioning of non-native Buddhists was also noted by Moran (2004) in his study of Western travelers interested in Tibetan Buddhism in Kathmandu, Nepal.

7 Embodying meditation

The Thai Buddhist meditation retreat format offers opportunities for learning and practice beyond meditation. These opportunities include interactions with the meditation teachers and other daily activities such as eating, cleaning, dressing, ceremonies, and all movements throughout the day. As we saw in Chapter 6, some of these practices within the meditation retreat for international meditators are intentionally not performed or are deemed unnecessary. This chapter explores particular adaptations and translations focusing on ways of using the body and cultivating the self. In contrast to the ideal ways the self is meant to be cultivated in tradition-specific ways in a *vipassanā* retreat, international meditators, through a selective and translated retreat model, are able to insert the retreat into their own repertoires matching their personal imaginaries and following the modern religious trend of self-authority.

International meditators often arrive at the meditation retreat with an autonomous, authoritative idea of the self. Anthony Giddens (1990) and Charles Taylor (1989) argue that a key aspect to the creation of modernity is the increasingly reflexive nature of the self. Giddens defines the reflexivity of modernity as "directly involved with the continual generating of systematic self-knowledge" (Giddens 1990, 45) and "consists in the fact that social practices are constantly examined and reformed in the light of incoming information about those practices, thus constitutively altering their character" (Giddens 1990, 38). This reflexive, modern self is thus able to question society and one's identity through awareness of other worldviews and cultures within a plurality of possibilities. Because of the recognition of other options, attention turns to one's own values, identity, and biography, and creates greater agency in defining and constructing one's own religiosity. Taylor (1989) identifies a 'massive subjective turn' and its emergence in the seventeenth and eighteenth centuries as a new kind of selfhood where one becomes more aware of one's own experiences, generating self-awareness and reflection. Reflexivity allows an inner awareness of oneself and increases the importance of reflection on one's own experiences and self-exploration (Taylor 1989, 211). In this way the autonomy of the self is the context through which international meditators approach the meditation retreat. This reveals an important window to explore assumptions that affect the translation and interpretation of the meditation retreat.

150 *Embodying meditation*

Buddhism, and especially its meditation practice, has been pulled into the orbit of these ideas of an interior and reflexive religiosity. Meditation becomes an inner, private, and personal experience unrelated to any institutional, devotional, or ritualistic form of religion (McMahan 2008, 251). This idea of the sovereign self significantly holds that the interior is ultimately more significant than the exterior, and the idea of the self is in contrast to what has been called the 'technologies' or 'practices of the self'— a distinction I will elucidate in the following section. These practices of the self cultivate the external self in order to produce an inner self one seeks. The monastic life, meditation retreats, and other religious training often utilize the body to cultivate the self in this external way. I argue that this contrast is a fruitful way to understand the differences between the *vipassanā* meditation retreat and international meditators' purposes and goals. This contrast does not reveal any problem or tension between the internal or external modes, as both are viable ways to approach the retreat.

As a consequence of enacting the retreat in different ways, questions of religious identity and conversion do not arise. These categories of identity or conversion are not as relevant in this context as more appropriate terms like repertoire, which allow for multiple religious influences rather than definitive changes in identification. The history of Buddhist missionizing in Thailand reveals similar approaches of incorporation rather than conversion. Missionizing in Thailand incorporates spirit cults and other pre-Buddhist religious complexes while international meditation centers draw from modern discourses of self-reflexivity and creative selective engagement in their retreat programs. I discuss this incorporation through examples of international meditation center teachers who have experience with teaching multi-faith groups.

Practices of the self

Practices of the self refer to bodily actions and performances that can be traced to early Greco-Roman philosophy. These practices are intended to create change in the behaviors and characters of those who enact them. External practices working on the body make one fit for spiritual development and eventual transformation into the desired state of ethical perfection or happiness. Michel Foucault delineates how both ancient philosophy and Christian asceticism were preoccupied with the constant practice of the care of oneself (Foucault 1988, 21). This care was manifested in persistent social practices, attention to the body, and modes of behavior that required reflection and discussion (Foucault 1976, 45). Foucault traces this history in order to understand how care of the self has been obscured by the idea of finding one's 'true' self. Because the modern West respects external law as the basis for morality, in this cultural context, he argues, care and respect for the self have become less important (Foucault 1988, 22). However, practices of the self continue to be an important mode of religiosity today not only through the *vipassanā* meditation retreat but also Christian monasticism and recent Islamic piety movements.

In order to understand these practices of the self in relation to the religiosity of international meditators, I outline here the major scholarly works and arguments from the Christian, Muslim, and Buddhist world. Talal Asad is concerned with the practices of the self as they relate to Christian monastic disciplines. He describes how religious discourses construct religious selves, and particular to Christian monasticism, how an obedient will is formed through guiding virtuous desires (Asad 1993, 125). The monastic program of disciplinary practices is aimed at reorganizing desire and humility toward obedience to God (Asad 1993, 134). The practices of the self in which Christian monks engage, such as manual labor and disciplinary techniques, become part of an external training of the self that creates a desire for obedience. Catholics participate in subject formation, which utilizes practices of the self. Rebecca Lester (2005) writes of the formation process of first year postulants within a Mexican convent, which is designed to create a particular experience of the self. Lester's ethnography describes bodily practices used for the reshaping of the subjective experience. Throughout their year of training, these postulants learned how to experience the body as a medium to understand their relationship with God. At the end of this first year postulants experienced themselves as transformed, their subjectivities reformulated. The postulants reach the goals of this process through the company of others in their community, managing their physical bodies and placing themselves in the service of authority. Through this formation "institutional priority became individual ones, gradually producing willing subjects of transformation" (Lester 2005, 22) by training "the body to be obedient to external elements rather than internal instincts and desires" (Lester 2005, 178). International meditators do not have the same particular, unified, or singular goal in their participation in the meditation retreat. Because of the limited time and engagement, international meditators do not necessarily go through a significant transformative process.

Religious movements such as the modern piety movement in Islam have revitalized the practice of caring for the self for Muslims. This is an important point of comparison for the experiences of international meditators in the mass lay meditation movement. Scholars Saba Mahmood (2005) and Charles Hirschkind (2006)[1] have studied the constitution of the self in Islamic contexts. Mahmood's study of the female mosque movement in Cairo focuses on how the bodily performance of virtue both creates and expresses desired traits (Mahmood 2005, 30). Ethical practices then shape the subject through a range of bodily and religious practices within everyday life. For example, Mahmood discusses informants who want to cultivate the quality of shyness. They do this through bodily acts such as wearing the veil and conducting themselves modestly in order to create an internal tendency toward shyness (Mahmood 2005, 158). In this way exteriority produces desired habits of interiority of a pious self, which aims to transform their conduct to be consistent with the standards of Islam. The *vipassanā* meditation retreat offers these opportunities to behave with attention so that one can cultivate a mindful self.

Charles Hirschkind (2006) investigates the ways Muslims in Cairo use tape recordings of sermons to "offer a portable, self-administered technology of moral health and Islamic virtue, one easily adapted to the rhythms, movements, and social contexts characteristic of contemporary forms of work and leisure"

152 *Embodying meditation*

(Hirschkind 2006, 73). For Hirschkind, the senses help to cultivate the self, as the act of listening becomes a ritual that leads to religious development. The sermons represent a 'technology of the self' through which individuals work on their selves to attain an ethical ideal (Hirschkind 2006, 39). This creation of the ethical self is acquired not through the rational mind but personal experience (Hirschkind 2006, 175). Hirschkind's work on recorded sermons also demonstrates how the body functions to work towards a change in behavior. As practitioners listen to cassette tapes they do not just hear the tape but demonstrate careful listening though bodily comportment and vocal responses, lip-syncing along with the preacher, and gesturing as one follows the argument.

Within Islamic revival movements, early Christian monasticism, and *vipassanā* meditation retreats, the constant vigilance and monitoring of one's own practices is how practitioners embody these practices of the self. Pierre Bourdieu (1977, 1993) uses the term habitus to illustrate how conditions of society, including religion and culture, are ingrained through practice and unconsciously marked in the bodies of each person. The main medium of the integration of the habitus is through bodily practices. One of the goals of the *vipassanā* meditation retreat program is to create a new habitus governed by the principles of Buddhism.

In Theravāda Buddhism there is an apparent contradiction between transcending of the self and the quest for *nibbāna* motivated by the self. The self must be examined and reflected upon in *vipassanā* meditation in order to understand what habits and tendencies need to be explored or reshaped. As one progresses along the path to *nibbāna* one creates a self that aligns with Buddhist ascetic and ethical ideals. Against the backdrop of the Indian Brahmanical world that aimed to cultivate control of the self, the Buddha denied the existence of such an entity and the possibility of such control (Collins 1990, 96). The doctrine of non-self then was articulated within specific historical and social contexts in the midst of soteriological debates about the nature of the self. When practicing *vipassanā*, one realizes selflessness through investigating the body and mind, coming to understand its impermanence and the impossibility of control or a constant self. In these ways, technologies of the self aim to cultivate various virtues dependent on particular religious doctrines. Throughout Thailand, *vipassanā* meditation centers utilize practices of the self in similar ways to reach particular goals of the retreat program specific to the Buddhist tradition.

Along with the *vipassanā* retreat, the Buddhist monastic life also utilizes these practices of the self. Steven Collins (2012) discusses Pāli practices of the self among monastics and meditators who embody particular modes of being that create a change in one's existential and social status. Correct physical decorum of monastics in Theravāda Buddhism is a requirement for public recognition and legitimation. Their social position requires their reputation and performance of Buddhist doctrines to be judged through "carefully composed deportment, and through social interaction where they are treated as revered superiors" (Collins 1997, 198). This significance is portrayed in the Vinaya of monastics with seventy-five 'Training Rules' concerned with dress, deportment, etiquette, and clothing (Collins 1997, 198). Therefore the inner mental condition is reflected

Embodying meditation 153

in the physical and verbal behavior of the person that consists of "private self-control and self-supervision required by the expected public body-image" (Collins 2000, 199). The daily life of monastics therefore reinforces Buddhist normative values. Monastics demonstrate the extent to which they have cultivated themselves through their behavior and outward performance.

These practices of the self are also cultivated through the Buddhist practice of *vipassanā* meditation itself, where Buddhist doctrines, principles, as well as communities dictate the desired ideal Buddhist self. Joanna Cook (2010) has recently examined the ways the self is made meaningful for modern Thai monastics and how their subjectivity is formed through religious experience (Cook 2010, 7). These 'technologies of the self' demonstrate how meditators remake themselves in ways consistent with their religious doctrines. The point then of *vipassanā* is to realize and experience the truth of Buddhist doctrines (Cook 2010, 9). Cook delineates how Pāli language can affect meditation practice. Although not understood conceptually or intellectually, the use of Pāli brings about an internal experience of Buddhist truths, demonstrating the kind of knowledge desired—a deep experiential one rather than intellectual or conceptual. She writes, "Use of Pali in the retreat process is understood as an aspect of the formation of the capacity by which people come to perceive religious truths in their bodies, senses and emotions" (Cook 2010, 102). This attention to the body and its behavior indicates the detailed and varied ways the retreat program aims to cultivate the self.

There are dozens of small rituals—formal and informal—within the retreat process, such as those described in earlier chapters, like opening and closing ceremonies, mealtimes, and the proscribed movements to begin and end meditation sessions. These seemingly insignificant practices within the retreat contribute to the cultivation of Buddhist ideals of non-self, suffering, and impermanence. The ritualized structure aims to create religious practitioners through the internalization and reproduction of values. Catherine Bell writes that the "series of physical movements within ritual practices serve to construct an environment which ingrains these movements upon the bodies of participants" (Bell 1997, 98). Within *vipassanā* meditation retreats the environment is constructed so that mindfulness and meditation become a part of one's experience within each moment. Slow, controlled movements signal to retreatants that this is time spent outside of ordinary life. The space of the *vipassanā* meditation center provides the context in which to enact Buddhist principles through the environment of a temple setting, in community with other participants reminding one to keep silent, and a separate space removed from unnecessary external stimuli.

The retreat program structures its environment through these proscribed physical movements that mold the participants, validating and extending the Buddhist doctrines they are intended to internalize. Mediation retreats therefore are meant to produce people anew who embody Buddhist doctrines, both lay and ordained. Buddhists are meant to embody their religion, not on a cognitive level, but to perform according to the doctrines and expectations of their religious culture so that religion will regulate conduct, action, emotions, and perceptions. The retreat program within the meditation centers aims to regulate the body and one's daily

154 *Embodying meditation*

schedule in order to produce a particular experience of awareness and control over particular activities participants will pursue. Meditators must learn to master the schedule, accommodation, food, clothing, and meditation practice—each of which has a purpose toward cultivating a mindful body. Clothing reinforces modesty and sets one apart, marked as part of a larger project of meditation and the self. The amount of food one chooses to eat and how one eats indicates one's level of mindfulness. Learning to sleep a limited number of hours on a hard surface and following the rhythms of the day through mindful meditation constitutes an initial process of intellectual understanding that transforms into one that is revealed in the body. One must give up agency and control over time and space. The retreat program aims for a reordering of the self through a technology of embodiment, an ongoing process of meaning-making and transformation. This subject formation, however, is rooted within particular cultural understandings. These actions therefore are both individual and societal/cultural as Buddhism is transmitted and reproduced through practice.

Thai lay meditators do not always have a thorough understanding of the Buddhist truths *vipassanā* meditation is meant to reveal. However, there is still a distinction between international meditators and Thai meditators, because the latter have a social and cultural frame of reference for *vipassanā* meditation within the context of Buddhism. Thai monastics and Buddhist laity strive for tradition-specific goals, an act which conforms to Buddhist cosmology, ethics, and social dimensions. Through making aspects of the retreat optional or translating them into modern Buddhist discourses that do not include practices of the self, international meditators may not be cultivating the self in this embedded way, rooted in the Buddhist tradition. Instead, international meditators have the ability to cultivate the self in ways related to their own religious and cultural repertoires.

International meditators' practices of the self

It is important to emphasize that the meditation retreat is composed of practices including physical movements and bodily enactments of ideologies and doctrines that can be inserted into formats such as public activities of classes and retreats. Aspects of belief and doctrine emerge through these experiences so that practitioners themselves decide how deeply and with what motivations to interact with the world view of the religion. Charles Taylor writes, "first people are drawn to a pilgrimage, or a World Youth Day, or a meditation group, or a prayer circle and then later, if they move along in the appropriate direction, they will find themselves embedded in ordinary practice" (Taylor 2009, 516). It is clear that a significant way people enter religious faiths in modernity is through forms of practice. These practices are structured and accessed in ways that are individualistic, inclusivist, ecumenical, and include loose hierarchies of authority.

Because of this, international meditators, even though practicing in a Buddhist context, are not, for the most part, striving for tradition-specific goals. International meditators often do not fully reproduce the comportment, dress, and orientation usually adhered to by Thai meditators to meet the aims of the meditation retreat. In this way a tradition-specific subjectivity is not formed among international meditators as they often place *vipassanā* within other religious or secular frameworks. Certainly some foreign meditators become deeply informed by meditation and Buddhist truths—however, because of the modern Buddhist discourses that divorce meditation from its Buddhist framework, many are experimenting and sampling the practice as a new way to 'discover' the self. As mentioned in Chapter 5 the distinction between 'knowing' oneself and 'finding' oneself is difficult to translate to international meditators. During the 'sharing session' at the closing of the monthly foreigners retreat at the International Dhamma Hermitage, international meditators describe how the course helped them to find their 'true selves,' to recharge in nature. At the *wan phra* ceremony at Wat Rampoeng, occasionally international meditators are asked to reveal their motivations for partaking in a retreat in Thailand. Similar motivations are repeated such as getting away from all responsibilities and finding or discovering oneself. In this way many international meditators exhibit an understanding of a self that is created internally. Because of this, the inner practice and transformation is given more value than outward demonstrations of the training.

This valuing of inner practice is demonstrated through specific practices adapted for international meditators. The international meditator orientation is translated especially conspicuously at Wat Umong. Here international meditators are not asked to participate in any type of opening ceremony. Thai meditators need to prepare the flowers, candles, and incense necessary for this ritual, but foreigners begin their practice without this formal ceremony. The head of the international meditation center has decided not to conduct the opening ceremony for foreigners in order to make it easier for them. One of the teachers of the international meditators found that they come to Wat Umong only to practice meditation and often do not care to participate in ceremonial and ritual activities. From my interview with the head of the international meditation center of Wat Umong, I wrote:

> [F]oreigners don't formally take precepts like Thais because they ask foreigners to follow the precepts on their own. It is not necessary to receive the precepts from a monk, just knowing how to follow is enough. The eight precepts are listed in the residence halls in English so foreigners can read this.

This translation of the retreat format for international meditators serves to remove part of the Thai Buddhist practice and replace it with a do-it-yourself attitude. At this meditation center, there is no formal reception of precepts so the international meditators must read and internalize the rules on their own without a ritual marking their entrance into a retreat and an ascetic lifestyle. Therefore the assumed preference of international meditators for practicing meditation without ritual creates a retreat experience that privileges an inward practice. International meditators are expected to direct their practice from the inside out instead of participating in the external, embodied practices of the retreat.

156 *Embodying meditation*

As discussed in Chapter 6, rituals have become devalued within modern religiosity. Instead religion is connected with psychology while non-scientific characteristics such as magic are repressed. Personal, inner religion and disenchantment marginalize public, communal rituals, as there is little belief that words and practices have any efficacy to act in the world. Charles Taylor discusses how the West came to value expressive individualism. He finds that this is tied to the realm of consumerism, where the customer is encouraged to express her or his particular identity through purchases (Taylor 2003, 80-81). One's particular religious practices also demonstrate one's eclecticism and cosmopolitanism to society. Instead of collective ritual, Taylor finds that through the Romantic expressivism of the later eighteenth century, individuals value non-conformity or any model that was discovered by oneself (Taylor 2003, 83). People will still join new religious communities but only because this is where their individual search for 'authenticity' leads them (Taylor 2008, 112). An interest in meditation may lead into more formal engagement with Thai Buddhism as seen in the Chapter 4 discussion of long-term international meditators. But those who become devoted disciples enter the practice through similar modes, privileging the interior.

Another example of translations for international meditators' orientation toward internal transformation is the daily schedule at Wat Umong. Here, Thai and Western meditators' schedules list the same morning and evening periods for group practice, but the groups are taught in separate meditation halls by different monk teachers. During the international group meditation period, Phra Viriya enters and bows to the Buddha statue. He then conducts a short chanting session and leads meditation. Here is what I wrote in my fieldnotes concerning Phra Viriya's perceptions of the international meditators during this session:

> Phra Viriya has found that there is no major resistance to bowing or chanting. He doesn't instruct his students to bow to the Buddha statue. As he bows the international meditators can follow him if they wish. They can also bow to him, their teacher, if they want. Phra Viriya teaches that this has the effect of creating respect for the teacher and cultivating a flexible mind. Most like chanting because Pāli words are interesting. Some foreigners want to get a recording of the chanting or copy the chanting book so they can keep it for themselves.

Here Phra Viriya reveals that outward performances such as bowing serve to create inner respect. However, since international meditators are not instructed to do this, it remains optional and not an explicit practice. As discussed in Chapter 6, international meditators are left to choose their level of participation in external practices. One of the consequences of this translation is that international meditators are not compelled to cultivate respect or participate fully in the goals of the meditation retreat. At Wat Doi Suthep, Ajan Buddhasak explicitly discusses bowing with his international students. From my interview with him, I recorded the following fieldnotes:

> [A]jan Buddhasak has had some foreign meditators who told him that they feel uncomfortable with some of the devotional aspects of the retreat. He responds

by instructing them not to worry because Buddhism isn't about the external, but is about the internal—it's not out but in. But it doesn't matter because it's only ceremony.[2]

Here Ajan Buddhasak demonstrates his understanding of international meditators; he does not expect them to perform the Buddhist religion externally, even overtly stating that Buddhism primarily concerns the internal and eschewing ritual and ceremony as unnecessary practices that do not help to cultivate an inner transformation.

Other instances of accommodating international meditators' reticence to participate in external practices occur in international meditation centers where international and Thai meditators participate together. At Wat Chom Tong, international meditators can practice with Thai meditators within the temple complex but also have their own separate space located just outside the main temple area. Because of this there are separate rules of dress depending on whether international meditators are in the shared or international section of the center. International female meditators must wear the *sabhai*, a white scarf that wraps around the chest, while in the temple areas. This serves to both cultivate modesty as well as adding an extra layer of covering in public spaces. But when females return to the international meditation center area, they can remove it, thus emphasizing that this cultivation of modesty is not necessary and is only for maintaining appropriateness in the Thai public spaces. International meditators are told that this is a Thai custom, therefore the instructors do not emphasize external practices but rather inner transformation through meditation.

Figure 7.1 Meditation clothes

158 *Embodying meditation*

The practice of daily meditation interviews reveals the extent to which translations for the international meditators removes external practices. At Wat Chom Tong, international meditators usually bow to a Buddha statue when entering the reporting room. Because mostly foreign laity teaches here, international meditators only bow to the Buddha statue, not the teacher. If one does not understand the reason for bowing, this can be discussed and negotiated. It is possible for international meditators instead to bow to the corner of the room if they would rather not bow to the Buddha statue. This translation of the retreat format occurred because international meditators told the teachers at Wat Chom Tong that they were uncomfortable bowing—they wanted to rely on themselves, not on any teacher. They felt uneasy with this outward demonstration of devotion. In Wat Rampoeng, however, where international meditators are mixed with Thai meditators, there is a mandatory process when entering and exiting the reporting room where one must bow to the Buddha statue first and then the abbot. Thus when Thai and international meditators practice in the same area it is difficult to perform these translations. During interview sessions at Dipabhavan Meditation Center, there are only international meditators present. International meditators sit across from monks on the same level rather than below. This positioning visually demonstrates equality between teacher and student so that the student isn't necessarily relying on or paying respect to the teacher. This would seem strange to a Thai Buddhist who is accustomed to the process of bowing both before and after speaking with a monk, sitting below him, and keeping her or his hands in a respectful *wai* position while listening and speaking. Therefore, international meditators are not practicing the cultivation of humility and respect that these techniques are meant to generate. Instead, meditation is the only practice international meditators perform fully. International meditation center teachers find that their international students are more comfortable with this inner practice than the external ones.

International meditation center teachers state, and my own observations confirm, that international meditators often exhibit an individualistic, self-authoritative response to meditation retreats in Thailand. A quote from the Thai Visa Forum (2009) discussion titled "Help Me Choose Among 4 Centers for Meditation Retreat," demonstrates this point further. In answer to the question of which meditation retreat the discussion topic creator should attend, one commenter writes that Wat Rampoeng

> also has a good reputation it seems. But seems a bit heavy on the Buddhism influence. Just seems a little funny that I have to bring 11 lotus flowers, etc., and circle around a Chedi [stupa] 3 times and do all this chanting. Does that actually have any benefit?"[3]

The author of this quote wonders why he has to participate in these external practices when presumably meditation is about the mind and transforming oneself from the inside.

Jeremy Carrette and Richard King (2005) find that these ideas are a consequence of the pervasive New Age emphasis on the self. They argue that through this lens Buddhism becomes misrepresented as a religion for self-development to build up and make the self stronger and more secure. However, the idea of an autonomous individual self is the central problem in human life for Buddhism, manifested as egoism and selfishness. They write:

> [I]t is for this reason that the Buddhist tradition has so often been misread as being fundamentally individualistic in orientation—its focus is precisely to work on the problem of the individual self by exposing its contradictions and porous boundaries.
>
> (Carrette & King 2005, 101)

Through the decontextualization of meditation from its Buddhist worldview, the practice can be transformed into a philosophy centered on individual practice and inner transformation. Michal Pagis, in her study of meditation practitioners in the Goenka tradition, relates this increased interest in the modern Western understanding of the self to the popularity of *vipassanā* meditation. She notes with some irony:

> [I]n its [*vipassanā* meditation's] modern manifestation, people who have little to do with Buddhism who do not call themselves Buddhists go to silent meditation retreats where they practice renunciation and embodied introspection, entering a process meant to lead to the de-stabilization of the experience of a permanent, stable self.
>
> (Pagis 2008, vi)

Meditation practices for international meditators often resonate with the increased importance of the interior life and personal experience in modernity in contrast to practices of the self, which are apparent in Christian monastic and Islamic revival movements. Because international meditators' meditation practices are directed more toward other religious or secular goals, rather than tradition-specific Buddhist goals, it is common for them to experience the meditation retreat through these modern reflexive ideas of the self.

In some cases, international meditators do execute external practices of the retreat program. This often occurs through intellectual explanation of the purposes of practices outside of meditation. Because the retreat experience is set apart as special and elevated, it becomes an opportunity to create affective changes of new attitudes and emotional responses and values. Meditation as an embodied practice is ritualized in different ways in different centers for international meditators depending on their teachers. Ajan Buddhasak saw that an initial intellectual description of the purpose of external practices gave way to openness for some of his students, manifesting in changes in behavior. In the Ajan Tong method, a mindful prostration is a preparatory action to prepare the mind to settle and be aware of the present moment that all international meditators learn. At the International Dhamma Hermitage, dhamma friends remind meditators to take their time to sit slowly finding a comfortable posture, bending down and sitting

160　*Embodying meditation*

up with a straight back, taking a few deep breaths before beginning. These initial practices become associated with increased concentration and positive mental states, and link posture to concentration. The meditation retreat program is established so that one learns through one's body. When their teachers overtly explain this to international meditators, it is easier to understand the link between outward practices and inner cultivation. This is one strategy to help international meditators participate more closely in the tradition-specific goals of the retreat program.

However, international meditation center teachers are not translating the retreat program with the goal of conversion but use points of convergence as a tool to claim familiarity and modernity. As well many international meditators are not compelled to participate fully in the retreat, with external practices being optional or intentionally avoided. All of the ways international meditation center teachers translate the retreat, so that international meditators do not have to perform any outward devotion or cultivate respect through bowing, demonstrate how conversion and change in religious identity are not applicable terms. The rest of this chapter discusses more appropriate descriptions for modern religious experimentation and the ways international meditation center teachers accommodate and incorporate international meditators from other religions. I argue this is similar to the incorporation strategies of Buddhist missionaries used in Thai history.

Conversion and religious identity of international meditators

Conversion has been an important topic within religious studies, especially in the psychology of religion.[4] Significant work has been done to theorize the nature of religious identity and conversion (Robbins 2011, 2009; Keane 2007; Rafael 1998). Conversion has been described as a transformation of worldview and a rupture from a religious past to a new religious future. This is of course not a definitive break, as there often exists tension with the previous religion and societal norms. Diane Austin-Broos, in a chapter concerning the anthropology of conversion writes that

> [T]o be converted is to reidentify, to learn, reorder, and reorient. It involves interrelated modes of transformation that generally continue over time and define a consistent course. Not mere syncretism, neither can conversion involve a simple and absolute break with a previous social life.
>
> (Austin-Broos 2003, 2)

In this way, conversion is not a one-time decisive moment that necessitates a clear dichotomy between the old religion and the new. Therefore religious adherents continually work toward maintaining this change in themselves. Robert Hefner (1993) labels the most important feature of conversion as the acceptance and adjustment of one's self-identification as a new reference point. He states that "conversion need not reformulate one's understanding of the ultimate conditions of existence, but it always involves commitment to a new kind of moral authority and a new or reconceptualized social identity" (Hefner 1993, 17). In

Embodying meditation 161

her ethnography of Samoan Christian conversions to newer forms of Christianity, Ilana Gershon (2007) analyzes how "shifts in meaning and morality were often also shifts in reflexivity—people were learning to carve out different personhoods through these conversions as well" (Gershon 2007, 149). Therefore these scholars argue that conversion eventually results in a set of new beliefs, a new worldview and sense of identity. These descriptions, although not describing conversion as something entirely new and different immediately for the adherent, all label conversion as a change in perception of oneself toward tradition-specific goals.

The project of international meditation centers is in contrast with this. A meditation retreat is practice oriented as opposed to belief oriented. The goal of the retreat is to gain enough insight through direct observation of one's mind that one is transformed physically as well as mentally. This can be detected through the way a meditator walks, carries oneself, speaks, and generally acts. Although the goal of most international meditation center teachers is to help their students reorder and reorient their daily lives and lived realities, few meditators would call themselves converts, as their experiences are limited, temporary, and often do not involve all of the external practices meant to cultivate Buddhist goals. Teachers' ultimate aim for students is to experience insight at a deep level that will ultimately transform them. However, at the same time they reinforce international meditators' assumptions about Buddhist meditation as a global religious practice, which can be added to other worldviews without conflict.

This is possible because of Buddhist attitudes towards conversion and religious identity. Buddhists are identified as such by being part of a community, taking precepts and the Three Refuges, having a particular teacher, or ordaining. However, these practices and creating a Buddhist identity are not necessary to attain Enlightenment. Jonathan Walters writes that it is "unproblematic (as far as Buddhists are concerned) to continue practicing previous religions, save perhaps in terms of their unproductiveness in the Buddhist context" (Walters 2005, 6080). In this way Buddhist ideas of religious identification and conversion are contrasted sharply with Abrahamic religious traditions. Thomas Tweed is one of the only scholars to theorize about Buddhist religious identification (Tweed 2002). His terms 'night-stand Buddhists' and 'Buddhist sympathizers' are helpful in understanding the nature of engagement with Buddhism in the contemporary world. Buddhist sympathizers and night-stand Buddhists are those who have an affinity toward the religion but do not identify with it fully or exclusively (Tweed 2002, 20). Using these terms, most of the international meditators who participate in retreats in Thailand would identify as sympathizers through their interest in meditation and living in a Buddhist temple. In this way, international meditators often approach the meditation retreat not interested in conversion, a shift in worldview, or new identity, but displaying cosmopolitanism[5] and experiencing something exotic and different.

Instead of conversion and religious identity, I follow Justin McDaniel's (2011) discussion of repertoires. One does not have to identify with a single religious tradition but instead can engage in a number of practices inconsistently, allowing for contradictions. Like Tweed and McDaniel, I am not interested in the normative

162 *Embodying meditation*

view of religious identity that creates a binary distinction between adherents and non-adherents. I am also not concerned about the inner state of conversion as this is beyond my purview. Instead of theorizing about religious identity and conversion in a categorical way, I am investigating a subtler manifestation, which assumes a diversity of forms, consisting of translations that are influenced by a multi-valent interplay of historical circumstances and cultural exchange. Sociocultural dynamics such as imaginings of Buddhism and meditation in popular culture, Orientalism, and tourist imaginaries of Thailand create new ways of engaging with Buddhism that do not result in conversion or a change in religious identity.

Conversion is affected by modernity, one's social location, as well as cultural context. We therefore have to consider the possibilities available for interna-tional meditators. They have the modern possibility of self-conscious selection and adoption of various elements into one's identity. Talal Asad reminds us that modernity serves to create, define, and control choices as well as offering a vari-ety of religious options and modes of exploration (Asad 1996, 263). The ability to select and integrate a plurality of religious elements is due to the opening of possibilities in modernity that was previously beyond the scope of religious imag-ination. Therefore I am not speculating on the religious identity of international meditators but instead analyzing their engagement with Thai Buddhism within the particular religious and cultural context of the meditation retreat. Historically, Buddhist missionary practices in Thailand lend themselves to theorizing about religious identity in a similar way to what I have just described.

Missionizing Buddhism

Within Thailand, other historical and ethnographic conversion accounts help to illuminate the context of international meditation centers. Missionizing practices in Thailand occurred in the 1960s when Buddhist monks, as part of a program cre-ated by the Thai Sangha and supported by the government, sought out indigenous peoples and villages attempting to convert them to Buddhism. The Dhammacarik (wandering dhamma) Bhikkhu Program (DBP) began in 1964 with the aim to convert indigenous groups[6] outside Central Thailand. These conversion efforts were aimed toward reigning in outside groups into the Thai national body. The purpose of the DBP was to integrate and enable indigenous people to become Thai citizens, teach the dhamma, and how to follow the Buddhist way of life (Wongprasert 1988, 127). The monks who took part in this program were asked to complete training before being assigned to a location of service where they would interact with and teach the indigenous people. This was a program sponsored by the government, which was an obvious attempt at promoting national interests, and an example of a more typical missionary endeavor. However, it is still an example of Thai Buddhist conversion of non-Buddhists.

Examples of the DBP from the 1960s by Charles Keyes (1993) and of wandering tudong monks of the forest tradition of Luangpu Mun by Kamala Tiyavanich (1997), who interacted with indigenous non-Buddhist groups throughout the 1930s, demonstrate the incorporation model of Buddhist missionizing. Through their wandering, forest monks taught indigenous people about offering food to monks, meditation, and the Buddha's teachings (Tiyavanich 1997, 160–165). The wandering forest monks exposed indigenous people to Buddhism but Tiyavanich writes that they "made no attempt to change other people's convictions or convert them to their kind of Buddhism" (Tiyavanich 1997, 164). Through the DBP project Keyes found that indigenous people were especially impressed with the discipline of the monastic lifestyle when they learned they did not drink, eat in the evening, or even touch women (Keyes 1993, 264). Keyes writes that in order for villagers to become Buddhist "they had to have more sustained contacts with monks and to accept that their lives could be made more meaningful by adopting a Buddhist worldview" (Keyes 1993, 266). In addition to this it was hoped that they could attend and participate in Buddhist rituals. The first step for the indigenous people was to understand the Buddha as transcending local spirits and then to follow the teachings of the Buddha (Keyes 1993, 267). Therefore conversion to Buddhism did not require a radical rejection of previous beliefs (Keyes 1993, 268).

Although both Buddhists and Christians participate in missionizing activities in Thailand, the two groups enact these in differing ways. Steven Kemper writes that "one thing 'Buddhist missionizing' did not borrow from Protestantism was its emphasis on conversion proper" (Kemper 2005, 27). He argues that the Sri Lankan Buddhist leader, Anagarika Dharmapala, distinguished between conversion and bringing knowledge. Dharmapala believed that this distinction made Buddhism more palatable to Westerners so that Buddhist practices did not require an exclusive commitment (Kemper 2005, 30). The strategy of modern Buddhist missionaries like Dharmapala therefore aims not toward converting non-Buddhists but leading meditation sessions and offering teachings to those interested. These Buddhist missionizing strategies lead to shifting, open-ended religious identities, and a continuation of this can be seen today in Thailand's international meditation centers.

Instead of conversion and concern with religious identity, international meditation centers allow international meditators to selectively engage with the retreat program. Vicente Rafael's (1998) *Contracting Colonialism* explores the strategies of receiving the missionizing religion in the context of the early encounter between the Spanish and the Tagalogs in the Philippines from the late sixteenth to the early eighteenth centuries. Rafael concludes that the Tagalogs were able to select their conversion, appropriating only fragments of the Christian teachings that were understood, and subverting others. For example, Rafael writes how the repetition of the term *JesusMaria* was turned into a protective phrase. He finds,

> [W]hat this amounts to is a recasting of the Christian Sign into something that can be torn away from the linguistic commerce that originates from and returns to the Father. It is instead rendered into an amulet-like object that does not result in the subjection of the speaker to the language of God.
>
> (Rafael 1987, 328–329)

In this context, the sacraments of confession and death rites, untranslatable terms, and translations into the vernacular show the Tagalogs' agency and the plurality

164 *Embodying meditation*

of conversions that took place. Rafael argues that conversion happened rapidly because the Tagalogs did not fully understand the faith they were accepting; instead they placed what they could comprehend into their own cultural and religious repertoires. In fact the missionaries were soon frustrated by the lack of ability to effectively translate the sacraments. In this context intercultural and religious dialogue demonstrates the sometimes long and variable processes of learning and translating a new religion for a new cultural setting or audience. We have seen that through dialogue with their students, international meditation center teachers adjust the meditation retreat program so that they engage selectively, choosing the parts that resonate with modern Buddhist imaginaries of meditation and Thailand.

For international meditators, selective performance is certainly the norm where behavioral performances of respect and mindfulness are initially awkward and self-conscious. Rebecca Sachs Norris finds that conversion occurs because it connects with the convert's previously held ideas about truth and meaning. "Having found a tradition that satisfies specific needs, the concepts and practices of the adopted religion are filtered through the convert's language and associations," (Norris 2003, 179). These associations cause some converts or interested practitioners to accept only that which corresponds to their preexisting beliefs and attitudes. She writes,

> Given that cultural beliefs and practices shape experience, and that the meaning of religious language and ritual is grounded in embodied experience, converts initially understand the symbolism and language of their adopted religion through the filter of their original language and worldview.
>
> (Norris 2003, 171)

What is most significant within international meditation centers is not belief or doctrine but the ways the retreat program enters into one's repertoire. Many seek to add to their cultural and religious repertoire but not subtract or change their lifestyle to a large degree, and remain within the limits and boundaries of their cultural habitus. Meditation retreats are attractive for this reason—one can engage intensely for a short period with limited commitment or prior knowledge. International meditation center teachers hope that these practices will eventually lead or begin the path to the development of a moral, wise, and compassionate self.

International meditation center teachers do this through translating for international meditators the possibility for selective and creative engagement, similar to the translation for individual preferences of the retreat program discussed in Chapter 6. Specifically, they have developed strategies for international meditators who are not willing to accept the full retreat program because of their religious commitments. During the course of my fieldwork I asked more than thirty meditation teachers about their strategies for accommodating and teaching meditation to those international meditators who have other religious commitments, and many of them shared stories of these occurrences. Indeed, Venerable Piyabhaso,[7] former teacher of the International Buddhist Meditation Center at Wat Mahathat,

Bangkok, believes that there are two kinds of foreign meditators: those with no religion who are more open to participating in a variety of temple activities, and those with a religious affiliation who have restrictions on their participation and performance. Most of these restrictions include the outer performances of the retreat such as bowing to monks and Buddha statues, as discussed earlier in this chapter. However the meditation practice and teachings of the retreat are also translated for non-Buddhist groups.

Venerable Dhammananda Bhikkhuni[8] thoughtfully considers teaching Buddhism and Buddhist practice within a multi-faith environment. She uses Christian concepts to help her audience understand Buddhist ideas. For example, the recitation of the Three Refuges, "I take refuge in the Buddha, Dhamma, and Sangha," can appear like a statement of conversion to international meditators. Because of this, Ven. Dhammananda Bhikkhuni notifies foreign visitors when the three refuges are being chanted and warns them that they may wish to refrain from repeating these Pāli words. She explains how to understand the Three Refuges in a Buddhist context by placing it within a Christian framework,

> [V]ery much like the Christians, when you go for your Sunday mass . . . it is the time that you are reminded that you are to follow the spirit of Christ . . . that is how we as Buddhists take Buddhahood into ourselves, follow the path and make it real.
>
> (Dhammananda 2008, 84)

Along with placing Buddhist practices into familiar Christian terms, this kind of sentiment allows non-Buddhist international meditators to understand experiences from meditation retreats within Christian frameworks. Therefore Dhammananda Bhikkhuni enables the selective performance of international meditators, making the practice as familiar as possible and allowing them the choice about whether to follow chanting the Three Refuges.

In Ven. Dhammananda Bhikkhuni's pamphlet *Meditation for Buddhists and Christians* (no date), and her book about meditation, *Training the Monkey Mind* (2008), she directs her teaching of meditation explicitly to a non-Buddhist audience. She begins by delineating the many different meditation techniques and objects of concentration, emphasizing that each person can choose which one is most suitable. This signals, she believes, that Buddhism respects individual difference (Dhammananda 2008, 9). Thus one can practice according to individual preference, even as a Christian. Instead of reciting the mantra 'Buddha,' she suggests substituting 'breathing in' and 'breathing out' for non-religious participants and 'Jesus' and 'Christ' for Christian participants. She therefore demonstrates that she understands the selective performance that many international meditators prefer. Here is what I have written in my fieldnotes from our conversation:

> [V]en. Dhammananda Bhikkhuni uses the same technique of mindfulness of breathing for foreigners and Thai but when she hosts groups of American university students she doesn't say anything about Buddhism, only explaining

166 *Embodying meditation*

meditation as mental training. She tells Christians that they can concentrate on a cross or use a mantra of Jesus Christ because the outer form doesn't have to be Buddhist.

This modification of a meditation technique for non-Buddhists is not completely uncommon. A laywoman at Wat Pa Baan That, informs me that

> in practice, the late Luangpho Budh Thaniyo of Wat Pa Salawan, Korat [Nakhon Ratchasima], used to teach his Christian students to chant by heart 'Jesus' while the Buddhists were taught to chant 'Buddho', in his meditation class. As a result, the Christians attain *samadhi* [concentration] as well as the Buddhists. Luangpho said should he have Muslim students he would teach them to chant 'Allah' and he's sure they could get into *samadhi*[9] as well.[10]

Therefore, meditation practice is adapted so that non-Buddhists can use words and symbols from their own religions. Selective performance and translations facilitate this intercultural exchange including removing or making optional external practices such as chanting and bowing, and adjusting meditation practices to suit participation of non-Buddhist religious meditators during the retreat program.

In the present time Buddhist missionizing has continued in similar ways to those mentioned above for international meditators so that there is no indication of commitment or conversion to Buddhism. International meditation center teachers emphasize that Buddhist meditation methods work no matter the religious status of the meditation enthusiast. Buddhist missionaries of the DBP (Keyes 1993, 264) and the wandering forest monks (Tiyavanich 1997, 164) did not require converts to abandon their beliefs in spirits and today international meditation teachers do not require their students to give up their previously held religious or non-religious beliefs. The indigenous peoples' religious repertoires expanded through their exposure to Buddhist monks and their discipline. In the same way international meditators add the Buddhist practice of meditation to their repertoires. Instead of a radical break with one's religious or non-religious beliefs, or a statement of dissent and disengagement with one's culture, participating in a meditation retreat is considered a 'must do' on many travelers' itineraries.

Both Thai and international meditators draw from a wide range of components when understanding and making meaning out of a meditation retreat. Thai Buddhists continually draw from their own cultural repertoires including Buddhism and other cultural and global influences. Justin McDaniel finds that Thai Buddhist repertoires are characterized by security, heritage, graciousness, and abundance (McDaniel 2011, 13), while I have described international meditators drawing from therapy, Romanticism, secularism, universalism, self-reflexivity, and personal choice. Also like Thai Buddhists, whom McDaniel argues add to their individual repertoires but rarely subtract, international meditators add meditation to their own personal secular and religious ways of understanding their reality.

Conclusion

The meditation retreat is not a wholly inward project, but also contains external practices. Offering to a monk, bowing to a Buddha statue, chanting, and other activities can be a part of the meditation retreat program. These external practices serve to mark someone as having an overt commitment to the Buddhist tradition. Therefore the meditation retreat involves the body as much the mind, in which all senses are engaged. Internal practices of the retreat such as sitting and walking meditation, become so popular and significant not only because they are decontextualized from Thai Buddhism and portable, but also because they can be added onto one's preexisting cultural and religious repertoire without conflict. Because *vipassanā* meditation is an internal practice, there is no outer marker or demonstration to society about one's commitment or status.

The dynamics of the international meditation center, with interaction between international meditators and international meditation center teachers, illuminate the interstices of religion and modernity, where religious identity and conversion are not helpful categories. Many of the external practices of the meditation retreat are not performed or are deemed unacceptable or unnecessary by international meditation center teachers, their students, or both. The modern reflexive self is in opposition to the ways the self is cultivated through outward performance in the meditation retreat. International meditation center teachers are aware of this difference, sometimes intentionally, and further translate the retreat to remove or make optional any external practices outside of meditation. This removal furthermore serves to create a space for non-Buddhists to participate in the retreat without any change in religious identity or fear of conversion. The outward practices of a religion are those that mark one's identity to the outside world. International meditators exhibit a selective performance of the retreat, removing these outer marks and thus constructing a retreat program that adds to their preexisting repertoires.

Notes

1 Following Foucault (1978, 1988).
2 Interview with Phra Ajan Buddhasak, Wat Prathat Doi Suthep, May 1st, 2010.
3 See Thai Visa Forum Website: www.thaivisa.com/forum/topic/241648-help-me-choose-among-4-centers-for-meditation-retreat/page__st__25.
4 There have been systematic studies done on the process of conversion, perhaps most notably Rambo (1993), where he divides conversion into a seven-stage model. These include context, crisis, quest, encounter, interaction, commitment, and consequences.
5 Rocha (2006) has studied the relationship between Zen Buddhism and cosmopolitanism in Brazil. She finds that Brazilian elites have taken the practice of Zen as a symbol of cosmopolitan modernity. Modern Buddhist discourses that have aligned Buddhism with modernity have also given Buddhist practice a status of urbanity that can be seen in Brazil, Thailand, and other parts of the world.
6 The indigenous people are traditionally dry-rice farmers, including the Karen, Meo, Lahu, Lisu, Yao, Akha, Lua, Htin, and Khmu, who live mostly in the mountains of North Thailand but have dispersed throughout the country. They make up about 1.3 percent of the population and practice animism, while some are Christian and Buddhist. I have chosen to call them 'indigenous' instead of 'hill tribe' people because

168 *Embodying meditation*

this is the name these groups prefer (Erni 2008). Many of them have lived in Thailand for generations but some have crossed the border from Myanmar more recently.

7 Interview with Phra Piyabhaso Bhatsakorn, Wat Mahathat, June 13th, 2010.

8 My interview with Venerable Dhammananda Bhikkhuni of Wat Songdhammakalyani, took place on March 8th, 2010. Ven. Dhammananda Bhikkhuni, formerly known as Chatsumarn Kabilsingh, is well-known in Thailand and abroad for her progressive stance on women and Buddhism. She was the first Theravāda *bhikkhunī* (fully-ordained nun) in Thailand, and her temple in Central Thailand, Wat Songdhammakalyani, is the first to train and create a group of female novices and monastics. Through this establishment, she has guided other Thai women through ordination in Sri Lanka, where she became a *bhikkhunī*. In my work, I am interested in Ven. Dhammanada Bhikkhuni as a meditation teacher and host to foreign visitors.

9 These teachers refer to *samādhi* meditation as a universal practice, rather than *vipassanā*, which has more tradition-specific goals.

10 Email correspondence March 24th, 2011.

8 The future of Thailand's international meditation centers

Throughout this work I have discussed the particular imaginaries of international meditators, as well as the imaginaries of meditation, Buddhism, and Thailand. For some international meditators, the engagement is limited and their imaginaries do not shift. But for others, the retreat experience makes a lasting impression, creating new networks for Thai meditation lineages abroad. Those who wish to take the practice to their home countries invite and host their international meditation center teachers to give teachings and meditation retreats. This is a serious undertaking with arrangements made for supporting the teacher, space for living and teaching, as well as engaging friends, family, and the wider community to participate. Examples of networks created abroad include not only students inviting teachers but also authorized lay meditation teachers creating or being appointed to teach at a branch center in their home countries. Therefore these international meditation centers in Thailand can have lasting effects, creating new communities.[1] In this chapter, I first highlight the features of these new communities abroad with specific examples used throughout this book of trajectories for teaching abroad.

Reflecting the diversity of international meditation center teachers in Thailand, foreign meditation teachers help to create networks through teaching in or near their home countries. The Ajan Tong method from Wat Chom Tong, Chiangmai, has extended into an international lay lineage as teachers have created centers in Israel, Mexico, Canada, and Germany. Phra Ofer, long-term meditator highlighted in Chapter 5, teaches in both his native Israel and Germany. Hildegard Huber is an example of a student who brought the Ajan Tong method to Germany. Since being a student of Ajan Tong in 1992, she organized courses in Europe for retreats within this lineage. She was authorized to teach in 1998 and established a meditation center near Munich in 2006.[2] Other authorized teachers such as Edward Kooij and Asher Gill teach in the Germany center and in Israel. International meditation centers thus create new communities abroad in non-Buddhist peripheries. These peripheries also bring students to Thailand. For example, during my retreat at Wat Chom Tong, a serious young female student from Mexico had arrived in order to participate in a long retreat, as well as to meet Ajan Tong and gain closer access to the lineage of the technique she had been practicing for many years.

170 The future of international meditation

The international meditation center teachers who do not come from an established lineage or have foreign lay disciples are at times invited to teach abroad by their students. These students, who have experienced their teachings in Thailand, want to spread the dhamma to their home communities and expose their teacher to a wider audience. After a retreat in Thailand, students want to share the experience with those who cannot or do not want to make the trip to Thailand. Mae Chii Brigitte of Wat Prayong in Bangkok visits Europe and, more recently, America each year through connections made with international students. Mae Chii Brigitte spends about half the year with these teaching obligations abroad, giving dhamma talks and short meditation retreats in people's homes, churches, clinics, schools, galleries, and meditation centers. Mae Chii Brigitte receives all of her invitations from students who have attended a retreat at Wat Prayong. In Europe she has been traveling to Austria, Germany, Switzerland, the Netherlands, and Spain since 2001. Following an invitation from many of her students she took several three-month journeys with her teacher, Phra Ajan Tippakorn, in 2001, 2002, and 2004. In 2003, Mae Chii Brigitte was the temporary head of the Buddhavihara Meditation Center in Amsterdam for three months while the head teacher attended a solitary retreat in Myanmar. She began teaching in the USA in 2013 and plans to go again in 2014 with the sponsorship of Mark Sawyer, an author and religious seeker who brings many teachers from Asia to America.[3]

Usually students find Mae Chii Brigitte's website when they are interested in meditation and planning a trip to Thailand. When they return to their home countries and hear that Mae Chii Brigitte is traveling and teaching, they invite her to their area. Once she arrives in Europe or the USA more invitations come as people discover her teachings. The donations from participants easily cover her travel expenses and the rest goes to her social projects, aiding other *mae chiis* within Thailand. These connections abroad could foster more interest in Thai Buddhism and a trip to the center of the Thai Buddhist meditation lineage that new students are learning about. Mae Chii Brigitte estimates that about 15 percent of the first-time participants of her overseas retreats visit her temple in Thailand, but about 60 percent continue to attend her overseas retreats in their areas. Many of her students who have attended her retreats in Thailand and abroad bring their friends and family members on return trips to Wat Prayong. Therefore these teachers and teachings abroad lead to a connection with Thailand and a particular teacher and meditation lineage that continues to expand.

At Wat Tam Doi Tohn, Phra Ajan Nawi Piyadassi has made important connections with students in America. He visited Thai communities in 2007, 2008, 2011, and 2012, and was able to travel to New Mexico, Florida, California, Massachusetts, Vermont, Connecticut, Minnesota, and Louisiana. Through these Thai diasporic communities, however, interested Americans from non-Thai backgrounds joined, by way of connections with these Thai-American residents, either by coincidence or through advertised retreats. Through these connections Phra Ajan Nawi has built an international community, with five to eight international meditators usually attending his monthly retreats in Mae Wang, despite needing an interpreter. Americans who received his teachings in

The future of international meditation 171

their home communities travel to Thailand for these monthly retreats or come to practice on their own for months at a time. Indeed, when I entered Wat Tam Doi Tohn in January 2014, there was a Swiss group of ten people staying at a nearby guesthouse and visiting the temple and Phra Ajan Nawi daily. There were also two American novice monks and an American lay meditator and French lay meditator who come every year to practice at this space under the guidance of Phra Ajan Nawi.

One of these students, Doug, met Phra Ajan Nawi in the summer of 2007 and acted as his assistant, continuing to travel with him for the same period the next year as well. Doug happened to be visiting a Buddhist temple in Massachusetts when the Thai group hosting Phra Ajan Nawi asked him to join them. After Phra Ajan Nawi left the USA, Doug visited Thailand, sitting a long course at Wat Tham Doi Thon in January 2009. After that he became a part of the community, ordaining as a novice monk. He typically spends the monthly retreat period of seven days for his own meditation and works for the temple the rest of the month. Doug was looking for a practice and direction for his life and feels lucky to have chanced upon Phra Ajan Nawi and his Thai followers.

Some of these dedicated followers take the legacy of their teacher and establish a meditation center abroad. This is of course a rare occurrence but possible for those with a deep connection with their teacher and Thai Buddhism. Santikaro, translator of Buddhadasa Bhikkhu's work, has created a meditation retreat center called Liberation Park, in Wisconsin, USA, in homage to his late teacher. Liberation Park is a translation of Suan Mokkh, the name of the temple that Buddhadasa Bhikkhu established and where he was abbot from its founding in 1932 until his death in 1993. In 2006 Santikaro began this project in southwestern Wisconsin, which continues to grow through volunteer labor and donations. Liberation Park is a retreat center where meditators can reserve a space in this natural forested area and meditate on their own or with some guidance by Santikaro in the tradition of Suan Mokkh and Buddhadasa Bhikkhu. In this way Santikaro attempts to recreate his teacher's vision in his home country, dedicating this space to providing a natural setting for retreat and study.[4] As well, Santikaro teaches group retreats at centers throughout the USA. However, Santikaro does not follow the model of the International Dharma Hermitage, the retreat center connected with Wat Suan Mokkh that began after Buddhadasa Bhikkhu died. Instead, Santikaro follows a model more like that of Wat Suan Mokkh, providing an unstructured practice space rather than a regimented retreat schedule.

Other foreign meditation teachers who wish to move back to their home countries after teaching in Thailand, use connections with their students to continue their teaching. Rosemary and Steve Weissman of Wat Kow Tahm held their last retreat there in 2013, after twenty-five years of monthly retreats. Through email correspondence with them and some of their former students I learned of the ways their teaching continues abroad while they transitioned out of teaching in Thailand. Since then they have taken their unique lineage to Australia and offer retreats there and in Europe. Steve and Rosemary represent a unique trajectory of meditation lineages that is a mix of their Thai teachers, but does not follow

172　*The future of international meditation*

a particular one exclusively. They have taken their ten-and twenty-day retreat formats outside of Thailand, while the Wat Kow Tahm International Meditation Center still holds similar retreats with different teachers. The Weissmans have developed a wide network of students who have created a variety of ways to host their retreats in their home countries. Most of Rosemary and Steve's overseas retreats began with a former student inviting them to their home country to teach in their community. Some previous students worked at established centers and encouraged the managers to invite Steve and Rosemary. Others who had attended many retreats created the teaching opportunity for their teachers by renting facilities. While others still had only attended one retreat but were inspired to host Rosemary and Steve abroad and learn more.

Two students in particular, a couple who had acted as assistants for retreats at Wat Kow Tahm, Felix and Kathrin, established retreats in their native Switzerland by locating and renting a center when they moved back in 2012. Through their experience helping to organize and run the meditation center at Wat Kow Tahm, they felt confident they could manage a retreat in their home country. Old students of Rosemary and Steve as well as new students interested in meditation from Switzerland and other European countries attended. In this way connections with former students are crucial for teaching abroad and creating new communities. In fact when they arrived in Switzerland, Felix and Kathrin founded a 'Steve and Rosemary meditation group' in the first few weeks. The group has been growing ever since, with six to eight members attending on a regular basis. There are also Facebook pages created for past participants of the retreats at Wat Kow Tahm led by Rosemary and Steve. This is a way for participants with a common experience to keep in touch and support each other. This is also a way for supporters to come together to manage, administer, and find participants for Steve and Rosemary's retreats abroad. Members of the groups post about their newest retreats with Rosemary and Steve, let them know of upcoming retreats, and request help managing and organizing.

Besides establishing connections with previous students, new networks and communities can be created through media. The Middle Way Retreat, the international retreat outreach program of Wat Dhammakaya, has also created networks outside of Thailand. They do this through technology that appeals to modern discourses and makes the practice familiar. Anyone can attend their free online meditation sessions every Monday via live streaming on their 'iPeace Channel.' One official center was opened in 2013 in Iloilo, Philippines, where they hold meditation seminars, workshops and retreats. In addition to this, Dhammakaya Temple also has networks throughout the world, many of which are not temples but meditation centers offering Middle Way retreats.[5] Since 2013 these online sessions have been held every month to an average of twenty-five participants, most of whom have already participated in a Middle Way Retreat, while a minority found the online sessions through social media like Facebook. Making meditation available online and in centers outside of Thailand are some of the ways The Middle Way retreat keeps former participants involved and practicing when they are not living in Thailand. Weekly emails, monthly newsletters, and

The future of international meditation   173

an accessible website aim to make the retreat experience more than a one-time opportunity.

All of these examples illustrate how individual connections of student and teacher or even just a one-time participation in a retreat allow meditation methods and lineages to spread outside of Thailand. A single meditation practitioner can chance upon a center and teacher and create a relationship that leads to an annual meditation retreat in their home country. The availability of international meditation centers multiplies the circumstances in which Buddhism can adapt to new contexts, generating new interpretations and practices. These networks not only highlight the decreased significance of borders, but how new ideas and communities form. They illustrate that foreign travel among these teachers confers prestige and status. Especially for Thai teachers, the opportunity to have foreign students who sponsor their trips abroad and value their teachings enough to bring them to their home country, suggests that these teachers have important knowledge through effective teaching practices.

Propagating the *sāsana*

I have discussed missionization and propagation of Buddhism briefly in Chapters 6 and Chapter 7; however, here I wish to highlight the role of international meditation center teachers and their students in spreading meditation outside of Thailand within the context of Theravāda Buddhism. International meditation centers, along with opening the practice to foreigners from a Theravāda Buddhist perspective, help to protect and propagate the teachings, institutions and practices of Buddhism (*sāsana*). Although this is not explicitly addressed in materials surrounding international meditation centers, I argue propagating the *sāsana* constitutes the backdrop of the creation of these centers.

Within Theravāda Buddhism the idea of decline of the *sāsana* is pervasive. It is thought that the *sāsana* will eventually disappear, but it is also believed that the process can be slowed. In the Gotami Sutta[6] and the Saddhamapatirūpaka Sutta[7] the Buddha explains that the *sāsana* will not last forever. The exact time of this decline could be hastened or abated depending on the ways individuals, countries, and institutions enact Buddhist religiosity in their behavior and learning (Braun 2013, 70). Within Pāli texts there are numerous narratives discussing this point. One popular way to view the decline of the *sāsana* is within a 5,000 year scheme where every 1,000 years one of five things disappears: inability to attain insight, lack of monks living according to the *Vinaya*, loss of textual knowledge, lack of adherence to ascetic life, and disappearance of the Buddha's relics (Carbine 2011, 36). This scheme is found in the Visuddhimagga and has become authoritative in the Theravāda Southeast Asian world. The Sixth Buddhist Council held in 1954 marked the halfway point of the 5,000-year period and mainly discussed how to protect, sustain and propagate the *sāsana*. Ways to slow this decline include studying the scriptures, maintaining proper monastic practices, rituals, and ordinations, but also teaching and spreading Buddhism beyond the boundaries of one's community. In Southeast Asia rituals

174 *The future of international meditation*

such as ordination are performed not only so that a male can enter the monastic life but also to support the *sāsana*.

Support for international meditation centers is also a way to protect and propagate the *sāsana*. When laity supports these centers through donations that help build new accommodation, supply food for the meditators, or provide for the livelihood of the meditation teachers, they maintain centers of Buddhist practice and allow them to remain open and available for more international meditators. If Buddhist practice is spread throughout the world then the religion will not be in decline but instead thrive through this new audience. In a similar way that higher ordination is thought to prevent this decline through more people understanding and propagating the *sāsana*, in international meditation centers the *sāsana* is being spread beyond Theravāda Buddhists. International meditators, of course, cannot be considered to be on the same path as fully-ordained monks, but the idea of propagating the *sāsana* through ordination and through international meditators can be seen in similar ways.

As we saw in Chapter 2 in the context of Burma, lay meditation practice was thought to protect the *sāsana* during uncertain times of British rule. The colonial history of British rule and exile of the king in 1885, the most important promoter of Buddhism in the country, created an unstable and difficult period for maintaining the *sāsana* in Burma. Because it was believed that the *sāsana* was rapidly declining in this period, Thomas Patton describes how lay associations formed to spread religious educational programs and erect pagodas (Patton 2013, 119). This common purpose of spreading the *sāsana* was seen to be the most productive way to slow the decline of the *sāsana*. Erik Braun describes an example of this in his work on the Burmese monk Ledi Sayadaw, describing his attempts to strengthen the *sāsana* through writings and teachings to the laity about Buddhist philosophy and meditation (Braun 2013, 70). Ingrid Jordt writes that in Burma the *vipassanā* movement's "aim was to stem the decline itself by means of purifying the laity's own actions and mental intentions" (Jordt 2007, 25). In Thailand, lay meditation constituted a revival for the Mahanikai sect. Based on the replicable meditation method and Mahasi Sayadaw's meditation center model, Mahanikai branch temples throughout the country offered meditation teachings. Laity, through the rise of literacy and education in the middle class, had an interest in practicing meditation and becoming more involved in Buddhist practice (Cook 2010, 31). In Chapter 7 I discussed the relationship between missionizing practices in Thailand and the project of the international meditation center. Their connection lays in the ways both wandering forest monks and international meditation center teachers do not ask their audiences to convert or to give up any other religious or cultural practices. This follows the strategies of leading Buddhist figures such as Thich Nhat Hanh and the Dalai Lama who have not been known to engage in interreligious dialogue concerning theology or soteriology. Linda Learman affirms that instead they talk about world peace and other common goals of religious persons (Learman 2005, 4).

Buddhist missions have been characterized not by zeal or large-scale movements; rather individual monks have historically spread the Buddha's teachings and participated in conversion to a new worldview. Jonathan Walters asserts that compassion (*karuna*), not conversion, is the driving force of teaching Buddhism (Walters 2005, 6079). International meditation center teachers can be considered to transmit Buddhism within the accommodationist-assimilationist mode, which Richard Payne defines as a method "in which missionaries and congregations attempt to bring their own tradition into better consonance with the surrounding society" (Payne 2005, 102).[8] However, international meditation center teachers are not bringing the meditation practice to their students, but the international meditators come to their Thai Buddhist temples and receive a translated retreat program. As we saw earlier, however, some of this international travel of international meditators leads to teachers' journeys abroad to propagate to foreign communities.

In this way international meditation center teachers can be considered to be Buddhist missionaries, localizing the tradition for the international meditators. This interaction between student and teacher reveals that the international meditation center project aims not at converting non-Buddhists but encouraging them to experiment with meditation and imagine an alternative way of living. To do this international meditation center teachers must have not only some knowledge of English or an interpreter, but also a solid grasp of modern Buddhist discourses and other religious traditions. This propagation, as we have seen, requires innovative strategies of interpretation for these new audiences. In turn their students can also become propagators of the *sāsana* upon returning home.

The future of international meditation centers

In order to become a global practice, meditation had to be removed from its Buddhist worldview. The effects of this process can be seen in new combinations of meditation within non-Buddhist contexts. Wade Clark Roof writes that religion in the modern world "is often loosened from its traditional moorings—from history, creeds and doctrines, from broad, symbolic universes, from religious community" (Roof 1999, 109). Decontextualized forms of meditation have shaped the perception of Buddhism in modern global contexts. Scholars have found that as Buddhist teachings and movements globalize, specific strategies for inserting practices into new contexts need to be employed. Sor-Ching Low observes about the growth of the Soka Gakkai[9] movement and its global prominence that "this process of hermeneutical revisioning and remapping is part of a historical process of re-interpretation within tradition" (Low 2010, 28). Low argues that remapping and revisioning Buddhist concepts as well as decentering rituals from the historical and cultural specificity of its religious tradition serve to transcend the local in the midst of the effects of globalization (Low 2010, 28). Reimaginings of Buddhist meditation portrays a 'universal' practice, one that can be inserted into modern discourses throughout the world. Modern Buddhist writing often divides Buddhism into 'cultural' and 'universal' forms, and the most significant 'universal' aspect of Buddhism is its meditation practice. This opens up a way for practitioners to practice meditation as an abstract element of the tradition—divorced from other so-called 'cultural' practices. By taking part in a retreat while traveling abroad, one can easily add

176 *The future of international meditation*

vipassanā meditation to one's cultural or religious repertoire. Instead of locating Buddhism within a particular space, institution, belief system, or group of people, this work has demonstrated that imaginaries of Buddhism are central in creating and reinforcing modern Buddhist discourses.

As international meditation centers in Thailand continue to grow, they represent an important way that non-Buddhist tourists and travelers engage with the religion and culture. The history of the mass lay meditation movement demonstrates the trajectories through which international meditation centers became popular. The centers were created within these contingent historical conjunctures. A particular field of engagement became popular for international meditators through tourism patterns in Central, Northern, and Southern Thailand. Narratives of these tourists reveal that both Romantic and Rational Orientalism remain important motivations for engagement and for generating imaginaries of meditation. The importance of nature and meditation used for the purposes of therapy and well-being is seen within the particular ways international meditators engage with the retreat program of these centers. Long-term meditators illustrate the possibility of shifting imaginaries that more closely reflect those of Thai Buddhists. Promotional materials for meditation parallel these Orientalist imaginaries with advertisements indicating that meditation embodies both Romantic and Rational Orientalist discourses at the same time. This commodification of meditation allows for more creative possibilities and opportunities of practice for international meditators.

International meditation center teachers are an important component of the experience for international meditators. Student-teacher interactions comprise the first actual experiences of the meditation retreat, reflecting reality instead of an imaginary of meditation. As much as these teachers attempt to reflect modern Buddhist discourses through various pedagogical strategies, there are some aspects of the retreat that remain unexplained. This leaves room for subversion and dissent from the retreat model. As we have seen, international meditators do not always participate fully in the retreat. Because of the translation from the Thai retreat model for the international meditators, they are not compelled to embody the retreat fully. They often do not participate in the external activities such as bowing and chanting meant to cultivate humility and respect, although participating in devotional activities can aid in creating mindfulness apart from formal walking and sitting meditation. Many hours of meditation are the most significant part of the retreat, however, these minor aspects add up to create an experience of Thai Buddhism and the cultivation of values that meditation aims for. Through the selective performance of international meditators and translation of the retreat by their teachers to remove outward practices, international meditators are easily able to add *vipassanā* meditation to their religious and cultural repertoires. Rather than conversion, the international meditation center project aims at incorporation, of which there are many examples throughout Buddhist history.

International meditation centers continue to maintain their importance and increase their significance in Thai society and in Buddhist circles worldwide. Many centers where I have conducted research have waiting lists for group retreats and continue to add more accommodation in the mixed international and

The future of international meditation   177

Thai retreats. These centers affect Thai Buddhism abroad and help to shape the imaginaries of meditation. Although Thai Buddhists do not fully understand the motivations of their international counterparts, spreading lineages abroad and missionizing Buddhism to create new Buddhist communities are important results of the international meditation center project.

Notes

1 Pattana Kitiarsa discusses the transnationalization of Thai Buddhism through the entwined forces of "(1) the overseas Buddhist missionary policy and activity sponsored by the Sangha and the Office of National Buddhism under the Ministry of Culture (formerly known as the Department of Religious Affairs); (2) the growth of Thai migrant communities abroad and their strong ties to homeland; and (3) the growing global interest in Buddhism, particularly in Australia, Europe, and North America and subsequent travel and exchanges concerning Buddhist ordination and meditation as well as 'religious commodification.'"(Kitiarsa 2010, 111). This chapter looks at this third force in describing the transnationalization of Thai Buddhism.
2 More information on Hildegard Huber can be found here: www.vipassana-dhammacari.com/hilde_eng.html.
3 His personal website is www.marksawyersworld.com.
4 The website for this practice center is www.liberationpark.org.
5 More information on Wat Dhammakaya's international networks can be found here: www.dhammakaya.net/modules/centers/worldwide-centers.
6 This sutta is located in the Anguttara Nikāya, or The Numerical Discourses of the Sutta Pitaka of the Pāli Canon (AN 8.51).
7 This sutta is located in the Sutta Nipata, or The Sutta Collection of the Sutta Pitaka of the Pāli Canon (SN 16.13).
8 Payne lists other ways missionaries transmit Buddhism including "conservationist, in which missionaries and congregations attempt to retain what they perceive to be essential to their faith; [and] propagationist, in which missionaries attempt to draw in new disciples, revitalize existing adherents, or simply retain current members, by emphasizing the uniqueness and the superiority of what they have to offer over what is available in the surrounding community" (Payne 2005, 102).
9 Soka Gakkai is a new Buddhist religious movement started in Japan with practitioners and centers throughout the world. See Seager (2006).

Bibliography

Ahmad, Rafiq. 2011. "Orientalist Imaginaries of Travels in Kashmir: Western Representations of the Place and People." *Journal of Tourism and Cultural Change* 9 (3): 167–182.

Alabaster, Henry. 1971. *The Wheel of the Law: Buddhism*. Taipei, Taiwan: Ch'eng-Wen Publishing.

Almond, Philip. 1988. *The British Discovery of Buddhism*. Cambridge, MA & New York: Cambridge University Press.

Analāyo, Bhikkhu. 2008. *Satipatthana: The Direct Path to Realization*. Birmingham, UK: Windhorse.

Anderson, Benedict. 2006. *Imagined Communities*. Rev. ed. London & New York: Verso.

Appadurai, Arjun. 1986. "Introduction: Commodities and the Politics of Value." In *The Social Life of Things: Commodities in Cultural Perspective*, ed. Arjun Appadurai. Cambridge, UK: Cambridge University Press, pp. 3–63.

Arnold, Edwin. 1879. *The Light of Asia*. London: Trubner & Co.

Asad, Talal. 1993. *Genealogies of Religion: Discipline and Reasons of Power in Christianity and Islam*. Baltimore, MD: Johns Hopkins University Press.

_____. 1996. "Comments on Conversion." In *Conversion to Modernities: The Globalization of Christianity*, ed. Peter Van der Veer. New York: Routledge, pp. 263–274.

_____. 2003. *Formations of the Secular: Christianity, Islam, Modernity*. Stanford, CA: Stanford University Press.

Aupers, Stef & Dick Houtman. 2010. "Religions of Modernity: Relocating the Sacred to the Self and the Digital." In *Religions of Modernity: Relocating the Sacred to the Self and the Digital*, eds. Dick Houtman & Stef Aupers. Leiden, Netherlands & Boston, MA: Brill, pp. 1–30.

Austin-Broos, Diane. 2003. "The Anthropology of Conversion: An Introduction." In *Anthropology of Religious Conversion*, eds. Andrew Bucker & Stephen Glazier. Oxford & Lanham, MD: Rowman & Littlefield Publishers, pp. 1–12.

Azurra. 2007. "My Suan Mokkh Experience" Travel Pod Website. www.travelpod.com/travel-blog-entries/azurra/se_asia_2007/1194878220/tpod.html. Accessed 5/20/2011.

Baltruschat, Dieter. 2007. "Meditation in Southeast Asia." Katharina Titkemeyer, trans. www.retreat-infos.de/Download/RFAE2007.pdf. Accessed 5/1/2011.

Bangkok Post, no author. 2009. "Meditation Hub Planned for Thailand". www.bangkokpost.com/business/tourism/24718/meditation-hub-planned. Published 09/29/2009 at 12:00am. Accessed 5/1/2011.

Baudrillard, Jean. 1998. *The Consumer Society: Myths and Structures*. London & Thousand Oaks, CA: Sage Publications.

Baumann, Martin. 1994. "The Transplantation of Buddhism to Germany: Processive Modes and Strategies of Adaptation." *Method & Theory in the Study of Religion* 6 (1): 35–61.

Bibliography   179

_____. 1995. "Creating a European Path to Nirvana: Historical and Contemporary Developments of Buddhism in Europe." *Journal of Contemporary Religion* 10 (1): 55–70.

_____. 1997. "Culture Contact and Valuation: Early German Buddhists and the Creation of a 'Buddhism in Protestant Shape.'" *Numen* 44 (3): 270–294.

_____. 2001. "Global Buddhism: Developmental Periods, Regional Histories, and a New Analytical Perspective." *Journal of Global Buddhism* 2: 1–43.

_____. 2002. "Protective Amulets and Awareness Techniques, or How to Make Sense of Buddhism in the West." In *Westward Dharma: Buddhism Beyond Asia*, eds. Martin Baumann & Charles S. Prebish. Berkeley, CA & London: University of California Press, pp. 51–65.

_____. 2012. "Modernist Interpretations of Buddhism in Europe." In *Buddhism in the Modern World*, ed. David McMahan. New York: Routledge, pp. 113–136.

Bell, Catherine. 1992. *Ritual Theory, Ritual Practice*. Oxford: Oxford University Press.

_____. 2007. *Ritual: Perspectives and Dimensions*. Oxford & New York: Oxford University Press.

Bender, Courtney. 2010. *The New Metaphysicals: Spirituality and the American Religious Imagination*. Chicago: University of Chicago Press.

Berkwitz, Stephen, Juliane Schober, & Claudia Brown. 2009. "Introduction: Rethinking Buddhist Manuscript Cultures." In *Buddhist Manuscript Cultures: Knowledge, Ritual, and Art*, eds. Stephen Berkwitz, Juliane Schober, & Claudia Brown. Abingdon & New York: Routledge, pp. 1–16.

Blackburn, Anne. 2010. *Locations of Buddhism: Colonialism and Modernity in Sri Lanka*. Chicago: University of Chicago Press.

Bodhi, Bhikkhu. 1988. "A Look at the Kalama Sutta." Access to Insight Website. www.accesstoinsight.org/lib/authors/bodhi/bps-essay_09.html. Accessed 4/14/2012.

Bond, George. 1988. *The Buddhist Revival in Sri Lanka: Religious Tradition, Reinterpretation, and Response*. Columbia, SC: University of South Carolina Press.

Boorstein, Sylvia. 1996. *That's Funny, You Don't Look Buddhist: On Being a Faithful Jew and a Compassionate Buddhist*. San Francisco: HarperCollins.

Boucher, Sandy. 2005. *Dancing in the Dharma: The Life and Teachings of Ruth Denison*. Boston, MA: Beacon Press.

Bourdieu, Pierre. 1977. *Outline of a Theory of Practice*. Cambridge, UK: Cambridge University Press.

_____. 1993. *The Field of Cultural Production: Essays on Art and Literature*. New York: Columbia University Press.

Bourdieu, Pierre & Loïc J. D. Wacquant. 1992. *An Invitation to Reflexive Sociology*. Chicago: University of Chicago Press.

Bowers, Jeffrey. 1996. *Dhammakaya Meditation in Thai Society*. Bangkok, Thailand: Chulalongkorn University Press.

Braun, Erik. 2008. "Ledi Sayadaw, Abhidhamma, and the Development of the Modern Insight Meditation Movement in Burma." Ph.D. Dissertation, Harvard University.

_____. 2013. *The Birth of Insight: Meditation, Modern Buddhism, and the Burmese Monk Ledi Sayadaw*. Chicago: University of Chicago Press.

Bruce, Steve. 1996. *Religion in the Modern World: From Cathedrals to Cults*. Oxford: Oxford University Press.

Bruner, Edward. 1991. "Transformation of Self in Tourism." *Annals of Tourism Research* 18 (2): 238–250.

Buddhadasa Bhikkhu. 2001. *Mindfulness with Breathing: A Manual for Serious Beginners*. Santikaro, trans. Chiangmai, Thailand: Silkworm Books.

180 *Bibliography*

Buddhaghosa, Bhandatacariya. 2011. *Visuddhimagga: The Path of Purification*. Bhikkhu Nanamoli, trans. Kandy, Sri Lanka: Buddhist Publication Society.

Buswell, Robert E. & Donald S. Lopez. 2013. *Princeton Dictionary of Buddhism*. Princeton, NJ: Princeton University Press.

Cadge, Wendy. 2005. *Heartwood: The First Generation of Theravada Buddhism in America*. Chicago: University of Chicago Press.

Campbell, Patricia. 2010. "Transforming Ordinary Life: Turning to Zen Buddhism in Toronto." In *Wild Geese: Buddhism in Canada*, eds. John S. Harding, Victor Sogen Hori, & Alexander Soucy. Montreal & Kingston, Canada: McGill-Queen's University Press, pp. 187–209.

———. 2011. *Knowing Body, Knowing Mind: Ritualizing and Learning at Two Buddhist Centers*. New York: Oxford University Press.

Carbine, Jason. 2011. *Sons of the Buddha: Continuities and Ruptures in a Burmese Monastic Tradition*. Berlin & New York: Walter de Gruyter.

Carrette, Jeremy & Richard King. 2005. *Selling Spirituality: The Silent Takeover of Religion*. New York & London: Routledge.

Carrithers, Michael. 1983. *The Forest Monks of Sri Lanka: An Anthropological and Historical Study*. New Delhi, India: Oxford University Press.

Casanova, Jose. 1994. *Public Religions in the Modern World*. Chicago: University of Chicago Press.

Cassaniti, Julia. 2006. "Toward a Cultural Psychology of Impermanence in Thailand." *Ethos: The Journal of Psychological Anthropology* 34 (1): 58–88.

Cate, Sandra. 2003. *Making Merit, Making Art: A Thai Temple in Wimbledon*. Honolulu, HI: University of Hawai'i Press.

Chakrabarty, Dipesh. 2010. "Foreword." In *The Ambiguous Allure of the West: Traces of the Colonial in Thailand*, eds. Rachel V. Harrison & Peter A. Jackson. Hong Kong: Hong Kong University Press, pp. vii–xviii.

Chatterjee, Partha. 2003. *The Nation and Its Fragments: Colonial and Postcolonial Histories*. Princeton, NJ: Princeton University Press.

Cheah, Joseph. 2004. "Negotiating Race and Religion in American Buddhism: Burmese Buddhism in California." Ph.D. Dissertation, Graduate Theological Union.

———. 2011. *Race and Religion in American Buddhism: White Supremacy and Immigrant Adaptation*. Oxford: Oxford University Press.

Chen, Kenneth. 1973. *The Chinese Transformation of Buddhism*. Princeton, NJ: Princeton University Press.

Cho, Francesca. 2012. "Buddhism and Science: Translating and Re-translating Culture." In *Buddhism in the Modern World*, ed. David McMahan. New York: Routledge, pp. 273–288.

Clasquin, Michel & J.S. Kruger, eds. 1999. *Buddhism and Africa*. Pretoria, SA: Unisa Press.

Clifford, James. 1997. *Routes: Travel and Translation in the Late Twentieth Century*. Cambridge, MA: Harvard University Press.

Cohen, Erik. 2001. *Thai Tourism: Hill Tribes, Islands and Open-Ended Prostitution*. Bangkok, Thailand: White Lotus Press.

Collins, Steven. 1990. "On the Very Idea of the Pali Canon." *Journal of the Pali Text Society* XV: 89–126.

———. 1994. "What Are Buddhists Doing When They Deny the Self?" In *Religion and Practical Reason: New Essays in the Comparative Philosophy of Religions*, eds. Frank E. Reynolds & David Tracy. Albany, NY: State University of New York Press, pp. 59–86.

———. 1997. "The Body in Theravada Buddhist Monasticism." In *Religion and the Body*, ed. Sarah Coakley. Cambridge, UK: Cambridge University Press, pp. 185–204.

_____. 2012. "Pāli Practices of the Self." Keynote Address of the Theravāda Civilizations Project, University of Toronto, Canada. March 10, 2012.

Confalonieri, Pierluigi, ed. 2006. *The Clock of Vipassana Has Struck: A Tribute to the Saintly Life and Legacy of a Lay Master of Vipassana Meditation*, 2nd ed. Isatpuri, India: Vipassana Research Institute.

Cook, Joanna. 2010. *Meditation in Modern Buddhism: Renunciation and Change in Thai Monastic Life*. Cambridge, UK: Cambridge University Press.

_____. 2012. "Power, Protection and Perfectability: Aspiration and Materiality in Thailand." In *Southeast Asian Perspectives on Power*, ed. Liana Chua. London & New York: Routledge, pp. 37–50.

Cousins, Lance. 1973. "Buddhist Jhāna: Its Nature and Attainment According to the Pali Sources." *Religion* 3 (2): 115–131.

_____. 1996. "The Origins of Insight Meditation." *The Buddhist Forum* 4: 35–58.

Cox, Laurence. 2013. *Buddhism and Ireland: From the Celts to the Counter-Culture and Beyond*. Sheffield, UK: Equinox Publishing Limited.

Crosby, Kate. 2000. "Tantric Theravāda: A Bibliographic Essay on the Writings of François Bizot and Others on the Yogāvacara Tradition." *Contemporary Buddhism* 1 (2): 141–198.

_____. 2005. "Devotion to the Buddha in Theravada and Its Role in Meditation." In *The Intimate Other: Love Divine in Indic Religions*, eds. Anna S. King & John Brockington. New Delhi, India: Orient Longman, pp. 244–277.

_____. 2013. *Theravada Buddhism: Continuity, Diversity, and Identity*. Malden, MA & Oxford: Wiley Blackwell.

Cummings, Joe. 1991. *The Meditation Temples of Thailand: A Guide*. Woodacre, CA: Spirit Rock Center.

Dann, Caron Eastgate. 2008. *Imagining Siam: A Travellers' Literary Guide to Thailand*. Victoria, Australia: Monash University Press.

Dann, Graham. 1996. "The People of Tourist Brochures." In *The Tourist Image: Myths and Myth Making in Tourism*, ed. Tom Selwyn. Chichester, UK & New York: Wiley, pp. 61–82.

Davies, Serena. No date. "Bliss Out with a Meditation Holiday in Thailand." iVillage UK Website.www.ivillage.co.uk/bliss-out-a-meditation-holiday-in-thailand/82575?field_pages=0. Accessed 5/21/2011.

Dhammanada, Bhikkhuni. No date. *Meditation for Buddhists and Christians*. Nakhon Pathom, Thailand: Wat Songdhammakalyani.

_____. 2008. *Training the Monkey Mind*. Bangkok, Thailand: KerdThai.

Dhammasakiyo, Phra Dr. Anil. 2010. "A Modern Trend of Study of Buddhism in Thailand: King Mongkut and Dhammayutikanikāya." https://sujato.files.wordpress.com/2010/02/mongkut-and-dhammayut-modern-trend.pdf. Accessed 12/10/2013.

Dipabhavan Meditation Center Website. No date. "Retreat Guidelines." www.dipabhavan.com/index.php?lay=show&ac=article&Id=538637615. Accessed 7/10/2010.

Eberhardt, Alfred. 2010. "Investigate Buddhism for Healthy Mind, Body." *The Nation*. Published 09/11/2010. www.nationmultimedia.com/home/Investigate-Buddhism-for-healthy-mind-body-30137727.html. Accessed 8/2/2011.

Eberhardt, Nancy. 2006. *Imagining the Course of Life: Self-Transformation in a Shan Buddhist Community*. Honolulu, HI: University of Hawai'i Press.

Edensor, Tim. 1998. *Tourists at the Taj: Performance and Meaning at a Symbolic Site*. London & New York: Routledge.

Edwards, Nicholas. 2009. "The Retreat at Wat Rampoeng." Travel Blog Website. www.travelblog.org/Asia/Thailand/North-West-Thailand/Chiang-Mai/blog-457594.html. Accessed 5/26/2011.

182 *Bibliography*

Ehrenreich, Barbara. 2010. *Bright-Sided: How Positive Thinking Is Undermining America*. New York: Picador.

Engler, Jack. 2003. "Being Somebody and Being Nobody: A Reexamination of the Understanding of Self in Psychoanalysis and Buddhism." In *Psychoanalysis and Buddhism: An Unfolding Dialogue*, ed. Jeremy D. Safran. Somerville, MA: Wisdom Publications, pp. 35–79.

Erni, Christian, ed. 2008. *The Concept of Indigenous Peoples in Asia: A Resource Book*. Copenhagen, Denmark and Chiangmai, Thailand: IWGIA and AIPP.

Essen, Juliana. 2005. *Right Development: The Santi Asoke Buddhist Reform Movement of Thailand*. Lanham, MD: Lexington Books.

Evrard, Olivier & Prasit Leepreecha. 2009a. "Staging the Nation, Exploring the Margins: Domestic Tourism and Its Political Implications in Northern Thailand." In *Asia on Tour: Exploring the Rise of Asian Tourism*, eds. Tim Winter, Peggy Teo, & T.C. Chang. London & New York: Routledge, pp. 239–252.

_____. 2009b. "Monks, Monarchs and Mountain Folks: Domestic Tourism and Internal Colonialism in Northern Thailand." *Critique of Anthropology* 29 (3): 300–323.

Featherstone, Mike. 2007. *Consumer Culture and Postmodernism*, 2nd ed. London: Sage Publications.

Flickstein, Matthew. 2012. *The Meditator's Workbook: A Journey to the Center*. Somerville, MA: Wisdom Publications.

Foucault, Michel. 1978. *The History of Sexuality*. Robert Hurley, trans. New York: Pantheon Books.

_____. 1988. "Technologies of the Self." In *Technologies of the Self: A Seminar with Michel Foucault*, eds. Luther H. Martin, Huck Gutman, & Patrick Hutton. Amherst, MA: University of Massachusetts Press, pp. 16–49.

Freeman, Paul. 2009. "My Experience of Wat Suan Mokkh's 10 Day Meditation Retreat in Thailand." http://voyage-of-the-odd-essay.com/2009/01/14/my-experience-of-wat-suan-mokkhs-10-day-meditation-retreat-in-thailand/. Accessed 5/10/2011.

Fuengfusakul, Aphinya. 2012. "Urban Logic and Mass Meditation in Contemporary Thailand." In *Global and Local Televangelism*, eds. Pradip N. Thomas & Philip Lee. New York: Palgrave Macmillan.

Garrett, Lee. 2008. "Meditation at Wat Rampoeng." Travel Blog Website. www.travelblog.org/Asia/Thailand/North-West-Thailand/Chiang-Mai/blog-395373.html. Accessed 5/20/2011.

Garrigan, Paul. 2009. "Wat Rampoeng: Vipassana Meditation Retreat in Thailand." Associated Content by Yahoo Website. www.associatedcontent.com/article/2258497/wat_rampoeng_vipisanna_meditation_retreat_pg2.html?cat=16. Accessed 5/11/2011.

_____. 2010. *Dead Drunk: Saving Myself from Alcoholism in a Thai Monastery*. Dublin, Ireland: Maverick House Publishers.

Geary, David. 2008. "Destination Enlightenment: Branding Buddhism and Spiritual Tourism in Bodhgaya." *Anthropology Today* 24 (3): 11–14.

Gershon, Ilana. 2007. "Converting Meanings and the Meanings of Conversion in Samoan Moral Economies." In *The Limits of Meaning: Case Studies in the Anthropology of Christianity*, eds. Matthew Engelke & Matt Tomlinson. Oxford & New York: Berghahn Books, pp. 147–164.

Gethin, Rupert. 1998. *The Foundations of Buddhism*. Oxford: Oxford University Press.

Giddens, Anthony. 1990. *The Consequences of Modernity*. Stanford, CA: Stanford University Press.

Goddard, Dwight. 1966 [1938]. *A Buddhist Bible*. Boston, MA: Beacon Press.

Bibliography   183

Goenka, S.N. 1998. "On Goenkaji's Return to Myanmar (Burma)." In *Sayagyi U Ba Khin Journal: A Collection Commemorating the Teaching of Sayagyi U Ba Khin*. Maharashtra, India: Vipassana Research Institute, pp. 173–178.

Goldstein, Joseph. 2003. *One Dharma: The Emerging Western Buddhism*. New York: HarperCollins.

Gombrich, Richard. 1983. "From Monastery to Meditation Center: Lay Meditation in Contemporary Sri Lanka." In *Buddhist Studies Ancient and Modern*, eds. P. Denwood & A. Piatigorsky. London: Curzon Press, pp. 20–34.

Gombrich, Richard & Gananath Obeyesekere. 1988. *Buddhism Transformed: Religious Changes in Sri Lanka*. Princeton, NJ: Princeton University Press.

Greene, Stephen Lyon. 1999. *Absolute Dreams: Thai Government under Rama IV, 1910–1925*. Bangkok, Thailand: White Lotus Press.

Griffiths, Paul. 1981. "Concentration or Insight: The Problematic of Theravāda Buddhist Meditation-Theory." *The Journal of the American Academy of Religion* 49 (4): 606–624.

Gunaratana, Ven. Henepola. 1995. *The Path of Serenity and Insight: An Explanation of the Buddhist Jhanas*. Delhi, India: Motilal Banarsidass.

Gutschow, Kim. 2004. *Being a Buddhist Nun: The Struggle for Enlightenment in the Himalayas*. Cambridge, MA: Harvard University Press.

Hallisey, Charles. 1995. "Roads Not Taken in the Study of Theravada Buddhism." In *Curators of the Buddha: The Study of Buddhism under Colonialism*, ed. Donald S. Lopez. Chicago: University of Chicago Press, pp. 31–62.

Hamilton-Merrit, Jane. 1986. *A Meditator's Diary: A Western Woman's Unique Experiences in Thailand Monasteries*. London: Unwin Paperbacks.

Harding, John, Victor Hori, & Alexander Soucy, eds. 2010. *Wild Geese: Buddhism in Canada*. Quebec & Ontario, Canada: McGill-Queen's University Press.

———. 2014. *Flowers on the Rock: Global and Local Buddhisms in Canada*. Quebec & Ontario, Canada: McGill-Queen's University Press.

Harrison, Rachel V. 2010. "Introduction: The Allure of Ambiguity: The 'West' and the Making of Thai Identities." In *The Ambiguous Allure of the West: Traces of the Colonial in Thailand*, eds. Rachel V. Harrison & Peter Jackson. Hong Kong: Hong Kong University Press, pp. 1–36.

Hart, William. 1987. *The Art of Living: Vipassana Meditation as Taught by S.N. Goenka*. San Francisco: HarperCollins.

Heelas, Paul. 1996. *The New Age Movement: The Celebration of the Self and the Sacralization of Modernity*. Oxford: Blackwell.

Heelas, Paul & Linda Woodhead, eds. 2005. *Spiritual Revolution: Why Religion Is Giving Way to Spirituality*. Malden, MA & Oxford: Blackwell Publishing.

Hefner, Robert W. 1993. "World Building and the Rationality of Conversion." In *Conversion to Christianity: Historical and Anthropological Perspectives on a Great Transformation*, ed. Robert W. Hefner. Berkeley, CA & Oxford: University of California Press, pp. 3–46.

———. 1998. "Introduction." In *Market Cultures: Society and Morality in the New Asian Capitalisms*, ed. Robert W. Hefner. Boulder, CO: Westview Press, pp. 1–40.

Heim, Maria. 2013. *The Forerunner of All Things: Buddhaghosa on Mind, Intention, and Agency*. Oxford: Oxford University Press.

Hirschkind, Charles. 2006. *The Ethical Soundscape: Cassette Sermons and Islamic Counterpublics*. New York: Columbia University Press.

Holt, John. 2009. *Spirits of the Place: Buddhism and Lao Religious Culture*. Honolulu, HI: University of Hawai'i Press.

184 *Bibliography*

Hori, Victor Sogen. 1994. "Sweet-and-Sour Buddhism." *Tricycle* 4 (1): 48–52.

Houtman, Gustaaf. 1990. "Traditions of Buddhist Practice in Burma." Ph.D. Dissertation, School of Oriental and African Studies, London University.

Ingram, Daniel. 2008. *Mastering the Core Teachings of the Buddha: An Unusually Hardcore Dharma Book*. London: Aeon Books.

Ito, Tomomi. 2012. *Modern Thai Buddhism and Buddhadāsa Bhikkhu: A Social History*. Singapore: National University of Singapore Press.

Iwamura, Jane. 2011. *Virtual Orientalism: Asian Religions and American Popular Culture*. Oxford: Oxford University Press.

Jackson, Peter. 2003. *Buddhadasa: Theravada Buddhism and Modern Buddhist Reform in Thailand*. Chiangmai, Thailand: Silkworm Books.

_____. 2010. "The Ambiguities of Semicolonial Power in Thailand." In *The Ambiguous Allure of the West: Traces of the Colonial in Thailand*, eds. Rachel V. Harrison & Peter Jackson. Hong Kong: Hong Kong University Press, pp. 37–56.

Johnston, William. 1997 [1971]. *Christian Zen*. New York, San Francisco, & London: Harper & Row Publishers.

Jordt, Ingrid. 2007. *Burma's Mass Lay Meditation Movement: Buddhism and the Cultural Construction on Power*. Athens, OH: Ohio University Press.

Keane, Webb. 2007. *Christian Moderns: Freedom and Fetish in the Mission Encounter*. Berkeley, CA, Los Angeles, CA, & London: University of California Press.

Kemper, Steven. 2005. "Dharmapala's *Dharmaduta* and the Buddhist Ethnoscape." In *Buddhist Missionaries in the Era of Globalization*, ed. Linda Learman. Honolulu, HI: University of Hawai'i Press, pp. 22–50.

Keyes, Charles. 1993. "Why the Thai Are Not Christians: Buddhist and Christian Conversion in Thailand." In *Conversion to Christianity: Historical and Anthropological Perspectives on a Great Transformation*, ed. Robert W. Hefner. Berkeley, CA: University of California Press, pp. 259–284.

King, Richard. 1999. *Orientalism and Religion: Post-Colonial Theory, India, and "the Mystic East."* London & New York: Routledge.

Kitiarsa, Pattana. 2010. "Missionary Intent and Monastic Networks: Thai Buddhism as a Transnational Religion." *Sojourn: Journal of Social Issues in Southeast Asia* 25 (1): 109–32.

_____. 2012. *Mediums, Monks, and Amulets: Thai Popular Buddhism Today*. Chiangmai, Thailand: Silkworm Books.

Knitter, Paul. 2009. *Without Buddha I Could Not Be a Christian*. Oxford: Oneworld Publications.

Kornfield, Jack. 1978. *A Brief Guide to Meditation Temples in Thailand*. Bangkok, Thailand: World Fellowship of Buddhists.

_____. 2001. *After the Ecstasy, the Laundry: How the Heart Grows Wise on the Spiritual Path*. New York: Random House.

_____. 2007. "This Fantastic, Unfolding Experiment." *Buddhadharma Magazine*. Summer, 2007, pp. 32–39.

_____. 2008. *Wise Heart: A Guide to the Universal Teachings of Buddhist Psychology*. New York: Bantam Books.

_____. 2009. *A Path with Heart: A Guide through the Perils and Promises of Spiritual Life*. New York: Random House.

_____. 2010. *Living Dharma: Teachings and Meditation Instructions from Twelve Theravada Masters*. Boston, MA & London: Shambhala Publications.

_____. 2011. *A Lamp in the Darkness: Illuminating the Path through Difficult Times*. Boulder, CO: Sounds True.

_____. 2012. *Bringing Home the Dharma: Awakening Right Where You Are*. Boston, MA: Shambhala Publications.

Lang, Pierre. 2007. "Suan Mokkh: Ten Days Retreat in Monastery." Travel Pod Website. www.travelpod.com/travel-blogentries/pierrelang/career_break_07/1176293940/tpod.html#ixzz1LuyDS5QV. Accessed 5/10/2011.

Learman, Linda. 2005. *Buddhist Missionaries in the Era of Globalization*. Honolulu, HI: University of Hawai'i Press.

Lester, Rebecca, J. 2005. *Jesus in Our Wombs: Embodying Modernity in a Mexican Convent*. Berkeley & Los Angeles, CA: University of California Press.

Lopez, Donald S. 1995. "Introduction." In *Curators of the Buddha: The Study of Buddhism under Colonialism*, ed. Donald S. Lopez. Chicago: University of Chicago Press, pp. 1–30.

_____. 2002. "Introduction." In *A Modern Buddhist Bible*, ed. Donald S. Lopez. Boston, MA: Beacon Press, pp. viii–xli.

_____. 2008. *Buddhism and Science: A Guide for the Perplexed*. Chicago: University of Chicago Press.

Low, Sor-Ching. 2010. "The Re-invention of Nichiren in an Era of Globalization: Remapping the Sacred." *Journal of Global Buddhism* 11: 27–43.

MacInnes, Elaine. 2003. *Zen Contemplation for Christians*. Lanham, MD: Rowman & Littlefield Publishers, Inc.

McAra, Sally. 2007. *Land of Beautiful Vision: Making a Buddhist Sacred Place in New Zealand*. Honolulu, HI: University of Hawai'i Press.

McDaniel, Justin. 2006. "Buddhism in Thailand: Negotiating the Modern Age." In *Buddhism in World Cultures: Contemporary Perspectives*, ed. Stephen Berkwitz. Santa Barbara, CA: ABC-CLIO, pp. 101–128.

_____. 2008. *Gathering Leaves and Lifting Words: Histories of Buddhist Monastic Education in Laos and Thailand*. Seattle, WA & London: University of Washington Press.

_____. 2011. *The Lovelorn Ghost and the Magical Monk: Practicing Buddhism in Modern Thailand*. New York: Columbia University Press.

McMahan, David. 2008. *The Making of Buddhist Modernism*. Oxford: Oxford University Press.

_____. 2010. "Review" *Buddhism and Science: A Guide for the Perplexed*, Donald S. Lopez, Jr. *Journal of the American Academy of Religion* 78 (3): 855–858.

Mahmood, Saba. 2005. *The Politics of Piety: The Islamic Revival and the Feminist Subject*. Princeton, NJ: Princeton University Press.

Marx, Karl. 1912. *Capital, a Critique of Political Economy*. ed. Frederick Engels, trans. Samuel Moore & Edward Aveling. Chicago: Charles H. Kerr & Co.

Mendelson, Michael, E. 1975. *Sangha and State in Burma: A Study of Monastic Sectarianism and Leadership*. Ithaca, NY: Cornell University Press.

Metcalf, Franz. 2002. "The Encounter of Buddhism and Psychology." In *Westward Dharma: Buddhism Beyond Asia*, eds. Martin Baumann & Charles Prebish. Berkeley & Los Angeles, CA: University of California Press, pp. 324–347.

Meyer, Walter. 1988. *Beyond the Mask: Toward a Transdisciplinary Approach of Selected Social Problems Related to the Evolution and Context of International Tourism in Thailand*. Saarbrucken, Germany & Fort Lauderdale, FL: Verlag Breitenbach Publishers.

Miller, Vincent, J. 2005. *Consuming Religion: Christian Faith and Practice in a Consumer Culture*. London & New York: Bloomsbury Academic.

186 Bibliography

Mollier, Christine. 2008. *Buddhism and Taoism Face to Face: Scripture, Ritual, and Iconographic Exchange in Medieval China*. Honolulu, HI: University of Hawai'i Press.

Moore, Henrietta. 2011. *Still Life: Hopes, Desires and Satisfactions*. Cambridge, UK: Polity Press.

Moran, Peter. 2004. *Buddhism Observed: Travelers, Exiles and Tibetan Dharma in Kathmandu*. London & New York: Routledge.

Naeb, Mahaniranonda. 1982. *The Development of Insight*. Bangkok, Thailand: Abhidhamma Foundation.

Ñāṇamoli, Bhikkhu. 2010. "Introduction." In *Visuddhimagga: The Path of Purification*, Bhadantācariya Buddhaghosa, Bhikkhu Ñāṇamoli, trans. Kandy, Sri Lanka: Buddhist Publication Society, pp. xxvii–lv.

Nanarama Mahathera, Sri. 2010. *The Seven Stages of Purification and the Insight Knowledges*. Kandy, Sri Lanka: Buddhist Publication Society.

National Identity Board (Prime Minister's Office). 1988. *A Brief Guide to Buddhist Meditation Centres in Thailand*. Bangkok, Thailand: World Fellowship of Buddhists.

Newell, Catherine. 2008. "Monks, Meditation and Missing Links: Continuity, 'Orthodoxy,' and the *Vijja Dhammakaya* in Thai Buddhism." Ph.D. Dissertation, School of Oriental and African Studies, University of London.

Norris, Rebecca Sachs. 2003. "Converting to What? Embodied Culture and Adoption of New Beliefs." In *The Anthropology of Religious Conversion*, eds. Andrew Buckser & Stephen Glazier. Lanham, MD: Rowman & Littlefield Publishers, pp. 171–182.

Noy, Chaim. 2004. "This Trip Really Changed Me: Backpackers' Narratives of Self-Change." *Annals of Tourism Research* 31 (1): 78–102.

Nyanaponika Thera. 1996 [1954]. *The Heart of Buddhist Meditation*. Kandy, Sri Lanka: Buddhist Publication Society.

Nyanatiloka Thera. 2004. *Buddhist Dictionary: Manual of Buddhist Terms & Doctrines*. Kandy, Sri Lanka: Buddhist Publication Society.

Ooi, Can-Sen. 2010. "Histories, Tourism and Museums Re-making Singapore." In *Heritage Tourism in Southeast Asia*, eds. Micheal Hitchcock, Victor T. King, & Michael Parnwell. Copenhagen, Denmark: NIAS Press, pp. 83–102.

Pagis, Michal. 2008. "Cultivating Selves: Vipassana Meditation and the Microsociology of Experience." Ph.D. Dissertation, University of Chicago.

Pandita, Sayadaw U. 2012. *In This Very Life: Liberation Teachings of the Buddha*. Somverville, MA: Wisdom Publications.

Patton, Thomas. 2013. "Bearers of Wisdom, Sources of Power: Sorcerer-Saints and Burmese Buddhism." Ph.D. Dissertation, Cornell University.

Payne, Richard, K. 2005. "Hiding in Plain Sight: The Invisibility of the Shingon Mission to the United States." In *Buddhist Missionaries in the Era of Globalization*, ed. Linda Learman. Honolulu, HI: University of Hawai'i Press, pp. 101–123.

Peyvel, Emmanuelle. 2011. "Visiting Indochina, the Imaginary of the French Colonial Period in Today's Touristic Vietnam." *Journal of Tourism and Cultural Change* 9 (3): 226–236.

Pratt, Mary Louise. 2007. *Imperial Eyes: Travel Writing and Transculturation*. New York & London: Routledge.

Prebish, Charles. 1999. *Luminous Passage: The Practice and Study of Buddhism in America*. Berkeley, CA: University of California Press.

Prothero, Stephen. 1996. *The White Buddhist: The Asian Odyssey of Henry Steel Olcott*. Bloomington, IN: Indiana University Press.

Queen, Christopher. 1999. "Introduction." In *American Buddhism: Methods and Findings in Recent Scholarship*, eds. Duncan Ryūken Williams & Christopher Queen. London & New York: RoutledgeCurzon, pp. xiv–xxxvii.

Bibliography 187

Queen, Christopher & Duncan Ryūken Williams, eds. 1999. *American Buddhism: Methods and Findings in Recent Scholarship*. London & New York: RoutledgeCurzon.

Quest. 2010. "10 Days of Silence, Meditation, and Monastic Life." Travel Pod Website. www.travelpod.com/travel-blogentries/quest/1/1270984065/tpod.html#ixzz1LuzGucw3. Accessed 5/10/2011.

Rafael, Vicente. 1987. "Confession, Conversion, and Reciprocity in Early Tagalog Colonial Society." *Comparative Studies in Society and History* 29 (2): 320–339.

_____. 1998. *Contracting Colonialism: Translation and Christian Conversion in Tagalog Society under Early Spanish Rule*. Ithaca, NY: Cornell University Press.

Rajyanvisith, Dr. Phra Barton. 2009. *The Heart of Dhammakaya Meditation: Volume 1*, 3rd ed. Rajburi, Thailand: Wat Luang Por Sot.

Rambo, Lewis. 1993. *Understanding Religious Conversion*. New Haven, CT: Yale University Press.

Ray, Reginald. 1994. *Buddhist Saints in India: A Study in Buddhist Values and Orientations*. New York: Oxford University Press.

Reynolds, Craig. 1972. "The Buddhist Monkhood in Nineteenth Century Thailand." Ph.D. Dissertation, Cornell University.

_____, trans. 1979. *Autobiography: The Life of Prince-Patriarch Vajiranana of Siam, 1860–1921*. Athens, OH: Ohio University Press.

Reynolds, Frank. 1977. "Civic Religion and National Community in Thailand." *Journal of Asian Studies* 36 (2): 267–282.

Rhys-Davids, Caroline. 1914. *Buddhist Psychology: An Inquiry into the Analysis and Theory of Mind in Pali Literature*. London: G. Bell and Sons, Ltd.

Robbins, Joel. 2011. "Crypto-Religion and the Study of Cultural Mixtures: Anthropology, Value, and the Nature of Syncretism." *Journal of the American Academy of Religion* 79 (2): 408–424.

Rocha, Cristina. 2006. *Zen in Brazil: The Quest for Cosmopolitan Modernity*. Honolulu, HI: University of Hawai'i Press.

Rocha, Cristina & Michelle Barker, eds. 2011. *Buddhism in Australia: Traditions in Change*. Abingdon, UK & New York: Routledge.

Roof, Wade Clark. 1999. *Spiritual Marketplace: Baby Boomers and the Remaking of American Religion*. Princeton, NJ: Princeton University Press.

Rubel, Paula & Abraham Rosman. 2003. "Introduction: Translation and Anthropology." In *Translating Cultures: Perspectives on Translation and Anthropology*, eds. Paula Rubel & Abraham Rosman. London: Bloomsbury Academic, pp. 1–24.

Said, Edward. 1978. *Orientalism*. New York: Pantheon.

Salazar, Noel. 2010. *Envisioning Eden: Mobilizing Imaginaries in Tourism and Beyond*. Oxford & New York: Berghahn Books.

_____. 2012. "Tourism Imaginaries: A Conceptual Approach." *Annals of Tourism Research* 39 (2): 863–882.

Salzberg, Sharon. 1999. *A Heart as Wide as the World: Stories on the Path of Lovingkindness*. Boston, MA: Shambala Publications.

_____. 2002. *Lovingkindness: The Revolutionary Art of Happiness*. Boston, MA: Shambala Publications.

Samuels, Jeffrey. 2003. "Establishing the Basis of the *Sasana*: Social Service and Ritual Performance in Contemporary Sri Lankan Monastic Training." In *Approaching the Dhamma: Buddhist Texts and Practices in South and Southeast Asia*, eds. Anne M. Blackburn & Jeffrey Samuels. Seattle, WA: BPS Pariyatti Publications, pp. 105–124.

Sanger, Annette. 1988. "Blessing or Blight? The Effects of Touristic Dance-Drama on Village Life in Singapadu, Bali." In *Come mek me hol' yu han': The Impact of Tourism*

188 Bibliography

on *Traditional Music*. Papers presented at ICTM Colloquium in Jamaica, 1986. Kingston, Jamaica: Memory Bank, pp. 89–104.

Santikaro, Bhikku. 2001a. "Translator's Introduction." In *Mindfulness with Breathing: A Manual for Serious Beginners*, Buddhadasa Bhikkhu. Chiangmai, Thailand: Silkworm Books, pp. xv–xx.

_____. 2001b. "Translator's Conclusion: Summary and Suggestions for Practice." In *Mindfulness with Breathing: A Manual for Serious Beginners*, Buddhadasa Bhikkhu. Chiangmai, Thailand: Silkworm Books, pp. 109–134.

Sayadaw, Mahasi. 1972. *Practical Insight Meditation*. Kandy, Sri Lanka: Buddhist Publication Society.

_____. 1994. *The Progress of Insight: A Treatise on Satipatthana Meditation*. Nyanaponika Thera, trans. Kandy, Sri Lanka: Buddhist Publication Society.

Schedneck, Brooke. 2010. "Sovereign Yet Subordinate: The Use of Buddhist Discourse during the Reigns of King Rama IV, V, and VI in Siam (1851–1925)." *Explorations: A Graduate Student Journal of Southeast Asian Studies* 10 (Spring): 23–31.

_____. 2013. "Enacting Female Buddhist Roles through *Vipassanā* Meditation Centers." Paper presented at the 13th Sakyadhita Conference on Women. Vaishali, India January 8, 2013.

_____. 2013. "Tourism, Nature, Healing, and Dissent: The Plurality of International Meditators in Thailand." *Rian Thai: International Journal of Thai Studies* 6 (3): 1–24.

_____. 2014. "Meditation for Tourists in Thailand: Commodifying a Universal and National Symbol." *Journal of Contemporary Religion* 29 (3): 439–456.

Schober, Juliane. 1995. "The Theravada Buddhist Engagement with Modernity in Southeast Asia: Whither the Social Paradigm of the Galactic Polity?" *Journal of Southeast Asian Studies* 26 (2): 307–325.

Scott, Rachelle M. 2009. *Nirvana for Sale: Buddhism, Wealth, and the Dhammakaya Temple in Contemporary Thailand*. Albany, NY: State University of New York Press.

Seager, Richard Hughes. 2006. *Encountering the Dharma: Daisaku Ikeda, Soka Gakkai, and the Globalization of Buddhist Humanism*. Berkeley & Los Angeles, CA: University of California Press.

Shankman, Richard. 2008. *The Experience of Samadhi: An In-Depth Exploration of Buddhist Meditation*. Boston, MA & London: Shambhala Publications.

Shapiro, Dani. 2010. "PS." In *Devotion: A Memoir*. New York: Harper Perennial, pp. 6–8.

Sharf, Robert. 1995. "Buddhist Modernism and the Rhetoric of Meditative Experience." *Numen* 42 (3): 228–283.

_____. 2002. *Coming to Terms with Chinese Buddhism: A Reading of the Treasure Store Treatise*. Honolulu, HI: University of Hawai'i Press.

Shaw, Sarah. 2006. *Buddhist Meditation: An Anthology of Texts from the Pāli Canon*. London & New York: Routledge.

Silananda, Sayadaw U. 2002. *The Four Foundations of Mindfulness*, ed. Heinze, Ruth-Inge. Boston, MA & London: Shambhala Publications.

Sinha, Vineeta. 2011. *Religion and Commodification: "Merchandizing" Diasporic Hinduism*. New York & London: Routledge.

Sirikanchana, Pataraporn. 2004. *A Guide to Buddhist Monasteries and Meditation Centres in Thailand*. Bangkok, Thailand: World Fellowship of Buddhists.

Sivaraksa, Sulak. 1992. *Seeds of Peace: A Buddhist Vision for Renewing Society*. Berkeley, CA: Parallax Press.

Bibliography 189

Skilton, Andrew. 2013. "Elective Affinities: The Reconstruction of a Forgotten Episode in the Shared History of Thai and British Buddhism—Kapilavaddho and Wat Paknam." *Contemporary Buddhism* 14 (1): 149–168.

Smith, Christian. 2003. *The Secular Revolution: Power, Interests, and Conflict in the Secularization of American Public Life*. Berkeley, CA: University of California Press.

Snyder, Tina & Stephen Rasmussen. 2009. *Practicing the Jhānas: Traditional Concentration Meditation as Presented by the Venerable Pa Auk Sayadaw*. Boston, MA & London: Shambhala Publications.

Soma Thera. 1967. *The Way of Mindfulness*. Kandy, Sri Lanka: Buddhist Publication Society.

_____. 1998. "The Way of Mindfulness: The Satipatthana Sutta and Its Commentary." Access to Insight Website (Legacy Edition). www.accesstoinsight.org/lib/authors/soma/wayof.html. Accessed 3/14/2014.

Soontravanich, Chalong. 2013. "The Regionalization of Local Buddhist Saints: Amulets, Crime, and Violence in Post World War II Thai Society." *Sojourn: Journal of Social Issues in Southeast Asia* 28 (2): 179–215.

Spuler, Michelle. 2003. *Developments in Australian Buddhism: Facets of the Diamond*. New York & London: RoutledgeCurzon.

Stewtchell, Jen. 2008. "Meditation Bootcamp: The Story of Two Meditation Dropouts." Living Spree Website. http://livingspree.wordpress.com/2008/11/14/meditation-boot-camp/. Accessed 5/20/2011.

Sutcliffe, Steven & Marion Bowman. 2000. *Beyond New Age: Exploring Alternative Spirituality*. Edinburgh, Scotland: Edinburgh University Press.

Swearer, Donald. 1989. "Introduction." In *Me and Mine: Selected Essays of Bhikkhu Buddhadasa*, ed. Donald Swearer. Albany, NY: State University of New York Press, pp. 1–13.

_____. 1995. "The Way of Meditation." In *Buddhism in Practice*, ed. Donald S. Lopez. Princeton, NJ: Princeton University Press, pp. 207–215.

_____. 2010. *The Buddhist World of Southeast Asia*. Albany, NY: State University of New York Press.

Tambiah, Stanley. 1984. *The Buddhist Saints of the Forest and the Cult of Amulets: A Study in Charisma, Hagiography, Sectarianism, and Millenial Buddhism*. Cambridge, UK & New York: Cambridge University Press.

Taylor, Charles. 1989. *Sources of the Self: The Making of the Modern Identity*. Cambridge, MA: Harvard University Press.

_____. 2003. *Varieties of Religion Today: William James Revisited*. Cambridge, MA: Harvard University Press.

_____. 2007. *A Secular Age*. Cambridge, MA: Harvard University Press.

_____. 2009. "Western Secularity." In *Rethinking Secularism*, eds. Craig Calhoun, Mark Juergensmeyer, & Jonathan Van Antwerpen. Oxford & New York: Oxford University Press, pp. 31–53.

Taylor, James. 1993. *Forest Monks and the Nation-State: An Anthropological and Historical Study in Northeast Thailand*. Singapore: Institute of Southeast-Asian Studies.

_____. 2008. *Buddhism and Postmodern Imaginings in Thailand: The Religiosity of Urban Space*. Surrey, UK & Burlington, VT: Ashgate Publishing.

Thai Visa Forum Website. 2009. "Help Me Choose Among 4 Centers for Meditation Retreat." Posted 8/4/2009. www.thaivisa.com/forum/topic/241648-help-me-choose-among-4-centers-for-meditation-retreat/page__st__25. Accessed 2/28/2010.

Thanissaro Bhikkhu. 2000. "Karma." Access to Insight Website (Legacy Edition). www.accesstoinsight.org/lib/authors/thanissaro/karma.html. Accessed 3/14/2014.

190 *Bibliography*

_____. 2005. "The Traditions of the Noble Ones: An Essay on the Thai Forest Tradition and Its Relationship with the Dhammayut Hierarchy." Paper presented at the Ninth International Thai Studies Conference, Northern Illinois University, Dekalb, IL.

_____. 2011. "One Tool among Many: The Place of Vipassana in Buddhist Practice." Access to Insight Website (Legacy Edition). www.accesstoinsight.org/lib/authors/thanissaro/onetool.html. Accessed 3/14/2014.

Tiyavanich, Kamala. 1997. *Forest Recollections: Wandering Monks in Twentieth-Century Thailand.* Honolulu, HI: University of Hawai'i Press.

Tong Srimangalo, Ajahn. 2004. *The Only Way: An Introduction to Vipassanā Meditation.* The Disciples, trans. Chiangmai, Thailand: Wat Chom Tong.

Tourism Authority of Thailand Booklet. 2003. "Experience Buddhist Meditation." Printed in Thailand by Advertising Production Division, Tourism Authority of Thailand.

_____. 2008. "Meditation in Thailand: The Path to Inner Peace and Well-Being." http://issuu.com/diethelmtravel/docs/meditation. Accessed 5/1/2011.

_____. 2010. "Meditation in Thailand: Learn and Practice Buddhist Meditation in the Traditional Thai Surroundings." www.tourismthailand.org/meditation/. Accessed 5/1/2011.

Tourism Authority of Thailand E-Magazine. no date. "Thailand: Centre of Buddhist Learning and Traditions." www.tatnews.org/emagazine/2146.asp. Accessed 5/1/2011.

Tourism Authority of Thailand Website. no date. www.tourismthailand.org/about-tat/. Accessed 7/1/2011.

Tsing, Anna. 2005. *Friction: An Ethnography of Global Connection.* Princeton, NJ: Princeton University Press.

Tweed, Thomas. 1992. *The American Encounter with Buddhism 1844–1912: Victorian Culture and the Limits of Dissent.* Bloomington, IN: Indiana University Press.

_____. 2002. "Who Is a Buddhist? Night-Stand Buddhists and Other Creatures." In *Westward Dharma: Buddhism Beyond Asia*, eds. Martin Baumann & Charles Prebish. Berkeley & Los Angeles, CA: University of California Press, pp. 17–33.

_____. 2008. *Crossing and Dwelling: A Theory of Religion.* Cambridge, MA: Harvard University Press.

Urry, John. 1995. *Consuming Places.* London & New York: Routledge.

_____. 2002. *The Tourist Gaze: Leisure and Travel in Contemporary Societies.* London & Thousand Oaks, CA: Sage Publications.

Van Esterik, John. 1977. "Cultural Interpretation of Canonical Paradox: Lay Meditation in a Central Thai Village." Ph.D. Dissertation, University of Illinois at Urbana-Champaign.

Vukonic, Boris. 2002. "Religion, Tourism and Economics: A Convenient Synthesis." *Tourism Recreation Research* 27 (2): 59–64.

Wallace, B. Alan. 2003. *Buddhism and Science: Breaking New Ground.* New York, Chichester & West Sussex, UK: Columbia University Press.

Walsh, Roger. 1981. "Speedy Western Minds Slow Slowly." *Revision* 4: 75–77.

Walters, Jonathan, S. 2005. "Missions: Buddhist Missions." In *Encyclopedia of Religion, Volume 1*, ed. Lindsey Jones. Detroit: MacMillan Reference USA, pp. 6077–6082.

Wannamethee, Phan. 2004. "Foreword." In *A Guide to Buddhist Monasteries and Meditation Centres in Thailand*, ed. Pataraporn Sirikanchana. Bangkok, Thailand: World Fellowship of Buddhists.

Ward, G. 2003. "The Commodification of Religion and the Consummation of Capitalism." *Hedgehog Review* 5 (2): 50–65.

Weir, Bill. 1991. *A Guide to Buddhist Monasteries and Meditation Centres in Thailand*, 3rd ed. Bangkok, Thailand: World Fellowship of Buddhists. www.hdamm.de/buddha/mdtctr01.htm. Accessed 5/1/2011.

Bibliography 191

Weissman, Steve. 2006. *Wise Reflection: The Importance of Yoniso Manasikara in Meditation*. Kandy, Sri Lanka: Buddhist Publication Society.

Weissman, Rosemary & Steve Weismann. 1999. *With Compassionate Understanding: A Meditation Retreat*. St. Paul, MN: Paragon House.

Wilson, Jeff. 2009. *Mourning the Unborn Dead: A Buddhist Ritual Comes to America*. Oxford: Oxford University Press.

Winichakul, Thongchai. 1994. *Siam Mapped: A History of the Geo-Body of a Nation*. Honolulu, HI: University of Hawai'i Press.

_____. 2000. "The Others Within: Travel and Ethno-Spatial Differentiation of Siamese Subjects 1885–1910." In *Civility and Savagery: Social Identity in Tai States*, ed. Andrew Turton. Richmond & Surrey, UK: RoutledgeCurzon, pp. 38–62.

Wongprasert, Sanit. 1988. "Impact of the Dhammacarik Bhikkhus' Programme on the Hill Tribes of Thailand." In *Ethnic Conflict in Buddhist Societies: Sri Lanka, Thailand, and Burma*, eds. K.M. De Silva, Pensri Duke, Ellen S. Goldberg, & Nathan Katz. Boulder, CO: Westview Press, pp. 126–137.

World Fellowship of Buddhists Website. no date. http://wfbhq.org/. Accessed 12/29/2011.

Yamashita, Shinji. 2003. *Bali and Beyond: Explorations in the Anthropology of Tourism*. Oxford & New York: Berghahn Books.

Zurcher, Erik. 2007. *The Buddhist Conquest of China*. Leiden, Netherlands: Brill.

Index

Abhidhamma 33, 38, 39, 71n
addiction 83
adjustment, international meditators 92
advertisements 103, 105, 106, 109–18,
    119–20, 124
Ahmon, Mae Chii 55
Alabaster, Henry 17
alcohol addiction 83
almsround ceremony 94
Americans 17, 64, 78, 127, 132, 170–1
amulets 18, 31, 39, 44n, 69, 105, 107–8,
    122n, 163
ānāpānasati 54, 117, 139
Ānāpānasati Sutta 27, 28–9, 41n, 54
anthropology of meditation 4–9
Appadurai, Arjun 4, 5
arhat 26, 28
ariya-puggala (Noble Ones) 26
Asad, Talal 3, 126, 151, 162
Australia 17, 171
'authenticity' 82, 105

Ba Khin, U 32, 34–6, 138
Bangkok 49–50
Bart, Phra (Barton Yanathiro, Khry (Khru)
    Baitika Dr.) 52–3, 72n, 131, 134, 136,
    147n
beaches 80–1
Bender, Courtney 18
bhavana meditation 31
blogs 76
BMI see Buddhist Meditation Institute
the body 28, 41n, 149–68
booklets 114–17
Bourdieu, Pierre 152

bowing 156, 158, 166
Braun, Erik 31, 32, 34, 35, 39, 122n, 129,
    147n, 173–4
breath: awareness of 29; long-breathing
    technique 83; mindfulness of 54
brochures see advertisements
Buddhadasa Bhikkhu 53–4, 88, 99, 138–9,
    171
Buddhaghosa 27, 29–30, 40n, 41–2n, 72n
Buddhasak, Phra Ajan 130–1, 147n, 156–
    7, 159, 167n
Buddhism: historical contexts 126–7;
    missionizing 160, 162–6, 174–5;
    modern 13–17; practices of the self 151
Buddhist Meditation Institute (BMI) 52–3
Burma (Myanmar) 32, 33–7, 39, 40n, 174

Carrette, Jeremy 158–9
Central Thailand 49–53
Chah, Ajan (Venerable Phra Bodhiñāna
    Thera) 49, 71n
chanting 93, 131, 156, 166
Cheah, Joseph 36–7, 126
choice, translation for 130–2, 143
Christianity: Buddhism comparison 4, 13,
    15, 139; conversions to 161;
    missionizing 163, 165; practices of the
    self 151–2, 159; translation and 135,
    140
Chulalongkorn, King 37
closing ceremony 9, 92, 95
clothing 157
Collins, Steven 41n, 137, 152–3
colonialism 10–11, 15, 33, 137
commodification 12–13, 23n, 103–23, 176

compassion (karuna) 175
consumerism 78, 107, 156
consumption, meditation 104–7
'contact zone', meditation translation
    124–5
conversion 160–2, 167n
Cook, Joanna 8–9, 153
cosmopolitanism 161
Crosby, Kate 25, 31, 40n, 41n, 72n
cultural differences 11, 70
Cummings, Joe 112, 123n
cycle of insight 14, 58, 141

daily practices 87–101
dāna 106, *see also* donations
DBP *see* Dhammacarik Bhikkhu
    Program
decontextualization: Buddhism 13, 159;
    meditation 3, 84, 175
defilements (kilesa) 25, 26, 32, 40n, 42n,
    118
determination period 89, 91
detox treatments 82
devotional activities 65–7, 77, 136, 140
Dhammacarik Bhikkhu Program (DBP)
    162, 166
Dhammakaya meditation 51–3, 72n
Dhammananda Bhikkhuni, Venerable
    165–6, 168n
dhammas, mindfulness of 28
dhamma talks 63, 93
Dhammavidu, Than 99
Dharmapala, Anagarika 129, 163
diet 93
difficulties with practice 91–2
dining halls 92–3
Dipabhavan Meditation Center 55–6, 65,
    81, 117, 139
discourse analysis, tourism 103–5
dissent 140–5
donations 66, 106

economy of merit 106, 121
early leaving, meditators 141–2
economy/meditation relationship 106–7
Eightfold Path 24
Eight Precepts 48, 71n, 131
embodying meditation 149–68
emotional trauma 83

engagement, international meditators
    45–74, 92
Engler, Jack 133
English instruction, temples 48
English language 48, 62, 93, 117
Enlightenment 24–7, 31, 32–4, 152
ethical practices 151
ethnography 3–5, 7–8, 128; meditation
    and 7–9, 151, 161
Euro–American meditators 64, 78
European meditators 17
exoticism: chanting 93; criticism and 95;
    imaginaries 11; meditation idea 89, 91;
    natural settings 82, 97
expectations, international meditators 88–90
experiential learning 128
external practices 157, 159

fear 90–1
feelings, mindfulness of 28
female teachers 63
field of engagement 45–74
fields of merit 66, 74n
fieldwork, author's experiences 5–6, 76
Five Hindrances 128, 147n
Five Precepts 31, 40n, 48, 131
flexibility, translations 126, 130
forest monks 38–9, 162–3, 166
forest tradition 37, 38–9, 41n, 43n, 44n,
    49, 60, 71, 162
Foucault, Michel 150
Four Foundations of Mindfulness 50–1,
    58, 128
Four Noble Truths 40n
Frank Gavesako, Phra 86

Giddens, Anthony 149
globalization 103, 146
Goenka, S.N. 36, 137–8, 147–8n
Gombrich, Richard 105
group retreats 53, 65, 96, 136
guidebooks, meditation 109–13

health 75, 82–4
Hirschkind, Charles 151–2
historical contexts: Buddhism's movement
    126–7; meditation centers 48–61;
    modern Buddhism 13, 15–17; vipassanā
    meditation 24–44

194 *Index*

Hoelscher, Reinhard 87
Holt, John 126
Houtman, Gustaaf 7

identities 22, 38, 104, 120, 149, 156;
   religious 3, 21, 22, 76, 130, 150, 160–3,
   167
images of meditation 118–20
imaginaries, meditation 9–12
impermanence (anicca) 26, 68
IMS *see* Insight Meditation Society
indigenous people 167–8n
individual choice, translation for 130–2
individualism 133–4, 158
individual retreats 65
inner practices 155
insight, cycle of 14, *see* cycle of insight
insight knowledge (ñana) 30, 128
Insight Meditation Society (IMS) 36
Insight Sharing 98–9
International Dhamma Hermitage 54–5,
   65, 77, 83, 87, 96–101, *see also* Wat
   Suan Mokkhabalarama
international meditation centers *see*
   meditation centers
international meditators 22n, 64–8;
   acceptance 112; changes for 146;
   conversion/religious identity 160–2;
   cultural differences 70; daily practices
   87–101; dissent/subversion 142–3;
   engagement with meditation centers
   45–74; experience narratives 75–102;
   interaction with teachers 8; interviews
   with 3, 6; make up of 1–2; other activity
   descriptions 92–5; practices of the self
   151, 154–60; regard for 68; researching
   17–19; translations for 125, 128
interviews 64, 92, 101n, 158
Islam 151–2, 159

jhāna states 25–7, 29, 40n, 102n
Jordt, Ingrid 8

kamma 66, 69, 73n, 74n, 106
Keane, Webb 140, 160
Keyes, Charles 162, 163, 166
King, Richard 158–9
Kitiarsa, Pattana 108
Kornfield, Jack 110, 122n, 132–3, 147n

language, culture and 126, *see also*
   English language
lay meditation/meditators: future of 176;
   lokkutara sphere 69; meditation centers
   47; popularity 2; practices of the self
   154; Thai meditators 64; vipassanā
   meditation 32–3, 35
lay teachers 62
lay understanding, Buddhism 18
learning, translations and 128
Ledi Sayadaw 34, 129
Lester, Rebecca 151
lineage 6, 15, 17, 25, 27, 36, 38, 41n, 43n,
   44n, 49, 51, 54–6, 61, 70–1, 144,
   169–71, 173, 177
listening 152
lokiya (worldly) sphere 69–70
lokkutara (world-transcending) sphere
   69–70
Lopez, Donald 14
Luangta, Ajan (Saayut Pannatharo, Phra
   Ajan) 60, 61, 62

McDaniel, Justin 19, 21, 108, 161–2, 166
McMahan, David 14, 22, 78, 130, 146
mae chii 8, 22n, 53, 63, 79, 85, 86, 99, 170
Mahabua (Ñānasampanno), Luangta 49
Mahanikai sect 37, 38
Mahasi Sayadaw 26–7, 32–4, 36, 38
Mahasi Thathana Yeiktha 8, 34–5
Mahmood, Saba 151
mantras (samma araham) 52
mass meditation movement 46
meditation centers: booklets 114, 116;
   concentration in Thailand 122n;; as
   'contact zone' 125; description of
   46–8; future of 169–77; guidebooks
   110–11; history/sites/meditation
   methods 48–61; international
   meditators' engagement with 45–74;
   origins 33; practices of the self 154;
   retreat pamphlets 117–18; sāsana
   propagating 173–4; teachers 61–4;
   tracking meditators 23n; translations
   within 126–8
meditation/economy relationship 106–7
meditation images 118–20
meditation methods 48–61; walking
   meditation 73n, 97, 143

meditation monks 31
meditators *see* international meditators
merit-making 65–7, 74n
middle classes 38
Middle Way Retreat 52, 86–7, 118, 121n, 172
mind: mindfulness of 28; states of 95
mindfulness 26, 28–9, 50–1, 54, 58, 128
missionizing Buddhism 160, 162–6, 174–5, 177n
modernity: Buddhism 13–17, 123n; conversion and 162; positive/negative aspects 115; reflexivity of 149; religion and 5, 130, 134, 137; secular translations 135; stress and 116; vipassanā meditation 24–44
monastics: ethnography 8; lokiya sphere 69; meditation center contrast 43n; merit-making 66; practices of the self 152–3; teachers 62–3; vipassanā meditation 31–2
Mongkut, Prince/King 15–17, 37
Moore, Henrietta 22, 103, 140
morality 24
Moran, Peter 105–6, 109, 122n, 148n
motivations, international meditators 88–90
mountain settings 80
Mun (Bhuridatta), Luangpu 39
Muslims *see* Islam
Myanmar (Burma) 32, 33–7, 39, 40n, 174

Naeb (Mahaniranonda), Ajan 49, 71n
narratives of meditation experiences 75–102
national symbol, meditation 103–23
nature 76–82, 96–8, 101
Nawi Piyadassi, Phra Ajan 59–60, 73n, 80, 139, 148n, 170–1
nervousness 90–1
nibbāna 24–7, 31, 32–4, 152
Noble Ones *see* ariya-puggala
non-self (anattā) 26, 68, 117–18
North America 17, *see also* Americans
Northern Thailand 56–61
Nu, U 34

Ofer (Adi), Phra (Phra Thiracitto) 85
online meditation sessions 172

opening ceremony 59, 68, 90–1, 155
ordination 85–6, 174
Orientalism 10–11; Rational Orientalism 10, 82, 84, 99, 114, 116; Romantic Orientalism 10, 103–4, 115–16
the Other 11, 89, 92, 97

pain 136–7
Pāli Canon 27–9
Pāli language 153
pamphlets 117–18, 119
Pau Auk Sayadaw 26
pedagogical techniques 124–48
Phimolatham, Phra 37–8, 44n
Pho, Ajan (Bodhi Buddhadhammo, Venerable Ajan) 53, 55, 72n, 80, 81, 139, 148n
piti (joy) 1, 25
Piyabhaso, Venerable 164–5
popular Buddhism 19
practices of the self 150–60
promotional materials 105, 109–18
propagating the sāsana 173–5
psychological translations 132–5
purifications 42n

Rational Orientalism 10, 82, 84, 99, 114, 116
reflexivity 149, 150
religion/religiosity: alternative forms of 3–4; anthropology of 5, 7; commodification 12–13; crisis of 132; expressions of 13; international meditators 19; modernity 130, 134, 137; practices of the self 151; reflexivity 150; rituals 156; temples 136; tourism and 12–13, 113; universal translation 138
religious differences, imaginaries 11
religious identity 160–2, *see also* identities
religious tourism 23n, 104, *see also* tourism
retreats: advertisements 120; Central Thailand 52; commodification 108–9; future of 171–2, 177; guidebooks 112; Northern Thailand 59; pamphlets 117–18; reflection on experience 95–6, 100–1; Southern Thailand 53, 55; types 65; vipassanā meditation 68, 124–6, 132, 135–6, 141–3

196 *Index*

Rhys-Davids, Caroline 129, 132
rituals, Buddhist 93–4, 136–7, 140, 153, 155–6
River, Luang Pi 86–7
Romantic gaze 120
Romanticism 75, 76–82, 97
Romantic Orientalism 10, 103–4, 115–16
rules, retreats 142–3

Salazar, Noel 4–5, 9, 109, 118
Salzberg, Sharon 36, 42n
samādhi 24, 27, 166, 168n
samatha meditation 25, 27, 29–31, 38
sampling meditation centers 86–7
Sander, Venerable 134, 147n
sangha 22n, 23n, 37, 42n, 162, 165, 177
Santikaro 171
sāsana 173–5
Satipaṭṭhāna meditation 27–9
Satipatthāna Sutta 41n, 50, 51, 54
schedule, International Dhamma Hermitage 98–9
Schrottenbacher, Mae Chii Brigitte 85–6, 170
science and Buddhism 115
secularization theory 3, 99
secular translations 135–7
selective performance 164, 165–6
self: practices of 150–60; psychological translations 133; sovereign self 150, *see also* non-self
self-authority 127, 144, 149, 158
shyness 151
sīla 24
silence 98, 142–4
Sinha, Vineeta 108
sleep 59, 98, 144–5
social backgrounds, teachers 61
social media 172
sotāpanna 26, 27, 33
Sot Chandassaro, Luang Por 51
Southern Thailand 53–6
spa treatments 82
spiritual marketplace term 130
stress 90, 116
student–teacher connections 170–3, 175–6
Suan Mokkh *see* Wat Suan Mokkhabalarama
subjectivities 5

subversion 140–5
suffering (dukkha) 26, 68
Sunno Bhikkhu *see* Kornfield, Jack
Suphan, Phra Ajan (Phrakru Bhavanavirach) 92, 95
Suputh Kosalo, Venerable Phra 50, 72n, 131
Switzerland 172
symbolism, meditation 103–23
sympathetic joy 56

tam bun 65–7, *see* merit-making
Tambiah, Stanley 12, 29, 31, 37–9, 44n, 58, 107–8, 122n
Taoism 127
TAT *see* Tourism Authority of Thailand
Taylor, Charles 135, 149
Taylor, James 12, 37, 38–9, 44n, 149
teachers: changes for international meditators 146; diversity of 169–70; experiences of 2; home countries 171–2; international meditators interaction with 8; interviews with 3; meditation centers 61–4; paying respect to 32; pedagogical techniques 125; propagating the sāsana 173; student connections 170–3, 175–6; translation strategies 129, 131, 134–6, 139–40; types of meditation teachers 6, 7, 27, 29–30, 38–9, 41, 48, 51, 62–4, 85, 128, 169; verification by 147n
teaching methods 49, 99
Ten Perfections 73n
Thailand: advertisements about 103, 106, 119–20, 124; history of mass lay meditation movement in 46; imaginaries of 9–12; meditation methods in 64–8, 119–20; tourism in 12–13, 103–23; vipassanā meditation in 68–70
Thai meditators 64–8, 119–20
Thammayut sect 15–16, 17, 37, 38
Theean Jittasubho, Luang Por 71n
therapy 82–4
Theravāda Buddhism 16, 24–44; countries 22–3n; merit-making 66; practices of the self 152; propagating 173; sources 27–30
Thipakorawong, Chao Phraya 17
Three Refuges 165

thudong (dhutanga) 38, 39, 44n
Tiyavanich, Kamala 16, 32, 37–8, 162–3, 166
Tong, Ajan Srimangalo 42n, 49, 51, 58–9, 65, 73n, 85, 86–7, 88, 102n, 144, 159, 169
tourism: commodification 23n, 103–23; imaginaries 9–10; international meditators 76–82; long-term meditation 85; meditation centers 6, 176; meditation and 89–90; patterns of 45, 49, 61; for personal change 102n; religion/commodification 12–13
Tourism Authority of Thailand (TAT) 109, 113–17, 123n
transformation, international meditators 155
translation: for individual choice 130–2; practices of the self 156, 160; psychological 132–5; secular 135–7; strategies 128–40; terminology 126; universal 137–40; vipassanā meditation 124–48; within meditation centers 126–8
transnationalization of Buddhism 177n
Tweed, Thomas 2, 4, 12, 103, 122, 132, 161

universal/national symbol, meditation 103–23
universal practice 175
universal translations 137–40
Urry, John 119, 120

Vajiravudh, King 16
vegetarian diet 93
Vinaya 16, 43n, 66, 152, 173
vipassanā meditation 24–44; Burma/ Myanmar 7, 24, 30, 32–6; history of modern practice 30–3; practices of the self 152–4; Thai Buddhist understandings of 68–70; Thailand 20, 24, 29–30, 37–9; translating 124–48
visualization methods 51
Visuddhimagga 27, 29–30, 32
volunteering 87

Wachirayan, Prince 16–17, 37
walking meditation 73n, 97, 143
wan phra (holiday) 93, 94
Wat Chom Tong 63, 77–8, 82, 84, 136–7
Wat Dhammakaya 51–2, 87
Wat Doi Suthep 58–9, 102n
Wat Kow Tahm International Meditation Center 55, 57, 81
Wat Luang Por Sot Buddhist Meditation Institute 52–3, see Buddhist Meditation Institute
Wat Mahathat 37–8
Wat Pah Tam Wua 60–1, 79–80
Wat Prathat Doi Suthep, see Wat Doi Suthep
Wat Prathat Sri Chom Tong, see Wat Chom Tong
Wat Prayong Gittivararam 51
Wat Rampoeng Tapotaram 58–9, 87, 88–96, 98
Wat Suan Mokkhabalarama 53, 77, 171, see also International Dhamma Hermitage
Wat Tam Doi Tohn 59–60
Wat Umong 59, 156
websites 6–7, 76
Weissman, Steve and Rosemary 55, 72n, 73n, 81, 106, 142, 171–2
well-being 75, 82–4
WFB see World Federation of Buddhists
wisdom (paññā) 24–6, 29–30, 40n, 60, 66, 73n, 105, 111, 115
wise-reflection meditation 56
women see female teachers
World Federation of Buddhists (WFB) 109–13

YBAT see Young Buddhists Association of Thailand
yoga 82, 101
Young Buddhists Association of Thailand (YBAT) 64–5

Zen Buddhism 167n

eBooks
from Taylor & Francis

Helping you to choose the right eBooks for your Library

Add to your library's digital collection today with Taylor & Francis eBooks. We have over 50,000 eBooks in the Humanities, Social Sciences, Behavioural Sciences, Built Environment and Law, from leading imprints, including Routledge, Focal Press and Psychology Press.

Choose from a range of subject packages or create your own!

Benefits for you
- Free MARC records
- COUNTER-compliant usage statistics
- Flexible purchase and pricing options
- All titles DRM-free.

Benefits for your user
- Off-site, anytime access via Athens or referring URL
- Print or copy pages or chapters
- Full content search
- Bookmark, highlight and annotate text
- Access to thousands of pages of quality research at the click of a button.

Free Trials Available
We offer free trials to qualifying academic, corporate and government customers.

eCollections

Choose from over 30 subject eCollections, including:

Archaeology	Language Learning
Architecture	Law
Asian Studies	Literature
Business & Management	Media & Communication
Classical Studies	Middle East Studies
Construction	Music
Creative & Media Arts	Philosophy
Criminology & Criminal Justice	Planning
Economics	Politics
Education	Psychology & Mental Health
Energy	Religion
Engineering	Security
English Language & Linguistics	Social Work
Environment & Sustainability	Sociology
Geography	Sport
Health Studies	Theatre & Performance
History	Tourism, Hospitality & Events

For more information, pricing enquiries or to order a free trial, please contact your local sales team:
www.tandfebooks.com/page/sales

www.tandfebooks.com